Minister of Finance Incorporated

Edmund Terence Gomez
with
Thirshalar Padmanabhan
Norfaryanti Kamaruddin • Sunil Bhalla
Fikri Fisal

Minister of Finance Incorporated

Ownership and Control of Corporate Malaysia

palgrave
macmillan

Edmund Terence Gomez
Faculty of Economics and Administration
University of Malaya
Kuala Lumpur, Malaysia

Norfaryanti Kamaruddin
INTROP
Universiti Putra Malaysia
Serdang, Malaysia

Fikri Fisal
Faculty of Economics and Administration
University of Malaya
Kuala Lumpur, Malaysia

Thirshalar Padmanabhan
Faculty of Economics and Administration
University of Malaya
Kuala Lumpur, Malaysia

Sunil Bhalla
Faculty of Economics and Administration
University of Malaya
Kuala Lumpur, Malaysia

The print edition is not for sale in Malaysia and Singapore. Customers from Malaysia and Singapore please order the print book from: GB Gerakbudaya Enterprise Sdn Bhd. [978-967-0960-80-7].

ISBN 978-981-10-4896-8 ISBN 978-981-10-4897-5 (eBook)
DOI 10.1007/978-981-10-4897-5

Library of Congress Control Number: 2017943817

Printed on acid-free paper

This Palgrave Macmillan imprint is published by Springer Nature
The registered company is Springer Nature Singapore Pte Ltd.
The registered company address is: 152 Beach Road, #21-01/04 Gateway East, Singapore 189721, Singapore

For Eshward

Foreword

The New Economic Model (NEM) was an important policy document published in the early years of the premiership of Malaysian Prime Minister Najib Razak. Officially released in 2010, it charts a plan to transform Malaysia into an advanced nation by 2020. Commenting on the role of government in business, the NEM says "Malaysia's economic engine is slowing. Since the Asian financial crisis of 1997... growth has been lower than other crisis-affected countries, while investment has not recovered. Private investors have taken a back seat.... In some industries, heavy government and government-linked company [GLC] presence have discouraged private investment." The NEM goes on to say that one of the "old" approaches that is still prevalent is "dominant state participation in the economy" and "large direct public investment (including through GLCs) in selected economic sectors". The NEM promises to change this situation.

Those responsible for drafting the document explained why they felt it was time to change the old approach of extensive government intervention in the business world. The NEM states that, while this old approach "may have served the country well in the past, it is unlikely to provide the dynamism needed to spur the country to developed country status." It argues that "the government as both business owner and regulator of industries faces conflicts of interest that can... give GLCs an unfair advantage over private firms".

This belief resulted in the NEM's policy objective that the role of government in business should be reduced. To spur private sector investment, the NEM says Malaysia will "divest GLCs in industries where the private sector is operating effectively.... Remaining GLCs will be required to operate on a commercial basis ... without government preferential treatment."

Subsequently, in 2011, the Performance Management and Delivery Unit (Pemandu), situated in the Prime Minister's Department, included in its economic transformation program a strategic reform initiative (SRI) called "Reducing Government's Role in Businesses". In its 2014 Annual Report, Pemandu stated that the government was committed to shifting the government's role in business from that of an investor to a facilitator. Pemandu also claimed it would do three things: clearly establish the government's role in business, develop a clear divestment plan and establish clear governance guidelines for government and state-owned companies.

However, just one year later, in its 2015 Annual Report, Pemandu's target of reducing the government's role in business was reduced to just a footnote, on page 10. This footnote read: "divestment had been completed by the 33 companies that had committed to do so at the launch of the SRIs in 2011". There was no mention of the three original targets it had stated the previous year. It appeared that the government was claiming that by 2015 it had succeeded in achieving its SRI of reducing its role in businesses.

Curious about the real extent to which the government had succeeded, I researched what had happened in the market. I found that the data did not support the claim that the government's role had been reduced to any appreciable extent. In fact, the opposite had happened. From 2011 to 2015, the government's share in the Kuala Lumpur Composite Index (KLCI) increased from 43.7% to 47.1%, indicating that the government had greater ownership of the equity of the largest companies in Malaysia in 2015, in contrast to the position in 2011 when the NEM was issued. The government had also increased its investments in private companies, whereas the number of disposals had not increased. The total value of GLC acquisitions was RM51.7 billion, and this dwarfed the total disposals of RM29.5 billion. A full analysis of these findings was published by the Institute for Democracy and Economic Affairs (IDEAS), for which I am currently CEO, in a paper entitled "Lesser Government in Business: An unfulfilled promise?" (April 2016).

Prior to that study, I was also involved in the Organisation for Economic Co-operation and Development (OECD) Network on Corporate Governance of State-Owned Enterprises. IDEAS attends the meetings organized by this global network, and since 2015 we have been the sole participant from Malaysia. The meetings of this network fascinate me, especially in terms of how much we still need to do in order to catch up with the rest of the world. Many countries that have a sizeable number of state-owned enterprises (SOEs) have a well-structured mechanism to monitor the governance and performance of these enterprises, usually in the form of a central government agency tasked with monitoring and evaluation. But, in Malaysia, there is no such effective body to undertake this task. Yes, we do have a division within the Ministry of Finance looking after government investment companies, but there is scant information on the scope of this division's powers. To give a simple example: I have been trying to determine the exact number of SOEs in Malaysia, but no one, not even senior officials at the Treasury, knows the answer. There is even uncertainty about the categorization of companies, whether certain companies should be classified as an SOE or not. If we do not even know how many SOEs exist in this country, can we really expect these companies to be well governed?

Within this context, we recently saw the national embarrassment that is 1Malaysia Development Bhd (1MDB). It baffles me how the chairmanship of the Advisory Board, a body that has no legal and fiduciary powers, can be given to the Prime Minister of Malaysia, the most powerful person in the country. How can anyone expect the company to be governed properly when the Board of Directors, the body that is supposed to hold all the legal and fiduciary responsibilities is, effectively, subservient to the Chairman of the Advisory Board? Does anyone really expect 1MDB Board members to say no to the Prime Minister? My bigger fear is that we do not know if the bad governance exemplified by 1MDB is more widespread and affects more than that one company. That is why I have been very keen to see more open and honest studies on the governance of Malaysia's SOEs. For this reason, I was delighted that Professor Edmund Terence Gomez of the University of Malaya agreed to conduct this study.

When we commissioned Professor Gomez to undertake the study I was not expecting a book. Our original intention was to have just a short paper outlining the state of governance of our GLCs. I still remember saying to Professor Gomez that I would be happy to get 5,000 words from the project. But the amount of data unearthed by Professor Gomez was so vast, particularly on the significance of Minister of Finance Incorporated (MoF Inc.), that we decided it would be inane to ignore the discovery. Hence, we now have this book that considers the wider political economy behind the governance of Malaysian GLCs, by focusing on the extensive reach of

MoF Inc. and therefore the Finance Minister. This is just the first output, as we are continuing with more work on this topic.

I believe that the government should act mainly as regulator and facilitator for the private sector. If there is a need for the government to be in business, then that need must be clearly specified so that we can judge when the necessity no longer exists. Where and when GLCs exist, their governance must be properly conducted and any weaknesses must be improved. But to design an effective improvement plan, we must first understand the current landscape. Professor Gomez and his team have done a sterling job in documenting a segment of the current landscape in this volume. There is, of course, a lot more that needs to be done. But, for now, I hope readers enjoy this book as much as I enjoyed reviewing and discussing the drafts with Professor Gomez.

Wan Saiful Wan Jan

Chief Executive
Institute for Democracy
& Economic Affairs (IDEAS)

Preface and Acknowledgements

This is a study of Malaysia's new political economy. It offers insights into corporate ownership patterns of the country's leading enterprises in 2013, controlled ultimately by the state of Malaysia through what have been classified as government-linked investment companies (GLICs). This book is the first in a series of studies to be published about the huge range of publicly listed and unquoted enterprises owned by these GLICs, commonly known as government-linked companies (GLCs). The reason for this publication at a time when research is still under way about the GLCs is that the authors and the institution responsible for this study, the Institute for Democracy and Economic Affairs (IDEAS), felt the pressing need to inform readers, particularly Malaysians, about the important role the GLICs play in the economy and in the corporate sector.

While undertaking the research, we were extremely surprised to learn that very few Malaysians, even well-informed academics and analysts of the economy, the political system and corporate governance, were aware of the existence of the GLICs and their extensive ownership and control of the corporate sector. This book serves to introduce the GLICs to the reader, outlining in the process why they were established and how they have come to secure their significant presence in the corporate sector. To stress why these government enterprises are such important actors in the Malaysian economy, this study also provides an overview of the GLICs' ownership and control of the leading publicly listed enterprises quoted on the domestic bourse, the Bursa Malaysia. Our focus is on the majority ownership that the GLICs have of the GLCs quoted among Bursa Malaysia's top 100 companies, as it stood in 2013.

Although this study was undertaken from early 2016, for this volume, the year 2013 was selected for assessment of corporate ownership ties. We focused on this year because it was then that Malaysian Prime Minister Najib Razak made an epochal announcement. Najib introduced his administration's version of affirmative action in business, an endeavour he christened the Bumiputera Economic Empowerment (BEE) policy. To achieve the BEE's primary objective of increasing Bumiputera[1] participation in business and ownership of corporate wealth, Najib made another important point. The Prime Minister announced he would employ Malaysia's top 20 GLCs as well as some GLICs to facilitate the transfer of corporate assets and business opportunities to Bumiputeras. Later that year, concerns began to emerge in the market about a government-linked company called 1Malaysia Development Bhd (1MDB). This company, closely associated with Najib, was subsequently enmeshed in major corporate controversies that involved its investments in Malaysia as well as a number of other countries. Given the important role of the GLICs and GLCs in the economy, these events necessitated urgent analysis of the corporate influence of these government-linked firms.

This study is arranged in five sections. While three chapters form the main body of the text, the remaining two provide an introduction to the issue at hand and review the implications of the GLICs' involvement in the corporate sector. The three long chapters trace, first, the history of the development of the GLICs. To understand the current state of Malaysia's political economy, one needs to understand the history of events leading up to this point where the GLICs have come to secure a dominant presence in the corporate sector. Situated in the second section is the empirical data uncovered in this project. This section focuses on the GLICs' *ownership* of corporate equity, particularly through their GLCs quoted in the Bursa's top 100. The third section provides an in-depth assessment of how the GLICs *control* the corporate sector. The study concludes with the political and business implications of the government's significant control of the corporate sector, particularly through its most important GLIC, the Minister of Finance Incorporated (MoF Inc.).

This study is written in an accessible manner for public consumption. We adopted this mode of presentation to reveal, with limited academic jargon, how the government has deployed the companies it owns, in different ways, to achieve different economic, social and political goals. Our aim here is to provide empirical evidence of GLIC–GLC presence in Malaysia's corporate sector. An in-depth and theoretically oriented study will be published after we have completed our assessment of a wider spectrum of GLCs. This broad-based study of GLICs and GLCs has just commenced and we plan to complete the project within two years.

A number of people have helped us to complete this study. My primary debt is to my co-authors, all my students who have contributed to the study. Jean-Marc Roda of CIRAD, the French Agricultural Research Centre for International Development, now concurrently based at the Institute of Tropical Forestry and Forest Products (INTROP) in Universiti Putra Malaysia, was a constant source of help when we approached him to prepare and decipher the corporate network graphics used in this study.

Research assistance was provided by a number of people. Maryam Lee helped write up material while our intern, Lesley Gabriel, worked diligently, sometimes over and beyond the call of duty, when she was assigned research tasks. Other members of the research team have asked that we do not mention their names, which is unfortunate given their enormous contribution to the project. We acknowledge the help provided by Khairil Yusof and his research team at Sinar Project. Khairil and his colleagues gathered important data we required about the directors of the GLICs and GLCs.

I am indebted to my team of researchers as they devoted much time to gathering the enormous volume of data provided in this study. The information presented here was obtained from the National Archives as well as the libraries of companies publishing major newspapers, specifically *The Star* and *The Edge*. We are grateful to the staff at these institutions who helped us gather the data we required. Further research was undertaken at Singapore's National Library and the National Archives of Singapore, where we compiled information about the history, shareholders and directors of the GLICs and GLCs. Since our primary focus was publicly listed GLCs, the team pored over the annual reports of these companies. A large body of information was obtained from the Companies Commission of Malaysia as well as two specific business information databases: Osiris and Oriana, provided by a Swedish company, Bureau Van Dijk, who specialize in company information and business intelligence. Oriana provides information about companies across the Asia-Pacific region. From the Osiris database, information was obtained about all publicly listed companies owned by or associated with the GLICs under study here.

The issues discussed here have been presented at numerous forums since July 2016 when a public lecture was first delivered, based on our preliminary findings. We have benefited enormously from the critical feedback we received during these forums.

I also acknowledge with much gratitude those who have taken the trouble to read the manuscript and provide important feedback. The two reviewers appointed by the publisher to read and comment on the manuscript provided important, insightful and detailed criticisms. I thank Mohd Sheriff Kassim, Latifah Merican, P. Gunasegaram and Elsa Satkunasingam for reading the manuscript and engaging me in a discussion about the research findings. I wish to thank Chris Leong, the former president of Malaysia's Bar Council, who read the manuscript and provided critical legal feedback.

Our final debt is to Wan Saiful Wan Jan and his colleagues, particularly Tricia Yeoh and Aira Azhari, at the organization he leads, IDEAS. This project began with my conversation with Wan Saiful about the need to assess the GLCs, though our discussion then focused on the topical matter of active government intervention in the economy. The issue of the extent of government intervention in the economy will be tackled in greater depth later, as this project continues over the coming years, since we hold differing viewpoints on the role of the state in the economy. IDEAS provided the funding to commence a study that focused on the GLICs. Funding was also provided by the Population Studies Unit (PSU) of the Faculty of Economics & Administration of the University of Malaya to cover research expenses. IDEAS has since secured additional funding to allow us to research the terrain of the GLCs, enterprises which now are an important presence in all sectors of the Malaysian economy.

While we are extremely indebted to all those mentioned here for their support, we, the authors, remain solely responsible for the contents of this book.

University of Malaya — Terence Gomez
1 March 2017

NOTE

1. Bumiputera, which means "sons of the soil", is the term used in reference to ethnic Malays and other indigenous peoples. Of Malaysia's 29 million multi-ethnic population in 2013, Bumiputeras accounted for 65%, Chinese 26%, Indians 8% and the rest comprising other ethnic groups.

Contents

Notes on Contributors

Sunil Bhalla obtained his undergraduate and postgraduate degrees from Universiti Putra Malaysia and the University of Malaya. He has worked for both the private and public sectors in Malaysia, including at Sime Darby and the Performance Management & Delivery Unit at Malaysia's Prime Minister's Department (Pemandu).

Fikri Fisal obtained his undergraduate degree in History and Actuarial Science from the University of Michigan, Ann Arbor, USA. He is now pursuing a Masters of Development Studies degree at the University of Malaya.

Edmund Terence Gomez is Professor of Political Economy at the Faculty of Economics & Administration, University of Malaya. He has held appointments at the University of Leeds (UK) and Murdoch University (Australia) and served as Visiting Professor at Kobe University (Japan) and at the Universities of Michigan (Ann Arbor) and California (San Diego) (USA). Between 2005 and 2008, he served as Research Coordinator at the United Nations Research Institute for Social Development (UNRISD), in Geneva (Switzerland). He is also a Senior Fellow at IDEAS. His publications include *Politics in Business: UMNO's Corporate Investments* (1990), *Money Politics in the Barisan Nasional* (1991), *Political Business: Corporate Involvement of Malaysian Political Parties* (1994) *Malaysia's Political Economy: Politics, Patronage and Profits* (1997), *Chinese Business in Malaysia: Accumulation, Ascendance, Accommodation* (1999), *Ethnic Futures: The State and Identity Politics in Asia* (Sage, 2000), *Political Business in East Asia* (2002), *The State of Malaysia: Ethnicity, Equity and*

Reform (2004), *The Politics of Resource Extraction: Indigenous Peoples, Multinational Corporations and the State* (Palgrave Macmillan, 2012), *The New Economic Policy in Malaysia: Affirmative Action, Horizontal Inequalities and Social Justice* (2013) and *Government-Linked Companies and Sustainable, Equitable Development* (2015).

Norfaryanti Kamaruddin is a research officer with the Institute of Tropical Forestry and Forest Products (INTROP), Universiti Putra Malaysia. She is preparing a doctoral dissertation on ownership and control of the plantations sector in Malaysia.

Thirshalar Padmanabhan graduated in 2015 from the University of Hull with a BA in Politics and International Relations. She is currently pursuing an MA in Development Studies degree at the University of Malaya.

List of Abbreviations

1MDB	1Malaysia Development Berhad
Agrobank	Bank Pertanian (M) Berhad
ASB	Amanah Saham Bumiputera (Bumiputera Unit Trust Scheme)
ASN	Amanah Saham Nasional (National Unit Trust Scheme)
ASNB	Amanah Saham Nasional Berhad
BCB	Bank of Commerce Berhad
BCIC	Bumiputera Commercial and Industrial Community policy
BEE	Bumiputera Economic Empowerment policy
BN	Barisan Nasional (National Front)
CDRC	Corporate Debt Restructuring Committee
CEO	Chief Executive Officer
CGC	Credit Guarantee Corporation (Malaysia) Berhad
DFIs	Development Financial Institutions
DRB	Diversified Resources Berhad
E&O	Eastern & Oriental Berhad
EPF	Employees Provident Fund
EPU	Economic Planning Unit
ETP	Economic Transformation Programme
EXIM Bank	Export-Import Bank of Malaysia Berhad
FAMA	Federal Agricultural Marketing Agency
FELCRA	Federal Land Consolidation and Rehabilitation Authority
FELDA	Federal Land Development Authority
FDI	Foreign Direct Investments
FGV	Felda Global Ventures Holdings Berhad
FIC	Foreign Investment Committee
GIC	Government Investment Companies Division
GLCs	Government-Linked Companies

GLICs	Government-Linked Investment Companies
GTP	Government Transformation Programme
HICOM	Heavy Industries Corporation of Malaysia Berhad
IPO	Initial Public Offering
JPA	Jabatan Perkhidmatan Awam (Public Service Department)
Khazanah	Khazanah Nasional Berhad
KLCCP	KLCC Property Holdings Berhad
KLK	Kuala Lumpur Kepong Berhad
KLSE	Kuala Lumpur Stock Exchange
KUB	Koperasi Usaha Bersatu Malaysia Berhad
KWAP	Kumpulan Wang Persaraan Diperbadankan (Retirement Fund Incorporated)
LRs	Listing Rules
LTAT	Lembaga Tabung Angkatan Tentera (Armed Forces Savings Fund)
LTH	Lembaga Tabung Haji (Pilgrims Savings Fund)
MAHB	Malaysia Airports Holdings Berhad
MARA	Majlis Amanah Rakyat (Council of Trust for Indigenous People)
MAS	Malaysian Airline System Berhad
MBSB	Malaysian Building Society Berhad
MCA	Malaysian Chinese Association
MD	Managing Director
MDeC	Multimedia Development Corporation Berhad
MIC	Malaysian Indian Congress
MIDF	Malaysian Industrial Development Finance Berhad
MINDA	Malaysian Directors Academy
MISC	Malaysian International Shipping Corporation Berhad
MITI	Ministry of International Trade and Industry
MMHE	Malaysia Marine and Heavy Engineering Holdings Berhad
MNCs	Multi-National Companies
MoF Inc.	Ministry of Finance (Incorporated)
MRCB	Malaysian Resources Corporation Berhad
MSM	MSM Malaysia Holdings Bhd
MUI	Malayan United Industries Berhad
NDP	National Development Policy
NEB	National Electricity Board
NEM	New Economic Model
NEP	New Economic Policy
NGO	Non-governmental Organization
NKRA	National Key Results Areas
NSTP	New Straits Times Press (Malaysia) Berhad
NVP	National Vision Policy
OECD	Organisation for Economic Cooperation and Development

Perkasa	Persatuan Pribumi Perkasa
Pernas	Perbadanan Nasional (National Corporation)
Petronas	Petroliam Nasional Berhad (National Petroleum Corporation)
PNB	Permodalan Nasional Berhad (National Equity Corporation)
Proton	Perusahaan Otomobil Nasional Berhad
PUNB	Perbadanan Usahawan Nasional Berhad
R&D	Research and Development
RIDA	Rural and Industrial Development Authority
RISDA	Rubber Industry Smallholders Development Authority
RPT	Related Party Transactions
SCC	Strongly Connected Component
Sdn Bhd	Sendirian Berhad (Private Limited)
SEDC	State Economic Development Corporation
SME Bank	Small Medium Enterprise Development Bank (M) Berhad
SMEs	Small- and Medium Scale Enterprises
SMIDEC	Small and Medium Industries Development Corporation
SOCSO	Social Security Organization
SOE	State-Owned Enterprise
SPV	Special Purpose Vehicle
SWF	Sovereign Wealth Fund
TEKUN	Tekun National Foundation
TIA	Terengganu Investment Authority
TRX	Tun Razak Exchange
UAB	United Asian Bank Berhad
UDA	Urban Development Holdings
UMBC	United Malayan Banking Corporation Berhad
UMNO	United Malays National Organization
VDP	Vendor Development Programme
YPB	Yayasan Pelaburan Bumiputera (Bumiputera Investment Foundation)

List of Figures

List of Tables

List of Boxes

List of Appendices

CHAPTER 1

Introduction

The Government's Business

In September 2009, a few months after Najib Razak was appointed Prime Minister, the Terengganu Investment Authority (TIA), a government-owned enterprise operating at the state level in the federation of Malaysia, was renamed 1Malaysia Development Bhd (1MDB). 1MDB came under the control of an opaque but extremely important company, the Minister of Finance Incorporated (MoF Inc.), under the jurisdiction of the federal government's Ministry of Finance. In one of the major anomalies of Malaysia's system of public governance, the Prime Minister has also served as the Minister of Finance since 2001, a situation that would emerge as a key concern when the 1MDB scandal broke a few years later.

In the early 2010s, 1MDB's reputation grew as it became a key player in major infrastructure projects and corporate activities. In July 2012, when Najib launched the first phase of the construction of the Tun Razak Exchange (TRX), the site of Malaysia's proposed international financial hub situated in the heart of the city of Kuala Lumpur, 1MDB was tasked with developing the project. 1MDB was also responsible for constructing Bandar Malaysia, a project on the single largest remaining tract of development land in Kuala Lumpur.[1] 1MDB went on to raise US$6.5 billion through three bond sales to fund investments in major energy-related projects. These bond sales were arranged and under-written between 2012 and 2013 by the international investment consultancy, Goldman Sachs (*Wall Street Journal* 7 June 2016).

E.T. Gomez et al., *Minister of Finance Incorporated*,
DOI 10.1007/978-981-10-4897-5_1

A few weeks after the third bond sale, Najib announced the dissolution of parliament in order to hold a general election on 5 May 2013. In this closely fought election, during which an enormous volume of funds was spent (Weiss 2013), Najib led the ruling Barisan Nasional (BN, or National Front) coalition to victory. However, the BN lost the popular vote, returning to power only because it had secured a simple majority in parliament, an outcome allegedly attributed to gerrymandering and the malapportionment of seats.[2]

Not long after this election, rather disconcerting reports about 1MDB began to emerge. When 1MDB's 2013 annual report was released, it was disclosed that the enterprise had debts amounting to RM36.3 billion (*Bloomberg* 2 February 2016). Important government-owned enterprises were linked to 1MDB's ventures. For instance, Lembaga Tabung Haji (LTH, or Pilgrims Fund Board), a prominent government-based savings institution, also known as a government-linked investment company (GLIC), offered to buy the TRX land, a transaction that eventually transpired in 2015. LTH reportedly acquired this land at an inflated price, approximately 43 times the price 1MDB had paid the government (*Malay Mail* 20 May 2015).[3] The government's pension-based scheme, Kumpulan Wang Persaraan Diperbadankan (KWAP, or Retirement Fund Incorporated), provided an RM4 billion loan in 2011 to SRC International Sdn Bhd, a company linked to 1MDB and owned by MoF Inc. (*New Straits Times* 6 April 2016).[4]

1MDB's business ventures also involved activities in a number of countries. The controversies surrounding 1MDB would eventually be described by the British *Guardian* newspaper (28 July 2016) as "the world's biggest financial scandal". When the United States' Department of Justice released a report on 1MDB, it alleged that US$3.5 billion had been misappropriated from this government-owned enterprise.[5] Prime Minister Najib, his close business allies and executives at Goldman Sachs were implicated in the controversy, while investigations on international financial flows linked to 1MDB commenced in numerous countries including in Singapore, Switzerland and the United States (*The Straits Times* 22 July 2016). While Malaysia's Attorney General exonerated Najib of any wrongdoing in the 1MDB controversy (see *Financial Times* 21 July 2016), investigations into the company's activities continue.

These controversial issues linking 1MDB and certain government-owned enterprises drew attention to a core issue: the important role of GLICs in Malaysia's corporate sector. The International Monetary Fund

(IMF) corroborated this point in a report it published in 2013,[6] which stated that the GLICs have substantial de facto ownership of the financial sector and are by far the most influential players in the Malaysian capital market, with significant interconnectedness. However, many Malaysians are unaware that the government operates enterprises classified as GLICs and that they have such a prominent role in the economy.[7] It is for this reason that this study focuses on GLICs, revealing how they have evolved, how they are now owned, controlled and employed, and the extent of their involvement in Malaysia's corporate sector.

Malaysia's GLICs

Seven institutions have been classified by the government as GLICs: in addition to MoF Inc., LTH and KWAP, they are Permodalan Nasional Bhd (PNB, or the National Equity Corporation), the Employees Provident Fund (EPF),[8] Khazanah Nasional Bhd and Lembaga Tabung Angkatan Tentera (LTAT, or Armed Forces Fund Board) (see Table 1.1).[9] These GLICs function in various forms—as a holding company, pension fund, special purpose fund, sovereign wealth fund and trust fund manager. While Khazanah and PNB were incorporated under the Companies Act, the other five GLICs are statutory bodies.

Four of the seven GLICs—EPF, KWAP, LTH and LTAT—are pension or special purpose funds. EPF and KWAP, pension funds for employees

Table 1.1 List of GLICs

1.	Minister of Finance Inc. (MoF Inc.)
2.	Permodalan Nasional Bhd (PNB)
3.	Khazanah Nasional Bhd (Khazanah)
4.	Employees Provident Fund (EPF)
5.	Lembaga Tabung Angkatan Tentera (LTAT) (Armed Forces Savings Fund)
6.	Lembaga Tabung Haji (LTH) (Pilgrims Savings Fund)
7.	Kumpulan Wang Persaraan Diperbadankan (KWAP) (Retirement Fund Incorporated)

Source: Ministry of Finance

of the private and public sectors respectively, have a long history, going back to the colonial period. LTH, whose roots can be traced to the early 1960s, is a special purpose fund for Muslims who intend to save for their hajj pilgrimage. LTAT was established in 1972 and serves as a pension fund for members of the armed forces. These funds were not created to act as the government's investment holding arms but would evolve to function in this manner. Two GLICs, PNB and Khazanah, were established after the government began intervening actively in the corporate sector to rectify social injustices. PNB functions to redistribute corporate wealth more equitably among all Malaysians, while Khazanah is the country's only sovereign wealth fund. MoF Inc., the government's most important GLIC, was incorporated in 1957 and functions as its investment holding company.

Table 1.2 indicates how the six men who have served as Prime Minister of Malaysia have employed the GLICs. The first three Prime Ministers, Tunku Abdul Rahman (1957–1970), Abdul Razak (1970–1976) and Hussein Onn (1976–1981), were responsible for establishing most of these GLICs and there is no evidence of any abuse of these enterprises. Razak used LTH for agriculture-focused investments while Hussein pursued the affirmative action-based New Economic Policy (NEP), initiated by Razak, by forming PNB. Mahathir Mohamad, the fourth Prime Minister, who served for 22 years, from 1981 until 2003, used the GLICs to nationalize foreign-owned firms while actively privatizing government companies, a number of which he eventually bailed out following the 1997 Asian currency crisis. Mahathir can be credited for Malaysia's rapid modernization, achieved through various means including through industrial development-based ventures that involved GLICs such as MoF Inc., PNB and Khazanah, which he incorporated in 1993. Abdullah Ahmad Badawi (2003–2009) inherited a large number of companies, owned primarily by the GLICs, popularly known as government-linked companies (GLCs), a legacy of the 1997 bailouts. Abdullah formulated a grand transformation strategy to improve the management and performance of the GLICs and GLCs, seeking in the process to turn them into global champions by increasing their business presence abroad. Najib's administration, however, is one that has been fraught with the use of the GLICs in contentious business deals. A number of these deals involved the controversial 1MDB, as indicated in Appendix 2.1,[10] in sharp contrast to his pledge on securing the premiership to deal with patronage and rent-seeking.

Table 1.2 Key use of GLICs based on major historical corporate actions, 1957–2016

Administration	MoF Inc.	EPF	LTH	LTAT	PNB	KWAP	Khazanah
Abdul Rahman	Created under MoF Inc. Act 1957	Created before Independence under the EPF Ordinance 1951	Created under Lembaga Urusan dan Tabung Haji Act 1969				
	Formed many GLCs						
Abdul Razak	Created Pernas to increase Bumiputera corporate ownership	Invests mostly in government securities	Pursues agriculture focused investments	Created under Tabung Angkatan Tentera Act 1972			
Hussein Onn	Transfer of assets to PNB				Created to increase Bumiputera corporate ownership; transfer of assets from Pernas to PNB		
Mahathir Mohamad	GLICs retain control over privatized companies						
	Transfer of assets to Khazanah; rescues Perwaja; takes over Bakun Dam project from Ekran Bhd	Rescues STAR LRT, Perwaja; finances Bakun Dam project	Major revamp due to mismanagement		Nationalization of Guthrie; rescue of Bank Bumiputra by Petronas	Created under Pension Trust Fund Act 1991	Creation of Khazanah in 1993
					Rescues Pernas; bails out financially-strapped companies in 1997	Rescues Time Engineering, MAS	Rescues Time Engineering, UEM, Bank Bumiputra
Abdullah Badawi		Rescues PTPTN			Mega-merger of Sime Darby, Golden Hope and Guthrie	Grows in function under Retirement Fund Act 2007	Goes through major revamp; Leads the GLC Transformation Programme
Najib Razak	Creates 1MDB	Purchases 1MDB bonds	Purchases TRX land and bonds from 1MDB	Purchases TRX land through Affin; receives 1MDB contract to develop Sg Besi Airport	Controversially takes over SP Setia	Purchases TRX land from 1MDB; gives huge loans to 1MDB's subsidiaries	
					Allegedly purchases 1MDB bonds		

When Najib came to power, his early policy pronouncements indicated his aim to continue the work Abdullah had put in place to professionalize the management of the GLICs and GLCs. His intent was clearly to privatize these companies and reduce the state's participation in the economy. Among Najib's first declarations as Prime Minister was his pledge to end "the eras of 'government knows best' and of excessive controls" (Ahmad Fauzi and Muhammad Takiyuddin 2014: 13). However, this agenda began to change after the 2013 election, when his BN coalition lost the popular vote.[11] Najib attributed the BN's dismal electoral performance to weak support by ethnic Chinese (Saravanamuttu 2016). A few months later, Najib announced his own affirmative action-based endeavour, the Bumiputera Economic Empowerment (BEE) policy, aimed at situating more of Malaysia's corporate holdings in the hands of this ethnic group.[12]

To attain the goals of the BEE, Najib further announced that he had instructed the GLICs and major publicly listed GLCs, or the G20, to play a lead role in the implementation of this policy.[13] It appeared that these government-linked businesses, while expected to function as well-managed, wealth-creating and employment generating enterprises, now also had a political agenda: to muster Bumiputera support for a Prime Minister who felt that his party's hold on power was under serious threat. This was an interesting development because one primary objective of the GLC transformation plan introduced by Abdullah was to remove politicians as members of the boards of directors of GLICs and GLCs.

Focus of Study: The GLICs

Defining GLICs and GLCs

The domineering presence of GLICs in corporate Malaysia can be seen in Table 1.3. GLICs have had, throughout their history, ownership of a range of quoted and unquoted firms, typical of large business groups. In 2013, a year of general election and change in the way government enterprises were to be employed, to include a political agenda, GLICs had majority ownership of 35 publicly listed firms. Table 1.3 lists the number of private and quoted companies associated with the GLICs. Table 1.3 further reveals that corporate ownership mechanisms, such as

Table 1.3 GLIC ownership of all companies, 2013

GLIC	*Subsidiary (50–100%)*	*Associate (20–49%)*	*Minority (1–19%)*	*Golden share*	*Total companies*
MoF Inc.	63	3	2	34	102
Khazanah	23	18	10	–	51
PNB	12	9	31	–	52
EPF	21	12	67	–	100
KWAP	5	1	38	–	44
LTH	36	11	15	–	62
LTAT	7	25	12	–	44
Total	167	79	175	34	455

subsidiaries, associate companies and minority interests, employed by these seven GLICs vary significantly. The use of the golden share to control companies is also evident in this table.

This study reviews the role of the GLICs in the corporate sector, and gives specific attention to their majority ownership of GLCs among Malaysia's top 100 companies, publicly listed on the domestic stock exchange, Bursa Malaysia, as it stood in 2013. Of these top 100 quoted companies, 35 were identified as GLCs. The list of the top 100 firms, organized by market capitalization, used in this study was obtained from Bloomberg. These 35 GLCs, discussed in greater depth in the chapters that follow, are major players in the corporate sector, constituting an estimated 42% of the total market capitalization of all listed companies in 2013. All seven GLICs also have an equity interest in a number of other publicly listed companies.

The Organisation for Economic Cooperation and Development (OECD), in its 2013 study of GLICs, provides a definition of these enterprises:

> Government-linked investment companies (GLICs) refer to investment companies in which the federal government has influence over the management by appointing and approving board members and senior management, who in turn report directly to the government. The government may also provide funds for operations or to guarantee capital (and some income) placed by unit holders. The Ministry of Finance or the Prime Minister's office are usually the government representatives on the board of GLICs and thereby play a role in the governance and investment decisions of these companies.[14]

In its definition of GLICs, the OECD goes on to add one other crucial point: "Representatives of GLIC beneficiaries (investors and pensioners) complement the board of directors". This is also the case with the Malaysian government in the running of its GLICs. This definition draws attention to a vital feature that allows the Ministry of Finance control over the GLICs: the appointment of its directors. While, according to this definition, the directors oversee the governance of the GLICs as well as investment decisions, the presumption of accountability does not necessarily follow given the structure of the Malaysian state where there is much concentration of political power. Moreover, the Minister of Finance also serves as the Prime Minister. Academics within the discipline of political science have referred to Malaysia's political system as one that is characterized as a single dominant party state,[15] an electoral authoritarian state,[16] a semi-authoritarian state[17] or a quasi-democratic state.[18] Where these studies share common ground is that they all view the Malaysian state as one that is under the hegemony of one party in the BN coalition, the United Malays National Organization (UMNO). Najib is the president of UMNO.

For this study, what constitutes a GLIC is based on the classification provided by the government.[19] A GLIC is defined by the government as an investment company linked to the federal government that allocates some or all of its funds to GLC investments.[20] The federal government is responsible for appointing the members of the board of directors of the GLICs as well as their senior management who in turn report directly to the government.[21]

The OECD provides a definition for the GLCs that operate in the Malaysian economy. This definition is adopted here, namely that GLCs are:

> companies that have primary commercial objective and in which the Malaysian government has a direct controlling stake, i.e. the ability to appoint board members and senior management, make major decisions (e.g. contract awards, strategy, restructuring and financing, acquisitions and divestments) for GLCs either directly or through GLICs. Hence, GLCs include companies where the government controls directly or collectively a controlling stake through state agencies… (and) includes companies where GLC themselves have a controlling stake, i.e. subsidiaries and affiliates of GLCs.[22]

The OECD's definition of Malaysia's GLCs is similar to that adopted by the World Bank in regard to such enterprises in general in its *Report on the Observance of Standards and Codes for GLCs.* In this report, the World

Bank defines GLCs as "companies where the government controls directly or collectively a controlling stake through state agencies".[23]

Companies under majority ownership of the government, specifically the seven GLICs, are defined as GLCs. If 20% or more of a company's equity is owned by one, or a collection, of GLICs, the enterprise is classified here as a GLC. Excluded in this definition of what constitutes a GLC is other forms of control such as the ability to appoint the members of the board of directors and senior management. A company in which the government has a golden share is classified as a GLC, provided no private enterprise or individual has a majority interest in the firm. This definition of a GLC would necessarily exclude privately owned publicly listed companies in which MoF Inc. has a golden share, such as Westports Bhd and Pos Bhd.

Key Themes: Ownership and Control

We provide a historical profile of the GLICs to trace how the Minister of Finance has come to obtain considerable influence over them and by extension over the publicly listed and private companies that they own. The GLICs in question, as well as a number of the large quoted enterprises they own, function as holding companies, emerging in the process as Malaysia's leading business groups. Since publicly listed firms are required to have a wide shareholding spread as defined by listing rules, it is common for a majority shareholder to reduce his shareholding while finding other mechanisms to retain control of the company.

For this reason, the concept of ownership and control requires careful definition. Control is defined here as the ability to determine the "basic long-term goals and objectives of the enterprise, and the adoption of courses of action and the allocation of resources necessary for carrying out these goals" (Chandler 1977: 13). Fligstein (2001: 128–129) notes that there are two bases for control, ownership and authority. Majority owners of large firms, and this includes a government with extensive interests in the corporate sector, are able to direct the course of these companies, but they have to "formulate a view of the world in order to take action" or "create a stable market where actors come to take one another's actions into account in the framing of their actions" (Fligstein 2001: 128–129).

Berle and Means (1932) stress the importance of control over ownership of corporate equity. For them, the separation of control from ownership can undermine the value of a company because managers who are not owners will not be guided by profit-maximizing motives. This argument is fortified by Jensen and Meckling (1976) who indicate that an imperfect alignment of incentives between managers and shareholders fosters a value-reducing agency problem. This problem can be mitigated if managers held stock of the company they run.

Berle and Means (1932) correctly note that in an enterprise with a large capital base, such as a publicly listed firms, a mere 10% equity ownership is sufficient to maintain control, particularly if there is considerable diffusion of share ownership. Berle and Means go on to distinguish five types of control: private ownership, majority control, minority control, management control and control through a legal device without majority ownership (this is evident in the case of the GLICs with their use of the golden share). For the last three types of control, majority ownership of a company's equity is unnecessary as relations among those with influence in the firm dictate decision-making. Domhoff (1983: 59) notes that control of a company can occur in three different ways: through the ability to (a) replace the top management; (b) maintain active involvement on the board of directors; and (c) influence mergers, acquisitions and growth strategies, all issues that prevail in the management of the GLICs and the GLCs.

Majority control differs from private ownership in that a number of shareholders are devoid of control because control is held by the owner(s) of a majority of the shares. Minority control refers to a situation where an individual or a group of associates owns enough stock to ensure control. Minority control ordinarily rests on a relatively even distribution of the remaining shares among many small shareholders, so that no rival has enough equity to successfully challenge the controlling stock owners.

The GLICs function primarily as investment holding companies, a business operation method adopted by corporations classified as business groups. The holding company structure serves as an important mechanism for one institution or actor to control a large number of enterprises. This system prevails when a parent or holding company holds more than half the issued share capital of another company, controls the composition of the board of directors or controls more than half the voting power. This definition is extended to include a company which is a subsidiary of a subsidiary. This pyramiding system allows the ultimate owner to maintain control over a number of companies with a relatively small investment.[24]

Bonbright and Means (1969: 10–11) define a holding company as "any company, incorporated or unincorporated, which is in a position to control, or materially to influence, the management of one or more companies by virtue, in part at least, of its ownership of securities in the other company or companies". Scott (1985: 135) notes that a holding company "is designed explicitly to control or influence other companies without taking full ownership of them". Scott (1985: 136) adds that holding companies can "dominate the flow of capital to other business enterprises".

Equity cross-holdings are common among holding companies. Numerous advantages accrue to the majority shareholder of a holding company from cross-holdings, a system that has no value for—and provides little protection to—minority shareholders of the firm. The cross-holding structure is also useful for enhancing—or distorting—the value of the equity of the holding company if it has ownership of profitable publicly listed subsidiaries or associate companies. This is crucial for the majority owner of a holding company as it allows him another means to gain access to bank loans, with the equity of profitable firms used as collateral. The main benefit of the cross-holding structure is that it allows the majority shareholder to protect his interests in profitable firms from hostile takeovers. By publicly listing a company, owners can use the company to buy other quoted and private enterprises, a process that can enable them to secure control over a diversified corporate empire, yet not hold stock in their own name. An increase in a quoted company's market capitalization can enable that firm to secure even more loans from foreign and local banks with equity as collateral.[25]

A number of quoted GLCs come under the umbrella of one holding company or a GLIC. These quoted GLCs, in turn, function as business groups, involving the use of a holding company—and, in some cases, cross-holdings and pyramiding—reflecting that this is an extremely important corporate control mechanism. Since GLICs function primarily as holding companies at the apex of a large number of quoted and unlisted firms, the concepts of business groups and pyramiding require thoughtful consideration. Leff (1978: 663) defines a business group as "a group of companies that does business in different markets under a common administrative or financial control". Granovetter (1995), in similar fashion, sees a business group as a corpus of firms, mutually bonded by varying degrees of legal and social connection, that transact in several markets under the control of a core firm.[26]

A pyramid corporate structure is defined as one where an ultimate owner creates a chain of ownership that allows it to control a number of firms, even the ones in which it has no direct ownership. In this pyramid, indirect ownership serves as a means to maintain control over a large group of companies (Bertrand and Mullainathan 2003).[27] In a pyramidal-type structure, the dominant owner is one well-endowed entity, usually a family company though in this study it is the government, through the Ministry of Finance. While GLICs actively employ pyramiding and cross-holdings, it is not for these reasons that such mechanisms are used by individual majority shareholders or families. The GLICs have joint shareholding of a range of publicly listed firms. However, in numerous cases one of the GLICs has majority ownership of a quoted GLC. Block shareholding, including through obscure private firms, of listed enterprises is common among the GLICs, particularly companies in Bursa Malaysia's top 100. Block shareholdings help shield the collectively majority ownership that GLICs have over major quoted companies. In a situation where a strong state, through GLICs, has ownership of listed companies, it is unlikely that private investors or even foreign enterprises will attempt to institute a takeover of these firms.

The owners of Malaysia's leading publicly listed enterprises, predominantly families, have managed to build corporate empires through effective use of holding companies that facilitate interlocking stock ownership of corporate equity. In this system, the holding company need not own a majority of the shares of a publicly listed company to control decision-making in it. A similar system prevails among the GLICs that function as holding companies with control over a number of quoted GLCs. These quoted companies in turn tend to own and control a large number of unlisted enterprises and usually operate as business groups with equity interests in a range of sectors.

Among government enterprises, the Ministry of Finance has control of the seven GLICs, each functioning as huge business groups, acting as a holding company with an equity stake in a large number of publicly listed firms which in turn own a huge volume of quoted and unquoted companies. This pyramid structure accords the Minister of Finance ownership and control over a large segment of Malaysia's corporate sector. The joint and cross-equity holdings within this pyramiding structure provides the shareholder at its apex, the Minister of Finance, enormous voting rights over quoted companies under the seven business groups. Moreover, the Minister is ultimately responsible for all board appointments, further augmenting his control over the companies. The government also employs golden shares, a mechanism it can use to veto decisions by the board of directors or instruct companies to act in a manner it deems necessary.

Ownership accords shareholder voting rights. According to Malaysian law, any person or institution with 5% or more equity ownership is considered a major shareholder and is required to disclose his or her identity.

GLICs, however, individually or collectively have more than 20% ownership of each of the country's leading quoted GLCs. When such large shareholdings are under the control of related institutions, an "insider system" of corporate ownership is said to prevail (Franks and Mayer 1997).[28] An insider system is one where the "corporate sector has controlling interests in itself and in which outside investors, while participating in equity returns through the stock market, are not able to exert much control" (Franks and Mayer 1997: 39).

The insider system can function more effectively when shareholders employ complex control and ownership arrangements designed to give them control, usually in excess of their equity ownership. Through blockholdings by the GLICs and a pyramid system that leads up to the Ministry of Finance, the Minister has enormous influence over the corporate sector. This insider system is further facilitated by directorship ties. Through directors with a link to a common institution or person, a company can also overcome information asymmetry by securing feedback to improve its position in the market (Mizruchi 1996). These ties can take a variety of forms and involve people with differing backgrounds.[29] An influential study by Useem (1984) argued that such closely connected directors serve to promote upper-class cohesion, creating a business elite that can be seen as an "inner circle" which determines how an institution should be run. The functioning of this inner circle is aided by the rise of a new managerial class, or professional elite.[30] In Malaysia, professionals from the private sector have been incorporated into government to serve as directors of the GLICs and the GLCs.[31]

Methodology

The primary objective of this study is to understand the structure of Malaysia's corporate structure as it relates to GLICs. The book provides an inside look at the GLICs, how they operate and the nature of the political and business worlds around which they have been constructed. The GLICs have widespread influence in the corporate sector, either by owning majority or minority equity positions in the largest publicly traded GLCs on Bursa Malaysia. Although the government has been encouraging the GLICs to internationalize themselves by investing actively abroad, particularly in developing economies of Southeast Asia, they derive most of their earning from domestic investments.

This volume reviews the incorporation and development of the seven GLICs, tracing how they have come to secure a huge presence in Malaysia's corporate structure. This historical profile will review the mechanisms the GLICs have employed to obtain ownership and control of the 35 GLCs in the top 100 in 2013. The study will also analyse the control mechanisms available to the GLICs when managing the GLCs. These control mechanisms include public policies, legislation, particularly statutory acts that give power to a majority of GLICs, directorships and investment panels, as well as their ownership of major banks and the media.

The sources for this study include the 2013 annual company reports of these GLICs, where available, and the 35 GLCs. The information about the shareholders and subsidiaries of the 35 GLCs were obtained from the Osiris and Oriana databases as well as the company records filed at the Companies Commission of Malaysia.[32] Further information was obtained from the archives in Malaysia and Singapore, while media reports were secured through searches at the libraries of national newspapers such as *The Star* and *The Edge*, and at the New Straits Times Resource Centre. Based on the voluminous data that was obtained from fieldwork and by producing a network mapping of the ownership patterns of the GLICs and their ties with the 35 quoted companies among the Bursa's top 100 in 2013, this study has been able to trace the extent of the government's corporate influence.

Before analysing this database, employing the concepts of ownership and control, what is first required is an understanding of how Malaysia reached the point where the GLICs have emerged as key actors in the corporate sector. This history of the GLICs is the subject of Chap. 2. In Chap. 3, the GLICs' ownership of the 35 GLCs listed in the top 100 is reviewed, while Chap. 4 analyses how these companies are controlled, ultimately by the Minister of Finance, through various mechanisms. The final chapter outlines the implications of the Minister of Finance's overwhelming control of the corporate sector, in a situation where a strong state exists and oversight institutions have inadequate autonomy to act independently.

Notes

1. Bandar Malaysia, with a gross development value of RM150 billion, is located on a former military airbase, and will serve as the city's integrated transport hub. This project, to run over the next 25 years, entails the construction of a mammoth underground city that will accommodate Mass

Rapid Transit lines and a commuter and express rail link. Some 12 highways will converge in Bandar Malaysia, the gateway for the proposed high-speed rail line between Kuala Lumpur and Singapore (*The Star* 17 June 2016).

2. For a discussion on the gerrymandering and malapportionment of seats that had contributed to BN's victory, see Ostwald (2013). Saravanamuttu (2016) and Gomez (2016) provide a comprehensive discussion of this controversial general election.
3. LTH also loaned 1MDB RM920.8 million (*The Sun Daily* 12 May 2015).
4. By March 2015, KWAP had invested a total of RM1.4 billion in 1MDB and its subsidiaries (*The Star* 19 May 2015).
5. For a copy of the full report by the Department of Justice, see: https://www.justice.gov/archives/opa/page/file/877166/download
6. See the International Monetary Fund's *Financial System Stability Assessment of Malaysia* (28 January 2013).
7. That many Malaysians, including academics, business analysts and policy planners, have little or no knowledge of the GLICs' widespread ownership and control of Malaysia's leading publicly listed enterprises became obvious to us during a public lecture that was delivered on this topic on 21 July 2016 at the University of Malaya.
8. EPF was also linked to 1MDB. However, EPF's direct investment in 1MDB was limited to RM200 million, one that is backed by a government guarantee (*The Edge* 11 June 2015).
9. For the Ministry of Finance's listing of these seven institutions as GLICs, see http://www.treasury.gov.my/index.php/en/contacus/faqs/gic.html
10. Appendix 2.1, in Chap. 2 of this volume which traces the history of the GLICs, provides a comprehensive list of major corporate controversies since Independence in 1957 to 2016.
11. The BN secured only 47.38% of the popular vote, but won 133 of the 222 seats in parliament. See Saravanamuttu (2016) for an in-depth and insightful discussion of this general election.
12. Najib's full speech on his BEE policy is available at http://www.malaysiaedition.net/bumiputera-economic-agenda-pms-speech/
13. The G20 refers to the top 20 publicly listed GLCs. The number of GLCs in the G20 has now been reduced to 17, due to mergers. The G20, comprising the17 quoted companies, will be discussed in further depth later in this study.
14. OECD Investment Policy Reviews: Malaysia 2013, p. 70 (Box 2.3).
15. See Gomez (2016) for an in-depth discussion of the key features of Malaysia's political system as a single dominant state.
16. Case (2009) provides a judicious analysis of the concept of an electoral authoritarian state and why its features conform to the nature of Malaysian politics.

17. Crouch's (1992) analysis was based on his assessment of Malaysian politics following restrictions on democratic space in the country, an outcome of a major feud in UMNO in 1987. See Shamsul (1988) for an in-depth assessment of this feud, which he referred to as a "battle royal".
18. Zakaria (1989) was the first academic to refer to the political system as one that functioned in a manner that was neither democratic nor authoritarian.
19. We are aware that other public institutions can function in this form, such as the Social Security Organization (SOCSO). This organization, created in 1971 to ensure the well-being of low income earners, operates two social security schemes with funds generated from monthly deductions from employers and employees (see http://www.perkeso.gov.my).
20. This definition is provided by the Ministry of Finance. See http://www.treasury.gov.my/index.php/en/contacus/faqs/gic.html
21. This point was made by the Putrajaya Committee on GLC High Performance, the government body formed in 2005 to implement the GLC Transformation Programme. See http://www.pcg.gov.my/FAQ.asp
22. OECD Investment Policy Reviews: Malaysia 2013, p. 70 (Box 2.3).
23. World Bank's Report on the Observance of Standards and Codes.
24. For a more in-depth discussion of the merits and de-merits of the holding company structure in the Malaysian context, see Lim (1981), Sieh-Lee (1982) and Gomez (1990).
25. Another source of money for a publicly listed company is foreign funds. For example, the enormous inflow of foreign funds as portfolio investments (FPI) and loans during the 1990s contributed appreciably to an increase in market capitalization of quoted stock, including that of the GLCs. Well-connected firms attracted substantial FPI, suggesting that foreign investors wanted to secure quick capital gains from their investments. Gomez and Jomo (1997) review the issue of FPI and its role in expanding the size of the domestic stock market in the 1990s.
26. The literature in the discipline of business define such groups in terms of their ownership and control by families, not the state. In fact, the literature on ownership and control by GLCs is extremely scant in spite of the growing number of countries that employ state-owned enterprises (SOEs). In definitions of privately owned business groups, Ghemawat and Khanna (1998: 35), for example, see them as "an organizational form characterized by diversification across a wide range of businesses, partial financial interlocks among them, and, in many cases, familial control", ideas that are applicable in an analysis of GLCs that function in this manner.
27. For a review of the pyramiding structure employed by huge business groups in Europe and Asia, see La Porta et al. (1999), Claessens, Djankov and Lang (2000) and Faccio and Lang (2002).

28. France and Germany have this system, also referred to as a "bank-based" system, characterized by a small quoted sector where shareholdings are not as dispersed as in the USA and the UK which have large stock exchanges and are seen as operating under a "market-based" system (Franks and Mayer 1997). In Germany and France, a number of companies have shareholders who have 25% equity or more, with these shareholdings held by families or other corporations (ibid.).
29. A core criticism of the use of interlocking or multiple directorates is that a person over-commits himself by sitting on the boards of numerous companies. Since directors need to monitor how managers run a company, a person with multiple directorships will inevitably not be able to devote full attention to his responsibilities, thereby undermining the trust of shareholders, particularly minority investors (Ferris et al. 2003). For a similar reason, politicians, particularly elected representatives, should not serve as directors of GLICs and GLCs.
30. James Burnham (1941) was the first to use the concept of the "managerial class", though this was with reference to emergence of a professional white collar segment of society.
31. Darity (1986) offers an insightful account of the professional managerial class that emerged in post-World War II United States through F.D. Roosevelt's New Deal. Darity notes, as we do here, the link between an interventionist state and the new managerial elite.
32. The Osiris and Oriana databases, a service run by Bureau Van Dijk, provide information about publicly listed and private limited companies.

CHAPTER 2

History of GLICs

The Minister of Finance Incorporated (MoF Inc.)

James Puthucheary's (1960) pioneering study of ownership and control of major firms in the 1950s revealed the overwhelming dominance that foreign enterprises had secured over the Malaysian economy. Puthucheary noted the ubiquitous presence of Chinese enterprises in rural and urban areas but correctly surmised that they had little influence in the economy and rarely posed a threat to the bigger, better-financed and politically favoured British firms. With his focus on foreign and Chinese enterprises, Puthucheary drew little attention to the presence of companies owned by the post-colonial government.

At independence in 1957, GLIC investments in the economy were small, mainly in government debt securities and companies in the trading, plantations and mining sectors. The government adopted a laissez-faire style of economic management but recognized the need to develop Malay-owned businesses to help this ethnic group secure a presence in the corporate sector. Moreover, the magnitude of rural Malay poverty necessitated some measure of government intervention in the economy. The British had hampered Malay involvement in key sectors of the economy, a core reason why this ethnic group had little presence in the corporate sector. Malays were compelled by the British to remain in rural economic sectors, particularly in rice and fish production. When Malay peasants ventured into rubber production, the British blocked their efforts through strict imposition of restrictive land cultivation regulations.[1] The colonial

E.T. Gomez et al., *Minister of Finance Incorporated*,
DOI 10.1007/978-981-10-4897-5_2

government feared Malay involvement in lucrative sectors of the economy because, by 1938, almost 93% of British capital in Malaya was in plantations and mines (Junid 1980: 18). The Chinese were not considered a threat as the British viewed them as mere sojourners in Malaya, only there to make money before returning home (Heng 1992).

To aid the expansion of Malay-owned enterprises, the Land Development Ordinance was enacted in 1956, paving the way for the creation of the Federal Land Development Authority (FELDA), a major scheme to open, develop and distribute land to the poor as a means to eradicate poverty. These parcels of land around the peninsula were developed as rubber and palm oil plantations, providing the settlers a decent livelihood. By the early 1970s, around 250,000 ha of land had been opened up in about 150 FELDA schemes (Young et al. 1980: 269).

But there were concerns among Malay leaders that the government policies to aid Bumiputera participation in business were far too inadequate. In 1965, when a Bumiputera Economic Congress was convened, then Prime Minister Tunku Abdul Rahman was critiqued for not having done enough for the Malays. A second Bumiputera Economic Congress was held in 1968. At these congresses, the government was urged to establish public enterprises and statutory bodies to accumulate wealth on behalf of the Bumiputeras. Another call was for Bumiputeras to be allotted an equity interest in new firms or when companies were expanding their capital base. These resolutions were enforced by the government and the Ministry of Trade and Industry was used to hold corporate equity on behalf of the Bumiputeras (Horii 1991: 290–291).

Majlis Amanah Rakyat (MARA, or Council of Trust for Indigenous People), Bank Bumiputra and Perbadanan Nasional (Pernas, or National Corporation) were major public enterprises that emerged in response to the congresses. MARA was authorized in 1966 to establish and manage new industrial enterprises for later transfer to the Malays (Gale 1981). MARA was originally known as the Rural and Industrial Development Authority (RIDA), established in 1950 to enhance Malay participation in business, the first concerted attempt to develop entrepreneurs from among members of this ethnic group by providing them with access to credit facilities and business training. By 1954, however, although RIDA had been converted into a public corporation and given enlarged responsibilities and funds, its efforts at promoting Malay businesses had not been successful (Golay et al. 1969: 366).[2]

In 1965, Bank Bumiputra was incorporated to provide Malays an avenue to obtain credit to develop start-ups. Pernas, a trust agency, was created in 1969 and, flush with funds from the government, was used to acquire leading foreign-owned publicly listed companies such as London Tin (now Malaysian Mining Corporation), the industrial-based Goodyear (M) Bhd and the plantations-based Sime Darby Bhd, Island & Peninsular Bhd and Highlands & Lowlands Bhd (Gale 1981). Bank Pertanian was established in 1969 to support the planting of paddy in the then extremely under-developed states of Kedah and Perlis. The Urban Development Authority (UDA) was formed in 1971 to increase Malay property ownership, though it also provides credit assistance to farmers. Other public enterprises established to help the Malays, particularly those in rural areas, were the Federal Agriculture Marketing Authority (FAMA), the Federal Land Consolidation and Rehabilitation Authority (FELCRA) and the Rubber Industry Smallholders Development Authority (RISDA). Alongside these federal institutions were the State Economic Development Corporations (SEDCs), established in almost all states in the federation to promote Malay welfare. The key institution that played a major role in developing these institutions during this period was the Minister of Finance Incorporated (MoF Inc.), as it owned a controlling interest in numerous developmental and investment trust-based agencies such as Pernas and UDA.[3]

MoF Inc., the most significant though least well known of the GLICs, was established through the Minister of Finance (Incorporated) Act 1957. The Government Investment Companies Division (GIC) within the Ministry of Finance was created to administer the companies owned by the British colonial government. These companies were channelled to MoF Inc., allowing it to function as the government's investment arm and holding company. This Act allowed the Minister of Finance to be represented by a corporate body, MoF Inc. Through MoF Inc., the ministry had the authority to enter into business contracts, acquire companies and manage tangible and intangible assets. This statutory body can be sued and sue other parties and can use a stamp bearing the inscription "Minister of Finance" in the absence of its own corporate seal. The Act also empowers the minister to sign all related documents on behalf of MoF Inc.[4]

By the early 2010s, MoF Inc. had direct majority shareholding of 63 enterprises, owned ordinary shares in private companies and had a golden share in a number of firms. This GLIC had, in total, an interest in 103 companies (see Table 2.1). The golden share grants MoF Inc. special rights

Table 2.1 MoF Inc.—related companies, 2016

Companies in which MoF Inc. has a golden share

#	*Company*	*Business activities*
1.	Aerospace Technology System Corporation Sdn Bhd	Aircraft maintenance
2.	Bintulu Port Holdings Bhd	Port management
3.	Bintulu Port Sdn Bhd	Port operator and services
4.	Boustead Naval Shipyard Sdn Bhd	Shipbuilding and maintenance
5.	Commerce Dot Com Sdn Bhd	E-commerce service provider
6.	Felda Global Ventures Holdings Bhd	Agribusiness
7.	FELDA Holdings Bhd	Agribusiness
8.	HICOM Holdings Bhd	Construction, automotive manufacturing
9.	Johor Port Bhd	Port operator and engineering equipment
10.	Konsortium Pelabuhan Kemaman Sdn Bhd	Port operator and services
11.	Kuantan Port Consortium Sdn Bhd	Port operator and services
12.	Malaysia Airport (Sepang) Sdn Bhd	Airport operator and services
13.	Malaysia Airport Holdings Bhd	Airport operator and services
14.	Malaysia Airports Sdn Bhd	Airport operator and services
15.	Malaysian Airline System Bhd	Airlines carrier
16.	Malaysian Maritime Academy Sdn Bhd	Shipping logistic services
17.	MARDEC Bhd	Managerial and technical consultancy services, rubber processing, trading and the manufacturing of value-added rubber and polymer products
18.	Medical Online Sdn Bhd	Healthcare multimedia services
19.	MISC Bhd	Shipping logistic services
20.	National Aerospace & Defence Industries (NADI)	Aviation maintenance, repair and overhaul, engines modifications and upgrades, aerospace parts manufacturing, avionics services and aviation services
21.	National Feedlot Corporation Sdn Bhd	Integrated livestock farming and production
22.	Northport (Malaysia) Bhd	Port operator and services
23.	Padiberas Nasional Bhd (Bernas)	Procurement and processing of paddy
24.	PDX.Com Sdn Bhd	Electronic government services
25.	Pelabuhan Tanjung Pelepas Sdn Bhd	Port operator and services
26.	Penang Port Sdn Bhd	Port operator and services
27.	Pos Malaysia Bhd	Postal delivery and related service
28.	Projek Lebuhraya Usahasama Bhd	Expressway operation services
29.	Sabah Electricity Sdn Bhd	Sabah state electrical utility

(*continued*)

Table 2.1 (continued)

Companies in which MoF Inc. has a golden share

#	Company	Business activities
30.	Senai Airport Terminal Services Sdn Bhd	Airport operator and services
31.	Syarikat Bekalan Air Selangor Sdn Bhd (Syabas)	Water Utility
32.	Telekom (M) Bhd	Telecommunication utility
33.	Tenaga Nasional Bhd	Electric utility
34.	Westports (M) Bhd	Port operator and services

Companies in which MoF Inc. holds direct majority shareholding

#	Company	Business activities
Commercial		
1.	1Malaysia Development Bhd (1MDB)	Strategic development
2.	Amanah Raya Bhd (ARB)	Trusteeship services
3.	Astronautic Technology (M) Sdn Bhd (ATSB)	Space and satellites technology services
4.	Cradle Fund Sdn Bhd	Early stage business investment
5.	Cyberview Sdn Bhd	Technology hub enabler
6.	FELCRA Bhd	Executing agency for agricultural development programmes
7.	Inno Bio Ventures Sdn Bhd (IBV)	Biopharmaceutical development and services
8.	Institut Terjemahan Dan Buku Malaysia Bhd (ITBM)	Translation services and book publisher
9.	Jambatan Kedua Sdn Bhd (JKSB)	Construction
10.	Khazanah Nasional Bhd	Sovereign wealth fund
11.	Kumpulan Modal Perdana Sdn Bhd (KMP)	Venture capitalist
12.	Malaysia Debt Ventures Bhd (MDV)	Technology financier
13.	Malaysia Kuwaiti Investment Corporation Sdn Bhd (MKIC)	Investment holding company in plantations and property
14.	Malaysian Venture Capital Management Bhd (MAVCAP)	ICT Venture capitalist
15.	MyCreative Ventures Sdn Bhd	Investment arm in creative industry
16.	Perbadanan Nasional Bhd (PNS, formerly Pernas)	Franchise industry development
17.	Petroliam Nasional Bhd (Petronas)	Oil and gas
18.	Prokhas Sdn Bhd	Financial and strategic advisory services

(*continued*)

Table 2.1 (continued)

Companies in which MoF Inc. holds direct majority shareholding		
#	*Company*	*Business activities*
19.	Rangkaian Hotel Seri Malaysia Sdn Bhd	Hospitality services
20.	Sarawak Hidro Sdn Bhd	Bakun Hydroelectric Project management
21.	Sepang International Circuit Sdn Bhd (SIC)	Motor racing facility operator and services
22.	SRC International Sdn Bhd	Renewable energy and resources management
23.	Technology Park Malaysia Corporation Sdn Bhd (TPM)	Provider of advanced infrastructure and services
24.	UDA Holdings Bhd	Property development
Non-Commercial Enterprises		
25.	Halal Industry Development Corporation Sdn Bhd (HDC)	Coordinates development of the halal industry
26.	IJN Holdings Sdn Bhd	Centre for cardiac health services
27.	Indah Water Konsortium Sdn Bhd (IWK)	Sewerage services
28.	JKP Sdn Bhd	Real estate developer
29.	Keretapi Tanah Melayu Bhd (KTMB)	Railway operator and management services
30.	Malaysian Biotechnology Corporation Sdn Bhd	Biotechnology support services
31.	Mass Rapid Transit Corporation Sdn Bhd (MRT)	MRT project developer and asset owner
32.	MIMOS Bhd	ICT technology provider
33.	Multimedia Development Corporation Sdn Bhd (MDeC)	ICT industry development and services
34.	Pembinaan BLT Sdn Bhd (PBLT)	Royal Malaysian Police quarters and facilities development
35.	Pengurusan Aset Air Bhd (PAAB)	Utility
36.	SIRIM Bhd	Water asset management
37.	Syarikat Perumahan Negara Bhd (SPNB)	Affordable homes developer
38.	Syarikat Prasarana Negara Bhd	Public transportation service
39.	MyHsr Corporation Sdn Bhd	High speed rail project development and promotion

(*continued*)

Table 2.1 (continued)

Companies in which MoF Inc. holds direct majority shareholding		
#	*Company*	*Business activities*
Development Financial Institutions (DFIs)		
40.	Bank Pembangunan Malaysia Bhd	Financial services
41.	Bank Pertanian Malaysia Bhd (Agrobank)	
42.	Export-Import Bank of Malaysia Bhd (Exim Bank)	
43.	Small Medium Enterprise Development Bank Malaysia Bhd (SME Bank)	
Special Purpose Vehicles (SPVs)		
44.	1Malaysia Sukuk Global Bhd	
45.	AES Solution Sdn Bhd	
46.	Aset Tanah Nasional Bhd	
47.	DanaInfra Nasional Bhd	
48.	GovCo Holdings Bhd	
49.	KL International Airport Bhd (KLIAB)	
50.	Malaysia Development Holding Sdn Bhd	
51.	Malaysia Sovereign Sukuk Sdn Bhd	
52.	Pembinaan PFI Sdn Bhd	
53.	Pengurusan Danaharta Nasional Bhd	
54.	Perwaja Terengganu Sdn Bhd	
55.	Piramid Pertama Sdn Bhd	
56.	Pyrotechnical Managers Holdings Sdn Bhd	
57.	SDE Solutions Sdn Bhd	
58.	Syarikat Jaminan Kredit Perumahan Bhd	
59.	Syarikat Jaminan Pembiayaan Perniagaan Bhd	
60.	Syarikat Tanah & Harta Sdn Bhd	
61.	Turus Pesawat Sdn Bhd	
62.	Wakala Global Sukuk Bhd	

(*continued*)

Table 2.1 (continued)

MoF Inc. shares in private companies			
#	*Company*	*% of shares*	
1.	Asean Potash Mining Public Co Ltd	9.61	Potash fertilizer manufacturer
2.	Danajamin Nasional Bhd	50.00	Financial guarantor
3.	International Rubber Development Consortium Ltd (IRCO)	22.22	Rubber industry policy regulator and marketing (Thailand, Indonesia, Malaysia)
4.	KUB Malaysia Bhd	22.55	Investment holding
5.	Syarikat Perumahan Pegawai Kerajaan Sdn Bhd	30.00	Real estate development services
6.	Permodalan Nasional Berhad	1 share	Investment vehicle

Source: Ministry of Finance: http://www.treasury.gov.my/index.php/en/contacus/faqs/gic.html

in the management of these companies. MoF Inc. also had an interest in about two dozen enterprises that function as development financial institutions (DFIs) which include the Small Medium Enterprise Development Bank (SME Bank), Agrobank and Export-Import (EXIM) Bank. DFIs include Islamic-based institutions such as Malaysia Sovereign Sukuk and 1Malaysia Sukuk Global and the Pengurusan Danaharta Nasional, created by the government following the 1997 Asian currency crisis to acquire non-performing loans from financial institutions and manage them. Table 2.1 provides a full list of companies under the control of MoF Inc. in 2016.

MoF Inc. has a golden share in companies that are in strategic areas such as logistics (airports and seaports), utilities and communications (Telekom Malaysia, Tenaga Nasional, Pos Malaysia and Sabah Electricity), agriculture and food suppliers (Bernas and National Feedlot Corporation) and healthcare, all sectors where the government has to protect national security and societal well-being. MoF Inc.'s direct majority interest is in a variety of companies (see Table 2.2). The first type, industry enablers, includes Cradle Fund, Inno Bio Ventures, MAVCAP, MyCreative Ventures, Agrobank and Cyberview. The second type is national investor companies which include the GLICs, Khazanah and PNB, as well as Petronas, Pernas, 1MDB, UDA Holdings and FELCRA. Khazanah, PNB, Petronas and Pernas have been used to acquire a number of firms. The third type of company that MoF Inc. has a stake in are corporatized agencies such as SIRIM, BiotechCorp and MDeC.

Table 2.2 Types of companies owned by MoF Inc.

Type	*Examples*	*Remarks*
Strategic Sectors	Tenaga Nasional Telekom Malaysia Bernas Pos Malaysia	Ownership of monopolies in key public services
Industry Enablers	Cradle Fund Inno Bio Ventures MAVCAP MyCreative Ventures Cyberview SIRIM BioCorp MDec Agrobank Bank Pembangunan	Private companies that serve to promote new industries (through specialized financing schemes) and support innovation in key sectors
National Investors	Khazanah PNB Petronas Pernas 1MDB FELCRA UDA Holdings	Private companies that invest in the economy with the aim of enhancing national wealth
SPVs	Danaharta Danainfra GovCo	Special purpose vehicles to help restructure companies and invest in specific government policies
Bond Issuers	1Malaysia Sukuk Global Malaysia Development Holdings	Bond issuing enterprises to raise financing for specific government objectives

The fourth type, listed as special purpose vehicles (SPVs), comprises corporations formed to execute specific projects that include corporate restructuring, for example, Danaharta, Danainfra and GovCo, and promote infrastructure development, such as MRT Corp and MyHSR Corp. They function primarily to implement government policies. The fifth type is bond-issuing companies such as 1Malaysia Sukuk Global, Malaysia Development Holding, Malaysia Sovereign Sukuk, Turus Pesawat and Wakala Global Sukuk. The funds from these bonds are used to finance government programmes.

Tables 2.1 and 2.2 indicate MoF Inc.'s important role in the development of Malaysia's economy, infrastructure and corporate sector. It owns companies specifically commissioned to nurture new technologies, support start-ups and offer financial services in niche areas, in rural industries, in Islamic-based industries and in the export sector. MoF Inc. deals with private sector inefficiencies through actions including taking over debt-ridden, ailing enterprises. Other types of company that support MoF Inc.'s role in developing the economy are the industry enablers, national investors and credit agencies.

Interestingly, MoF Inc. has ownership of companies that have been involved in corporate controversies. It owns a huge interest in a cooperative that was incorporated by UMNO, Koperasi Usaha Bersatu (KUB),[5] and wholly owns 1Malaysia Development Bhd (1MDB), which came to be embroiled in a major controversy in 2015, plagued as it was with huge debts. MoF Inc. has a golden share in food-based National Feedlot Corp, another company that was embroiled in a major scandal.

The Pension and Savings Funds

Of the seven GLICs, the Kumpulan Wang Persaraan Diperbadankan (KWAP) has the longest history, one that can be traced to a civil sector-based pension scheme that was introduced in 1875, the first of its sort in the country. In 1928, a consolidated pension scheme was launched for civil servants,[6] which eventually evolved into the Pensions Ordinance 1951, the predecessor to the current nationwide civil service pension scheme (Mohd. Saidatulakmal 2012: 121–122).[7] From 1957, the public pension was funded directly by the government and managed by the Pensions Department of the Jabatan Perkhidmatan Awam (JPA, or Public Service Department). Public pension remained under this department in the JPA until 2015, when KWAP took full responsibility for it.

In 1991, the Pensions Trust Fund Act was promulgated to create a reserve to financially assist the government in servicing its pension responsibilities. The Pensions Trust Fund, established through the act, fell under the responsibility of the Accountant General's office, situated in the Ministry of Finance.[8] A RM500 million grant was launched for this fund that was to function as a pure investment agency (*Malaysian Business* 1 September 2009). A Pensions Trust Fund council and an investment panel were created to administer the fund and their members were appointed by the Minister of Finance. By 2007, the fund size had grown to RM48 billion (*The Star* 21 December 2013).

Since the government had been registering consecutive fiscal deficits since 1997, it began to worry that it would not be able to service its huge and increasing pension liability.[9] To address this matter, the Pensions Trust

Fund was reconstituted as KWAP, or the Retirement Fund Incorporated, through the Retirement Fund Act 2007. All the powers, functions, activities, assets and liabilities of the Pensions Trust Fund were taken over by KWAP. Under this scheme, the federal government contributes 5% of the total annual budgeted emolument while statutory bodies, local authorities and agencies contribute 17.5% of their employees' salaries into KWAP.[10]

This reconstituted fund is no longer under the management of the Accountant General, but it remains under the jurisdiction of the Minister of Finance. The council was replaced by a board of directors while the investment panel remained. Members of both bodies were still appointed by the Minister of Finance. In effect, this meant that responsibility for the financing of the public pension was transferred from a bureaucrat, the Director General of JPA, and then the Accountant General, to a politician, the Minister of Finance, albeit a member of the government who is accountable to the Prime Minister and the Cabinet.

Following the incorporation of KWAP, which had its own investment panel and newly defined board of directors, this institution could now function like a GLIC. By 2013, KWAP had a fund size of RM100 billion and 0.16 million members.[11] KWAP owned an equity interest in about 90 publicly listed companies (*The Star* 21 December 2013).[12] In 2015, following an amendment to one clause in its Act, KWAP was allowed to function as a full-fledged pension fund. Another amendment in the Act that year resulted in Bank Negara, the central bank, removing its representation from KWAP's board. One justification for this was that an oversight institution such as the central bank should not have a representative on the board of pension funds like KWAP as it could lead to conflict-of-interest situations (*The Star* 11 April 2015).

While KWAP was established specifically to serve public-sector staff, the Employees Provident Fund (EPF), established via the Employees Provident Fund Ordinance 1951, was to function as a retirement savings fund that catered to workers from the private sector,[13] as well as civil servants who preferred this scheme instead of a public pension. Unlike KWAP, EPF's defined contribution scheme entails both the employer and employee having to contribute to its fund. The rate of contribution was originally set at 5% each for employers and employees. In 1975, the contribution rates were increased and, by 1995, the rate stood at 11 and 12% of an employee's base remuneration for employees and employers respectively (Doraisamy 2009: 203). Since August 1998, foreign workers have been included in this scheme (Mohd. Saidatulakmal 2012: 122).

EPF grew rapidly to become an extremely financially well-endowed savings institution. Within a year of its incorporation, EPF had half a million contributing members with funds totalling RM516.6 million. By 1994, its membership had increased to 7.2 million, with a fund size of RM7.25 billion. In 2013, EPF had 13.92 million members and a fund size of RM593.45 billion.[14] By 2016, EPF was reputedly the world's seventh-largest pension fund with assets amounting to about RM680 billion (*The Star* 25 May 2016; *Asia Asset Management* 17 January 2017).

Although the EPF was originally meant to meet the retirement financial requirements of its members, from 1968 it introduced its first partial withdrawal scheme. This scheme allowed members to withdraw up to one-third of their accumulated savings at the age of 50 to purchase a house or prepare for retirement. From 1994, withdrawals could be made for the purchase of property and for medical expenses (Sallehuddin 1995).

Like KWAP, when EPF was established, its funds were invested primarily—about 80%—in government securities which were employed for development projects (Ang 2008: 59). While EPF was required to invest more than 70% of it in government securities, this rule was relaxed in the 1990s. From the mid-1980s, EPF began increasingly investing in money markets and company equity, following the introduction of privatization and due to the extremely bullish trends of the domestic stock market (Sallehuddin 1995: 24–26). EPF invests in a large number of quoted and private companies, evidently functioning primarily as an investor. Since EPF has to declare high dividends to its members, it must invest in profit-registering enterprises. EPF is the biggest trader on the Bursa Malaysia as it needs to lock in profits before it can declare its annual dividends. From 1993, EPF entered joint-ventures and began financing projects, in line with privatization. In 1994, EPF was given government approval to invest abroad, though permission had to be obtained from the Minister of Finance for overseas investments (*The Star* 26 October 1994).

After the global financial crisis in 2008, which led to a recession in Malaysia, EPF focused far more on private equities, property and infrastructure ventures and pursued investments abroad, also part of the government's internationalization drive of its GLICs. By 2016, EPF's assets were in four main areas: government and corporate bonds, equities, money market instruments and assets that hedge against inflation (*The Star* 28 May 2016). Among its assets, EPF had huge direct stakes in major expressways such as the Projek Lebuhraya Utara Selatan (PLUS) Highway, Damansara Ulu Kelang Expressway (DUKE), Cheras-Kajang Highway and New North

Klang Straits Bypassway.[15] Toll-based highways guarantee consistent cash flow. When EPF began investing abroad more aggressively after 2008, its overseas assets base grew from 10% to 25% of all assets. These investments included joint-ventures with Goodman Group in Australia,[16] SP Setia and Sime Darby in the United Kingdom and GuocoLand Ltd. in Singapore, a company controlled by Quek Leng Chan, the Malaysian magnate who owns the well-diversified Hong Leong group. EPF has apparently created joint-venture ties abroad with privately owned Chinese companies of major repute.

The third pension fund, Lembaga Tabung Angkatan Tentera (LTAT, or Armed Forces Fund Board), is a retirement savings fund established in 1972 and financed through direct collections from its members, a process allowed for by an Act of Parliament introduced in 1973 (Norma et al. 2014). LTAT's primary objective is to provide retirement and other benefits to members of the armed forces who are compulsory contributors. The fund also enables officers and members of the volunteer forces in the service to participate in a savings scheme (Norma et al. 2014). In 1973, LTAT made it compulsory for all military personnel below the rank of commissioned officers, including warrant officers, non-commissioned officers and privates in the armed forces, to become LTAT contributors (Mohd. Saidatulakmal 2012: 126).[17]

The rate of a member's contribution to the fund is 10% of his or her monthly salary, with an additional 15% contribution from the government (Mohd. Saidatulakmal 2012: 126). The benefits accruing to LTAT members include a death and disablement scheme, where a lump sum compensation is made to a contributor if he is discharged due to illness or to his next-of-kin if he dies in service. Contributors can withdraw up to 40% of their savings to purchase a house. LTAT is required to invest not less than 70% of its funds in trustee investments (*Astro Awani* 30 March 2016). LTAT's fund size in 2013 was RM8.3 billion.

By 1990, LTAT had a majority interest in Boustead Holdings and Affin Holdings. In 2011, LTAT acquired, through Boustead, Malaysia's largest integrated local healthcare company and generic pharmaceuticals manufacturer Pharmaniaga.[18] Almost all other companies in the LTAT group are private enterprises in a diverse range of sectors such as plantations, communications and biotechnology. Thus, LTAT has no sectoral focus and it has numerous joint ownerships.[19]

Lembaga Tabung Haji (LTH, or Pilgrims Fund Board) is a special-purpose savings fund financed by direct collections from the public.

LTH's roots can be traced to two bodies responsible for the administration of pilgrimage matters, the Perbadanan Wang Simpanan Bakal-Bakal Haji (Prospective Pilgrims Fund Corporation) and the Pejabat Urusan Hal Ehwal Haji (Pilgrimage Affairs Management), the latter based in the state of Penang. The Prospective Pilgrims Fund Corporation was formed in 1962, an outcome of a working paper prepared in 1959 by a professor of economics, Ungku Aziz, based at the University of Malaya, entitled "Plan to Improve the Economy of Prospective Pilgrims". Ungku Aziz disclosed that a large number of Malay-Muslim small-scale low income farmers could not save sufficient funds for the pilgrimage. They had to resort to selling their land and livestock to raise funds to perform the hajj. These two bodies merged in 1969 to form Lembaga Urusan dan Tabung Haji (Pilgrims Management and Fund Board) through the Lembaga Urusan dan Tabung Haji Act 1969 (Omar et al. 2013). It was Malaysia's first Islamic financial institution. Through LTH, the government subsidizes the costs incurred for the pilgrimage. In 2016, the government absorbed about RM9,000 per person, keeping the cost borne by each pilgrim for the hajj to about RM10,000.

LTH's primary objective of strengthening the economy of Muslims in Malaysia was to be achieved by channelling funds principally to Islamic-permissible investments. In its early years, LTH invested mainly in the agriculture sector through its subsidiary, Syarikat Perbadanan Ladang-Ladang Tabung Haji Sdn Bhd (Mahfuz 1977). From the 1980s, its investment portfolio diversified, with an involvement in manufacturing, housing and agriculture. The introduction of the Tabung Haji Act 1995 was to diversify this GLIC's scope and functions. By 2013, LTH's fund size stood at about RM45.7 billion, with 8.3 million members.[20] Twenty percent of LTH's portfolio is in property investments, while equity investments comprise 50% (*Astro Awani* 31 March 2016). LTH also has property investments in Saudi Arabia and the United Kingdom.

LTH's business model is more interesting than those of the other GLICs because it is clearly attempting to create its own brand. Its core enterprises bear Tabung Haji's acronym, TH. The likely reason for LTH's aggressive strategy of entering numerous sectors is due to the rising popularity of Shariah-compliance in businesses in Malaysia. By utilizing its own brand when introducing Shariah-compliant products and services across many industries, it can secure a large clientele from among the Muslim-majority population. Internationalization of LTH is also a sensible strategy given the potential market of the large Muslim population abroad.[21]

LTH's constant access to funds is possible because this GLIC is in charge of hajj pilgrimage services in Malaysia. LTH is solely responsible for vetting and approving visa applications to enter Saudi Arabia. Moreover, all prospective Muslim pilgrims must create and deposit money in a Tabung Haji account to be eligible to perform the pilgrimage.

However, LTH's history is riddled with controversies. One prominent government leader, Nor Mohamed Yakcop, recounts in his memoirs how, in his capacity as economic advisor to the Prime Minister, he informed Mahathir Mohamad of LTH's serious financial problems following the 1997 currency crisis (Nor Mohamed 2016: xviii). In 2001, LTH was in the news over reports of fraudulent withdrawals amounting to RM9 million (Wong 2011: 413). In October 2001, when Mohd Bakke Salleh, a professional from the corporate sector, was appointed CEO of LTH to turnaround the GLIC, he noted that "as a first step to restore confidence, the Government formed an independent investment panel to review and monitor all investment proposals and projects" (quoted in Wong 2011: 414–415). Another corporate figure, Syed Anwar Jamalullail, was incorporated to chair this panel. A consultancy firm, PricewaterhouseCoopers, was appointed to advise on the restructuring of LTH. A key recommendation was that proposals approved by the investment panel could be overturned by the board of directors. However, the board could not approve proposals that were rejected by investment panel (Wong 2016: 415).[22] One major revamp was the public listing of the GLIC's plantations, a mechanism to ensure, according to Bakke, that "it would be professionally managed while Tabung Haji would be able to focus on its principle activities, which is serving the needs of the pilgrims" (quoted in Wong 2011: 415). Following these reforms, LTH's financial performance improved, with revenue increasing from RM109 million in 2001 to RM406.7 million in 2006, while the number of its depositors increased from 4.5 million to 5.2 million over the same period (Nor Mohamed 2016: 60). Syed Anwar served LTH for six years, while Bakke left the GLIC in November 2005 to take charge of a GLC, Sime Darby (Wong 2011: 415–416).

These pension and special purpose savings funds were created with the intention of providing optimal returns to their shareholders. In the immediate post-colonial period, their investments were small and until 1969, while the government had a laissez-faire market approach, they had little ownership of private businesses. It was from the 1970s that these GLICs began acquiring domestic equities and played the dual role of being pension funds and investment holding arms of the government, controlled ultimately by the Minister of Finance.[23]

Introducing the NEP (1970–1981): Creation of PNB

There were only 23 public enterprises in 1957 and by the late 1960s, though more had been created, these agencies had managed to acquire only about 2% of Malaysia's total corporate equity. Evidently, little had been achieved in terms of equitable distribution of corporate wealth among all communities. Two decades after Puthucheary's work, Lim Mah Hui's (1981) analysis of the top 100 quoted firms during the 1970s revealed that the corporate sector had undergone little structural change. A substantial degree of interlocking stock ownership through business groups prevailed, indicating that wealth remained concentrated in the hands of large foreign corporations and a few Chinese family-owned firms.

When the riots of 1969 occurred, this conflagration was attributed to wealth and social inequities that had not been redressed since independence. The government responded with the promulgation of the affirmative action-based New Economic Policy (NEP) in 1971. The NEP was a 20-year programme to redistribute wealth along ethnic lines through extensive government intervention in the economy. Public enterprises and trust agencies were entrusted to accumulate corporate equity on behalf of the Bumiputeras; these institutions were later renamed GLICs and GLCs.

The most important enterprise created during the two NEP decades was Permodalan Nasional Bhd (PNB), controlled by the Yayasan Pelaburan Bumiputera (YPB, or Bumiputera Investment Foundation) that was founded in 1978 by Prime Minister Hussein Onn. Very little is known about YPB and how it functions. Mahathir (2011: 466–476), who replaced Hussein as Prime Minister, provides important insights into why YPB was established. The government's growing concern by the mid-1970s was that the Bumiputeras were selling off the shares parcelled out to them under the NEP, primarily during the initial public offerings (IPOs) of companies seeking listing on the stock exchange. To deal with this problem, Mahathir proposed to Ismail Mohamed Ali, his brother-in-law who was serving as the Governor of Bank Negara, the central bank, the idea of employing the then novel method of unit trusts. Ismail proposed a "complex, three tier arrangement" that "practically guaranteed the investor would never lose money" (Mahathir 2011: 471). In this structure, YPB was established and given RM200 million to incorporate PNB which would use the funds to acquire shares that were transferred to a unit trust called Amanah Saham Nasional (ASN) and managed by Amanah Saham Nasional Bhd (ASNB). Bumiputeras could acquire ASN units, each costing RM1, as well as sell them back but at the same price. Another merit of this system was that the government effectively ensured that the acquired equity remained under its control. The RM1 units offered by ASNB further ensured wider dispersion of share ownership among Bumiputeras. PNB, as an investment house and fund manager, was to be professionally managed and dividends declared from funds generated through these investments were to be channelled back to the ASN unit trust holders (Mahathir 2011: 470–471).

When YPB was established, it was led by a board of trustees headed by the Prime Minister. YPB, apart from overseeing PNB, had another important goal: it served to develop opportunities for Bumiputera professionals to participate in creating and managing wealth (Ooi 2009: 253; Zainal 1991: 370). YPB has oversight of Perbadanan Usahawan Nasional Bhd (PUNB), established in 1991 to increase the quantity and enhance the quality of Bumiputera entrepreneurs.[24]

When PNB was incorporated in 1979, it took the form of a limited company. When launched in April 1981, PNB transitioned into an investment trust business, though initially it was particularly active in the acquisition of foreign-owned firms in Malaysia. PNB rapidly increased its stockholdings due to its ability to obtain interest-free and non-collateral loans through YPB (Salleh and Meyanathan 1993: 22).

PNB, which has MoF Inc. as a shareholder with one controlling share, benefited immediately when 13 prime assets owned by Pernas were transferred to it. Mahathir (2011: 472) also states that the Ministry of Trade and Industry "allocated more than RM2.5 billion worth of shares to PNB", though it is not certain when this happened. What is clear is that PNB began operations by taking over many of the assets owned by Pernas and various other statutory bodies, at cost—a factor that contributed to its rapid growth (*The Star* 7 September 1988).[25] Pernas' most important listed enterprises that were channelled to PNB were Sime Darby and Malaysia Mining Corporation Bhd (MMC). Later, other government-owned institutions such as MARA, UDA and some SEDCs were similarly compelled to transfer important assets to PNB. Major financial institutions that came under PNB's control were Malayan Banking Bhd, Bank Pembangunan Bhd and Komplex Kewangan (M) Bhd (Low 1985: 227).

As PNB's wholly owned subsidiary, ASNB managed these unit trust funds. By 1989, PNB had transferred to ASNB sizeable stakes in a number of listed firms involved in different sectors, including in mining, plantations and banking. These companies included, along with MMC and Sime Darby, Guthrie Corp, KFC Holdings Bhd, Malaysian Tobacco Company Bhd, Rothmans of Pall Mall Bhd and Malaysian Plantations

Bhd (Gomez and Jomo 1997: 34–35). PNB secured controlling interests in other major enterprises, such as the leading shipping firm Malaysian International Shipping Corp Bhd (MISC) and the auto motor giant, United Motor Works Bhd (UMW).

The ASN unit trust proved quite successful in terms of the number of holders that it had and subsequently Amanah Saham Bumiputera (ASB) was launched in 1990.[26] PNB quickly emerged as Malaysia's largest fund manager. According to Mahathir (2011: 472), within just over a decade, by 1990, ASN and ASB collectively had 4.3 million unit holders while the total volume of dividends that had been paid out amounted to RM4.15 billion. PNB went on to launch numerous other unit trusts: Amanah Saham Wawasan 2020, Amanah Saham Nasional 2, Amanah Saham Malaysia, Amanah Saham Didik, Amanah Saham Nasional 3 Imbang, Amanah Saham Gemilang and Amanah Saham 1Malaysia.[27]

Given the size of PNB's fund, this GLIC can serve as a mechanism to influence the stock market. Since PNB has a large presence on the Bursa Malaysia, its stock-trading affects the market. Theoretically, PNB can shore up share prices of the GLCs and other companies by actively acquiring a significant quantity of publicly listed equity. This serves PNB's interest because a high dividend yield generates more cash for ASNB. Importantly, too, the cash surplus can be stored to maintain the trust scheme's dividend yield, even in poor market conditions. PNB has investments in listed companies that generate a good annual dividend yield, such as Malayan Banking. This income funds ASNB's numerous trust schemes, allowing for consistent and rather high annual dividends for its investors. Since ASNB was formed to increase the savings of Bumiputeras and their ownership of domestic corporate equity, this trust scheme's effective performance is vital to garner electoral support. By 2013, ASN had 11.81 million members. For this reason, there is a strong pressure on ASNB to consistently declare high dividend yields.

PNB was also a major beneficiary through IPOs when non-Bumiputera companies were publicly listed, as the government had introduced a rule in 1975 that each quoted firm had to ensure that a minimum 30% of its equity was allocated to Bumiputera agencies or individuals. Other GLICs significantly benefited from this regulation as well. PNB, along with EPF, LTH and LTAT, became major equity shareholders. By 1983, just a few years after PNB's incorporation, Mehmet (1986: 111–17) noted that of the top 145 companies listed on the bourse, this GLIC was already the country's single largest shareholder; ASNB was the third largest.

LTAT similarly channelled its funds into profitable investments, emerging by 1983 as the 11th-largest stockowner of 145 listed companies on the stock exchange (Mehmet 1986). Mehmet (1986) would refer to the rise of these institutions as "distributional coalitions", that is cartel-like networks acting in collusion to concentrate wealth.

By 1980, the share of corporate wealth attributable to government agencies had increased by more than 10%, to 12.5%.[28] Foreign ownership of corporate equity had tumbled by over 20%, from 63.4% in 1970 to 42.9% in 1980. State-level governments, through their respective SEDCs, also began acquiring corporate equity. Some state governments, such as those in Johor and Sarawak, are now shareholders of major quoted firms through their investment arms.

Mahathir, Privatization and Incorporation of Khazanah

Mahathir's appointment as Prime Minister in July 1981 was an epochal moment in Malaysian history as he significantly reshaped the mode of implementation of affirmative action, introduced major industrialization-based policies and reconstructed the role of the GLICs and GLCs. Mahathir, a doctor by profession, was deeply immersed in the world of politics but he had also been active in business.[29] He had incorporated his own companies, albeit small enterprises, and had served as a director of GLCs such as Kumpulan FIMA.[30] Mahathir moved easily between the worlds of business and politics. As Prime Minister, he laboured tirelessly to merge these worlds through his policies, as his primary concern was the creation of Malay entrepreneurs. Only two months after taking office, in September 1981, the changed role of the GLICs in the economy was revealed with a much-publicized international acquisition, dubbed the "Dawn-Raid", when PNB took over the British-owned plantations company, Guthrie Corp, which was listed on the London Stock Exchange.

Mahathir's primary concern was the implementation of the Bumiputera Commercial and Industrial Community (BCIC) policy, a mechanism to redistribute wealth more equitably between ethnic groups. He had famously argued that "in trying to redress the imbalance, it is necessary to concentrate your efforts on the Malays to bring about more Malay entrepreneurs and to bring out, and to make Malay millionaires, if you like, so that the number of Malays who are rich equal the number of Chinese who are rich ... then you can say parity has been achieved" (quoted in

Chandra 1977: 171). The BCIC's focus was on fostering Bumiputera-owned small- and medium-scale enterprises (SMEs), including through vendor development programmes that tied small firms to large companies, foreign enterprises as well as the GLCs.

Mahathir drew his close confidant, businessman Daim Zainuddin, into government to help him create huge Malay-led companies. Daim, an unknown figure outside the business world, was appointed Minister of Finance in 1984. This announcement was unanticipated, even perplexing. However, since Daim had no support in UMNO and no political ambitions, he did not need to respond to demands from the party about the way policies were to be implemented and GLCs were to function. Crucially, too, for Mahathir, Daim was as deeply enamoured as he with the workings of the Kuala Lumpur Stock Exchange (KLSE), later renamed Bursa Malaysia, and saw it as an important avenue to quickly create large business groups.

When Malaysia registered negative growth rates during a major recession in 1986, the GLICs played a key role in stimulating the economy and the stock market. The government placed the NEP in abeyance, the economy was liberalized through a great degree of deregulation and foreign direct investments (FDI) were encouraged. Privatization became a keystone project. Mooted earlier by Mahathir in 1983 and with guidelines developed in 1985,[31] privatization was expedited but in tandem with the creation of the BCIC.

Privatization justified the transfer of government assets to private businesspeople. However, Mahathir was responsible for "picking the winners" when privatized concessions were awarded without tender, a system he defended by contending that the best way to build national champions was to disperse government-generated rents to those most adept at generating wealth. When government assets as well as licences, contracts and projects were channelled in a selective manner to well-connected businessmen, this practice soon led to serious allegations of cronyism. These privatized rents were acquired with loans from banks owned by the government and a number of them were quoted on the stock exchange, contributing huge returns to the recipients of these government-awarded concessions. This tripartite link between the government, private capital and financial institutions aided the rapid rise of well-diversified business groups.[32] For this tripartite government-private business-financial capital system to work efficiently, the government had to have significant control over the banking sector.[33]

Undoubtedly, after the NEP's introduction, the government had invested heavily in agencies and companies that were responsible for accumulating corporate assets on behalf of the Bumiputeras. According to one foreign press organ quoting senior civil servants, by the end of the 1990s, the government had invested RM21.7 billion in 1,109 quoted and unlisted companies, with most of these investments occurring in the 1970s (*Business Times* (S) 21 June 1994). To Mahathir's mind, the time had come for these companies to be transferred into private hands.

GLICs played an important role in the privatization of GLCs as they allowed the government to take these wholly owned companies private. However, the GLICs continued to retain majority ownership of numerous privatized companies. In fact, in 1993, at the peak of a stock market boom, precipitated also by the active public-listing of numerous major privatizations, a report by the magazine *Malaysian Business* disclosed an important point: the two top shareholders on the local bourse were two GLICs, MoF Inc. and PNB. Just these two GLICs collectively owned about one quarter of the stock market's total market capitalization of RM300 billion in November 1993 (quoted in *Business Times* (S) 3 December 1993). This trend of massive public ownership of private equity indicated that the government was hardly intent on relinquishing total ownership and control of these firms to members of the private sector.

Subsequently, these GLCs were instructed to incorporate joint-ventures with private sector firms. These joint-ventures were employed by the government to direct the mode of industrialization, to fill what it saw as "entrepreneurial gaps".[34] Joint-ventures in heavy industries involved foreign companies, a means to acquire insights into new technologies through knowledge transfer. One heavy industry venture where the government hoped technology transfer would occur was the national car project, Proton Saga. The Proton project involved Mitsubishi of Japan and a newly created GLC, Heavy Industries Corporation of Malaysia Bhd (HICOM).[35] Mahathir insisted that these GLC-foreign joint-ventures were imperative because private domestic firms were reluctant to participate in heavy industries for two reasons: the huge capital investments required and their limited technological expertise. Apart from Proton, HICOM collaborated with foreign companies to develop industries in steel (Perwaja Steel) and cement production (Kedah Cement). These enterprises failed to make an impact. Although Proton is now a firm under private ownership, it remains an enterprise in constant need of government support.

Meanwhile, the NEP, BCIC and privatization profoundly affected how the Chinese developed their enterprises. Interlocking stock ownership involving companies within business groups served as a mechanism to protect their corporate interests, a practice adopted by the Berjaya, Malayan United Industries (MUI), Hong Leong, Genting and Kuala Lumpur Kepong (KLK) groups (Gomez 1999). Chinese-owned business groups continued to prosper in spite of the NEP, but they increasingly needed to accommodate the government. A number of them productively employed the government-generated rents they had secured (Searle 1999). Other Chinese were able to develop their enterprises because they were forced to compete more effectively in an environment in which they were discriminated against.[36] The need for non-Bumiputera firms to adapt prudently in the economy became imperative when policies targeting Bumiputeras in business were continued after the NEP came to an end in 1990, with the introduction of the National Development Policy (NDP), implemented between 1991 and 2000, the National Vision Policy (2001–2010) and the Bumiputera Economic Empowerment (BEE) policy (since 2013).

Fifteen years into Mahathir's tenure as Prime Minister, huge business groups controlled by well-connected Malays had secured extensive ownership of companies in key sectors of the economy (see Table 2.3). The largest firms controlled by these Malays were linked to one of the then three most powerful politicians—Prime Minister Mahathir, Deputy Prime Minister Anwar Ibrahim and then former Minister of Finance Daim. These corporate captains included Halim Saad, Tajudin Ramli, Wan Azmi Wan Hamzah, Rashid Hussain, Shamsuddin Abdul Kadir, Azman Hashim, Ahmad Sebi Abu Bakar, Ishak Ismail, Mirzan Mahathir, Mokhzani Mahathir, Amin Shah Omar Shah and Yahya Ahmad. Well-connected non-Bumiputeras who quickly developed huge business groups with government patronage, specifically the award of privatized contracts, comprised Vincent Tan Chee Yioun, Francis Yeoh, Ting Pek Khiing, Jeffrey Cheah Fook Ling, Lin Yun Ling and T. Ananda Krishnan.[37] By the early 1990s, one key outcome of government intervention in the economy was that ownership and control of the top 100 companies was now in the hands of the government and well-connected business figures, including in key sectors of the economy such as banking, plantations, oil and gas, property development and construction and media (see Table 2.3).

Table 2.3 also highlights important corporate ownership transitions following the active implementation of the NEP, BCIC and privatization. Corporate equity ownership by foreigners had declined appreciably between 1971 and 1997. Prominent Chinese enterprises of the early 1970s

Table 2.3 Ownership and control of the top 100 companies in 1971 and 1997[a]

1971	*1997*
1. Aokam Tin (Foreign)	Tenaga Nasional (Government)
2. Asia Motor Co. (KL) (Phang family)	Telekom Malaysia (Government)
3. Associated Pan Malaysia Cement (Foreign)	Malayan Banking (Government)
4. Austral Amalgamated Tin (Foreign, Lee Loy Seng family, OCBC)	Sime Darby (Government)
5. Ayer Hitam Tin Dredging (Foreign)	Petronas Gas (Government)
6. BP Malaysia (Foreign)	United Engineers (Malaysia) (UEM) (Halim Saad)
7. Bank Bumiputra (Government)	RHB Capital (Rashid Hussain)
8. Batu Kawan (Lee Loy Seng family)	Resorts World (Lim Goh Tong)
9. Benta Plantations (Foreign)	Genting (Lim Goh Tong)
10. Berjuntai Tin Dredging (Foreign)	Rothmans of Pall Mall (Foreign)
11. Borneo Co. (M) (Foreign)	Renong (Halim Saad)
12. Boustead Trading (Foreign)	Berjaya Toto (Vincent Tan)
13. Bovis South East Asia (Foreign)	Malaysia International Shipping Corp (MISC) (Government)
14. Caltex Oil Malaysia (Foreign)	YTL Corp (Yeoh family)
15. Central Sugars (Foreign)	YTL Power International (Yeoh family)
16. Champion Motor (M) (Foreign)	Perusahaan Otomobil Nasional (Proton) (Yahya Ahmad)
17. Chartered Bank (Foreign)	Public Bank (Teh Hong Piow)
18. Chemical Company of Malaysia (Foreign)	AMMB Holdings (Azman Hashim)
19. Chung Khiaw Bank (UOB-Singapore)	Rashid Hussain Bhd (Rashid Hussain)
20. Cold Storage Holdings (Foreign)	Commerce-Asset Holdings (Halim Saad, through Renong)
21. Consolidated Plantations (Foreign)	Magnum Corp (T.K. Lim)
22. Cycle & Carriage (Chua family)	Heavy Industries Corp of Malaysia (HICOM) (Yahya Ahmad)
23. Cycle & Carriage (M) (Chua family)	Malaysian Airlines (Tajudin Ramli)
24. Dunlop Estates (Foreign)	Edaran Otomobil Nasional (EON) (Yahya Ahmad)
25. Dunlop Malaysian Ind. (Foreign)	Nestlé (Foreign)
26. East Asiatic Co. (Foreign)	Kuala Lumpur-Kepong (KLK) (Lee Loy Seng family)
27. Syarikat Eastern Smelting (OCBC Group-Singapore)	Malaysian Resources Corporation (MRCB) (Khalid Ahmad, Ahmad Nazri Abdullah, Abdul Kadir Jasin, Mohd Noor Mutalib, through Realmild)

(*continued*)

Table 2.3 (continued)

1971	*1997*
28. Empat Nombor Ekor (Lim Chooi Seng and family)	Berjaya Land (Vincent Tan)
29. Esso Standard Malaya (Foreign)	Golden Hope Plantations (Government)
30. Federal Flour Mills (Kuok family)	Oriental Holdings (Loh family)
31. Firestone Malaya (Foreign)	MNI Holdings (Government)
32. Folex Industries (Chan and Tan families)	Sarawak Enterprise Corporation Bhd (State Government of Sarawak)
33. Fraser & Neave (OCBC-Singapore)	Guthrie (Government)
34. Golden Hope Plantations (Foreign)	Cahya Mata Sarawak (Onn Mahmud)
35. Guinness Malaysia (Foreign)	MBF Holdings Bhd (Loy family)
36. Gula Perak (Government)	Hong Leong Credit (Quek Leng Chan)
37. Guthrie Ropel (Foreign)	Hong Leong Bank (Quek Leng Chan)
38. Guthrie Waugh Malaysia (Foreign)	New Straits Times Press (Khalid Ahmad, Ahmad Nazri Abdullah, Abdul Kadir Jasin, Mohd Noor Mutalib, through MRCB)
39. Harrisons & Crosfield (M) (Foreign)	Affin Holdings (Government)
40. Haw Par Brothers International (Foreign)	Tanjong (T. Ananda Krishnan)
41. Highlands and Lowlands Para Rubber Co. (Foreign)	Jaya Tiasa Holdings (Tiong Hiew King)
42. Highlands Malaya Plantations (Foreign)	TR Industries (TRI) (Tajudin Ramli)
43. Hock Heng Co. (Ng Quee Lam family)	Kwong Yik Bank (Government)
44. Hongkong & Shanghai Bank (Foreign)	Tan Chong Motor (Tan family)
45. Hume Industries (Far East) (Kwek family and OCBC-Singapore)	UMW Holdings (Government)
46. Inchcape (Foreign)	Innovest (Azrat Gull Amirzat Gull and Mohd Shariff Ahmad)
47. Joo Seng Rubber Co. (Low Beow Seng and Khor Siew Tong families)	Perlis Plantations (Robert Kuok)
48. Kempas (M) (OCBC-Singapore)	Konsortium Perkapalan (Mirzan Mahathir)
49. Kepong Plantations (Lee Loy Seng family)	Ekran (Ting Pek Khiing)
50. Kulim Group Estate (Government)	Berjaya Toto (Vincent Tan)
51. Lee Rubber (Selangor) (Lee Kong Chian family)	Multi-Purpose Holdings (MPHB) (T.K. Lim family)
52. Lee Rubber Co. (Lee Kong Chian family)	Malaysian Pacific Industries (Quek Leng Chan)
53. Lever Brothers (M) (Foreign)	Time Engineering (Halim Saad, through Renong)

(*continued*)

Table 2.3 (continued)

1971	*1997*
54. London Asiatic Rubber and Produce (Foreign)	Hume Industries (Quek Leng Chan)
55. Malayan Banking (Government)	Shell (Foreign)
56. Malayan Breweries (OCBC-Singapore)	Petronas Dagangan (Government)
57. Malayan Cement (Foreign)	Malayan United Industries (MUI) (Khoo Kay Peng)
58. Malayan Containers (Foreign)	Amsteel (William Cheng)
59. Malayan Flour Mills (Jerry Sung family)	Amcorp (William Cheng)
60. Malayan Sugar Manufacturing Co. (Kuok family)	IOI Corp (Lee Shin Cheng)
61. Malayan Tin Dredging (Foreign)	Malakoff (Khalid Ahmad, Ahmad Nazri Abdullah, Abdul Kadir Jasin, Mohd Noor Mutalib, through Realmild)
62. Malayan Tobacco Co. (Foreign)	MMC Corp (Government)
63. Malayan Weaving Mills (Foreign)	Gamuda (Lin Yun Ling)
64. Malayawata Steel (Foreign)	Arab-Malaysia Finance (Azman Hashim)
65. Manilal & Sons (M) (Patel family)	Lafarge (Foreign)
66. Metal Box Company of Malaysia (Foreign)	Highlands & Lowlands (Government)
67. Mobil Oil Malaysia (Foreign)	OYL (Quek Leng Chan)
68. North Borneo Timber Products (Foreign)	Malaysian Industrial Development Finance (MIDF) (Government)
69. Oversea-Chinese Banking Corporation (OCBC) (Lee family and numerous others—Singapore-based)	Sime UEP Properties (Government)
70. Pan Malaysia Cement Works (Nominee shareholder)	North Borneo Timbers (Aman Takzim Sdn Bhd)
71. Perak River Hydro Electric Power Co. (Foreign)	Metroplex (Chan Teik Huat and Lim Siew Kim)
72. Petaling Rubber Estate (Foreign)	Pan Malaysia Cement Works (Khoo Kay Peng, through MUI)
73. Petaling Tin (OCBC-Singapore)	Ramatex (Ma Wong Chin, Ma On May and Wong Lang Piow)
74. Rothmans of Pall Mall (M) (Foreign)	Berjaya Capital (Vincent Tan)
75. Selangor Dredging (Teh Kien Toh family)	Repco Holdings (Low Thiam Hock)
76. Shell Malaysia Trading (Foreign)	Carlsberg Brewery (Foreign)
77. Shell Refining Co. (Foreign)	Lingui Developments (Yaw Chee Ming)
78. Short Deposits Malaysia (Foreign)	Sungei Wei Holdings (Cheah Fook Ling)

(*continued*)

Table 2.3 (continued)

1971	*1997*
79. Sime Darby Holdings (OCBC-Singapore)	Pacific Bank (Foreign, OCBC)
80. Sime Darby Malaysia (OCBC-Singapore)	Hong Leong Properties (Quek Leng Chan)
81. Société Des Matières Premières Tropicales (Foreign)	Malayan Cement (Foreign)
82. Southern Kinta Consolidated (Foreign)	Ban Hin Lee Bank (Ahmad Sebi Bakar, through Advance Synergy)
83. Southern Malayan Tin Dredging (Foreign)	Southern Steel (Quek Leng Chan, through Hong Leong group)
84. Straits Steamship Co. (Foreign)	Leader Universal (H'ng family)
85. Straits Trading Co. (OCBC-Singapore)	Southern Bank (Tan Teong Hean)
86. Taiping Textiles (Foreign)	TA Enterprise (Tiah Thee Kian)
87. Tan Chong & Sons Motor (Tan family)	Hap Seng Consolidated (Lau Gek Poh, through Malaysian Mosaics Bhd)
88. Tan Chong Motor Holdings (Tan family)	IJM Corporation (Tan Chin Nam)
89. Tasek Cement (Tan Lark Sye family and Kwek Hong P'ng family)	Hong Leong Industries (Quek Leng Chan)
90. Textile Corporation of Malaya (Foreign)	Phileo Allied (Tong Kooi Ong)
91. Tractors Malaysia (OCBC-Singapore)	Pantai (Mokhzani Mahathir)
92. Tronoh Mines (Foreign)	KFC Holdings Malaysia (Ishak Ismail)
93. United Engineers (OCBC-Singapore)	Fraser & Neave Holdings (Foreign)
94. United Engineers (M) (OCBC-Singapore)	Cycle & Carriage Bintang (Foreign)
95. United Malayan Banking Corporation (Chang Min Thein)	ESSO (Foreign)
96. United Motor Works (M) Holdings (Chia Cheng Guan family)	Country Heights Holdings (Lee Kim Yew)
97. United Motor Works (M) (Chia Cheng Guan family)	Hock Seng Lee (Yu Chee Lieng, Yu Chee Hoe, Yii Chi Hau, Yii Chee Ming and Yii Chee Sing)
98. United Plantations (Foreign)	Uniphoenix Corp (Soh Chee Wen)
99. Wearne Brothers Ltd. (OCBC-Singapore)	Star Publications (MCA)
100. Wearne Brothers (M) (OCBC-Singapore)	Guinness Anchor (Foreign)

[a]The top 100 companies in 1971 in Table 2.3, prepared by Lim (1981: 126–128), are listed in alphabetical order and comprise quoted and unlisted companies. The companies listed under the year 1997 were ranked according to market capitalization

Source: Lim 1981: 126–128; Gomez 2009

did not figure among the Bursa's top 20 by the mid-1990s, suggesting their limited desire to invest in research and development (R&D) to continue to grow. The leading Chinese enterprises in 1997 were owned by businesspeople who had been privy to government rents. These companies included the well-connected Genting, Berjaya and YTL Corp groups. Chinese-owned business groups had done particularly well in the highly lucrative recession-free gaming industry, specifically Genting, which owned the only casino in Malaysia, while Berjaya owned the highly lucrative Sports Toto, controversially privatized in 1985,[38] and Magnum ran an extremely profitable four-digit numbers forecasting betting operation.[39] The government had ownership of Malaysia's top five enterprises, which included the utilities Tenaga and Telekom, the country's largest bank, Malayan Banking, as well as Sime Darby, one the largest plantations companies in the world. The number of Malay corporate captains had increased significantly with Halim Saad, Tajudin Ramli, Rashid Hussain, Azman Hashim and Yahya Ahmad now appearing as owners of major enterprises.

In September 1993, Mahathir established Khazanah Nasional Bhd, Malaysia's sovereign wealth fund (SWF).[40] Khazanah, now internationally known as a sovereign wealth fund of some repute, was incorporated under the Companies Act 1965 as a public limited company. It is wholly owned by MoF Inc. and is government funded.[41] Khazanah was established to manage commercial assets owned by the federal government as well as design strategic investments that would contribute to "nation building" (Lai 2012: 237). Khazanah's current Managing Director, Azman Mokhtar, sees the company as more than a sovereign wealth fund; for him, it is a "nation building institution" (*Enterprising Investor* 30 July 2013).

Khazanah was reportedly fashioned along the lines of one of Singapore's leading GLCs, Temasek Holdings, a body responsible for securing better returns on the assets of the country. When incorporated, it was envisioned that Khazanah would, unlike the other GLICs, embark on investments abroad, even initiate and lead them. Mahathir was of the opinion that since private companies had been extremely reluctant to invest in emerging markets, this was partly the reason why his South-South cooperation programme had not been very successful.[42] Khazanah, flush with the resources transferred to it, was to serve as Malaysia's vanguard company in foreign, particularly emerging economies. Through Khazanah, Malaysia was to be seen as a key investor in developing economies (*Business Times* (S) 8 April 1994). Among Khazanah's first foreign forays was a joint-venture involving a car project that included Japan and China, then a rapidly emerging economy.[43] Mahathir wanted Malaysian companies to invest in China, particularly enterprises owned by ethnic Chinese who could trace their ancestral roots to rapidly burgeoning provinces in the mainland. In 1993, Mahathir led a 300-strong delegation to China, with half his team comprising businessmen (Gomez 1999: 10–11).

Khazanah was introduced to take over the role of MoF Inc., then a major player on the local bourse, and was to be run by professionals, not bureaucrats. Khazanah was not meant to be an active trader on the stock market, though it was to use the RM7 billion worth of commercial assets it took over from MoF Inc. to raise funds (*Business Times* 14 July 1994; Lai 2012: 238). These commercial assets included 37 companies then under MoF Inc. (*New Straits Times* 16 September 1994).

Given the expectations the government had of its SWF, Khazanah's board of directors was chaired by the Prime Minister, with the Minister of Finance as deputy chairman. To ensure it was professionally managed, while keeping in mind its social obligations, Khazanah had six other directors, three each from the public and private sectors, all appointed by the government (*The Straits Times* 28 April 1994). Khazanah's first chief executive was Mohamad Sheriff Kassim, the secretary-general of the Ministry of Finance who was about to retire from the civil service.[44] The other senior civil servants appointed to Khazanah's board were the Governor of Bank Negara and the director-general of the Economic Planning Unit (EPU) in the Prime Minister's Department. The three private sector representatives were the prominent and well-connected banker, Rashid Hussain, Price Waterhouse's then executive chairman, Raja Arshad Tun Uda, and former Bank Negara deputy governor Lin See Yan, who was then the chairman of Pacific Bank Bhd (*The Straits Times* 10 August 1994).

Khazanah does not rely on public savings for funds. It raises money by issuing loan stocks, shares or other financial instruments in domestic and international markets as well as through the sale of investments (*Bloomberg* 2 December 2010). For example, in 1995, Khazanah sold a huge chunk of HICOM shares, a sale that contributed to a RM1.8 billion profit (*New Straits Times* 19 October 1995). However, in spite of the handover of MoF Inc.'s corporate duties to Khazanah, the former's role as an asset owner for the government has not diminished. After transferring its corporate assets to Khazanah, MoF Inc. went on to acquire another range of quoted and unquoted private companies (see Table 2.1).

Khazanah has also entered into ventures in areas deemed strategic by the government and in line with the policies of the Prime Minister. When agriculture became the core focus of the government in 2003, Khazanah helped develop this sector through its subsidiaries, Malaysian Agrifood Corporation, Blue Archipelago and Biotropics Malaysia. When the government launched five development corridors in the mid-2000s, an attempt to ensure more even-handed economic growth throughout the country, Khazanah played a vital role by leading the development of the South Johor Economic Region, better known as Iskandar Malaysia, through subsidiaries such as Iskandar Investment, UEM Land, Pulau Indah Ventures, Pinewood Iskandar Malaysia and Themed Attractions and Resorts. From the early 2010s, Khazanah spearheaded the government's desire to get GLICs and GLCs to function as major regional corporate players, possibly also with greater global presence.

Asian Currency Crisis 1997: GLICs to the Rescue

In many ways, the year 1997 was a critical juncture in Malaysian history. When the Asian financial crisis erupted that year, GLICs were used by the government to bailout businessmen who were severely over-leveraged as they were caught holding corporate stocks worth far less than their acquired value. This led to the fall of a number of corporate captains.[45] These bailouts by the GLICs led to their emergence as key corporate actors, after a long phase of privatization and much government focus on creating Bumiputera-owned business groups. Despite Mahathir's scrutiny of these preferentially selected and treated corporate captains, there had been little or no disciplining of them, probably because in some cases the business owners were only doing his bidding.

The companies bailed out included Halim Saad's Renong, which reputedly served to represent the rise of Malay-owned big business. Before Halim's takeover of the Renong group, its associated companies had been owned by UMNO and were privy to numerous lucrative privatized projects, including the multi-billion-ringgit North–South Highway. Proton had been privatized but had to be bought from the debt-ridden DRB-HICOM by the government's cash-rich petroleum firm Petronas.[46] The loss-registering and debt-ridden MAS, the nation's privatized airline, was renationalized to rescue it from imminent bankruptcy. MAS was controlled by the well-connected Tajudin Ramli, who also owned Celcom, the privatized mobile phone operator that was taken over by the telecommunications GLC, Telekom Malaysia. The government's acquisition of debt-ridden businesses owned by Mahathir's eldest son, Mirzan, was another issue that was mired in much controversy.

By 2001, no Bumiputera had ownership of a top 10-quoted firm. If Table 2.3 indicated the rise of Malay corporate captains, including the well-connected Halim and Tajudin, Table 2.4 shows their corporate demise after the 1997 crisis. Among the top 20 companies in 2001, only one was owned by a Malay, Rashid Hussain. Pertinently, even Rashid would lose ownership of his firm, RHB Capital, which owned RHB Bank, not too long later.[47] By 2001, the government had majority ownership of seven of the top 10 firms through the GLICs, due also to the partial nature of some privatizations, as well as half of the top 30. These firms included public utilities Telekom Malaysia and Tenaga Nasional, the leading bank, Malayan Banking, Petronas' gas producer, Petronas Gas, the national shipping line MISC, and the well-diversified Sime Darby. GLICs also had a majority stake in the third-largest bank, Commerce Asset-Holding, later renamed CIMB, after the privately owned Public Bank. CIMB was the outcome of a merger between government-owned Bank Bumiputra and Bank of Commerce, owned by UMNO. A decade later, by 2013, as Table 2.4 indicates, no significant change had occurred in terms of ownership and control of key firms, pointing to the now longstanding and important role of GLICs and GLCs in the corporate sector.

Table 2.4 further indicates that in the decade between 2001 and 2013, GLCs continued to occupy seven out of the top 10 positions, an indication that these companies had the capacity to perform well. An interesting phenomenon was the continued decline of Chinese-owned companies among Malaysia's leading enterprises. If there were two Chinese-owned enterprises in the top 10 in 2001, the number had fallen to one by 2013. While eight Chinese-owned companies figured among the top 20 in 2001, there were only six in 2013.[48] Public Bank, owned by Teh Hong Piow and widely recognized as a highly entrepreneurial enterprise, had emerged as the second-largest quoted company in Malaysia by 2013.[49] Another firm on the ascendancy was Ananda Krishnan's Maxis, a telecommunications enterprise. The well-connected Ananda Krishnan also had ownership of two other companies in the top 100, Astro (M) Holdings at number 29 and Bumi Armada that was ranked 32.[50]

Another factor contributed to the fall of a number of leading firms following the currency crisis. Since the rise of these businessmen was linked to the patronage of influential politicians, their fortunes depended on

Table 2.4 Top 100 quoted companies, by market capitalization, in 2001 and 2013

2001	*2013*
1. Tenaga Nasional (Government)	Malayan Banking (Government)
2. Telekom Malaysia (Government)	Public Bank (Teh Hong Piow)
3. Malayan Banking (Government)	Tenaga Nasional (Government)
4. Malaysia International Shipping Corp (MISC) (Government)	Axiata Group (Government)
5. Petronas Gas (Government)	CIMB Group Holdings (Government)
6. British American Tobacco (Foreign)	Sime Darby (Government)
7. Sime Darby (Government)	Petronas Chemicals (Government)
8. Public Bank (Teh Hong Piow)	Maxis (T. Ananda Krishnan)
9. Commerce Asset-Holding (Government)	Petronas Gas (Government)
10. Genting (Lim Goh Tong)	Digi Dot Com (Foreign)
11. YTL Power International (Yeoh family)	Genting (Lim family)
12. Resorts World (Lim Goh Tong)	IHH Healthcare (Government)
13. YTL Corp (Yeoh family)	Petronas Dagangan (Government)
14. TIME dotCom (Halim Saad, through Renong)	IOI Corp (Lee Shin Cheng)
15. Nestlé (Foreign)	Sapurakencana Petroleum (Shahril and Shahriman Shamsuddin)
16. Hong Leong Bank (Quek Leng Chan)	Kuala Lumpur Kepong (Lee family)
17. DIGI (Vincent Tan)	Hong Leong Bank (Quek Leng Chan)
18. RHB Capital (Rashid Hussain)	MISC (Government)
19. Kuala Lumpur-Kepong (Lee family)	Genting (M) (Lim family)
20. Golden Hope Plantations (Government)	AMMB Holdings (Foreign/Azman Hashim)
21. Malayan Cement (Foreign)	RHB Capital (Government)
22. Malaysian Pacific Industries (Quek Leng Chan)	Telekom Malaysia (Government)
23. Perusahaan Otomobil Nasional (Proton) (Government)	PPB Group (Robert Kuok)
24. Kumpulan Guthrie (Government)	British American Tobacco (M) (Foreign)
25. AMMB Holdings (Azman Hashim)	YTL Corporation (Yeoh Family)
26. Gamuda (Eleena Azlan Shah)	Felda Global Ventures Holdings (Government)
27. Malakoff (Government, through MRCB)	Hong Leong Finance (Quek Leng Chan)
28. Tanjong (T. Ananda Krishnan)	Nestle (M) (Foreign)
29. United Engineers (Malaysia) (UEM) (Halim Saad)	Astro (M) Holdings (T. Ananda Krishnan)
30. Hong Leong Credit (Quek Leng Chan)	UMW Holdings (Government)

(*continued*)

Table 2.4 (continued)

2001	*2013*
31. IOI Corporation (Lee Shin Cheng)	YTL Power International (Yeoh family)
32. Berjaya Sports Toto (Vincent Tan)	Bumi Armada (T. Ananda Krishnan)
33. Magnum Corp (T.K. Lim)	Malaysia Airports Holdings (Government)
34. Malaysia Airport Holdings (Government)	Gamuda (Government)
35. Oriental Holdings (Loh family)	UEM Sunrise (Government)
36. OYL (Quek Leng Chan)	KLCCP Holdings (Government)
37. Petronas Dagangan (Government)	MMC Corp (Syed Mokhtar Al-Bukhary)
38. Southern Bank (Tan Teong Hean)	Dialog Group (Ngau Boon Keat and Loy Ah Wei)
39. Malaysia Airlines System (MAS) (Government)	UWM Oil and Gas Corp (Government)
40. HICOM Holdings	Westports Holdings (G. Gnanalingam)
41. IOI Properties (Lee Shin Cheng)	Genting Plantations (Lim family)
42. Sime UEP Properties (Government, through Sime Darby)	IJM Corporation (Government)
43. Renong (Halim Saad)	Batu Kawan (Lee family)
44. Edaran Otomobil Nasional (EON) (Government)	SP Setia (Government)
45. PPB Oil Palms (Robert Kuok)	Alliance Financial Group (Foreign)
46. Sarawak Enterprise Corporation (Sarawak state government)	Lafarge (M) (Foreign)
47. MMC Corp (Government)	BIMB Holdings (Government)
48. TR Industries (TRI) (Tajudin Ramli)	Fraser & Neave Holdings (Foreign)
49. Highland & Lowland (Government)	Affin Holdings (Government)
50. Carlsberg Brewery (M) (Foreign)	AirAsia (Kamarudin Meranun and Tony Fernandes)
51. Malaysian Oxygen (Foreign)	Hap Seng Consolidated (Foreign)
52. UMW Holdings (Government)	Boustead Holdings (Government)
53. Northport Corporation (Government)	Malaysia Marine and Heavy Engineering Holdings (Government)
54. Star Publications (MCA)	DRB Hicom (Syed Mokhtar Al-Bukhary)
55. Powertek (T. Ananda Krishnan)	United Plantations (Foreign)
56. IJM Corp (Tan Chin Nam)	Hartalega Holdings (Ching family)
57. PSC Industries (Amin Shah Omar Shah)	Berjaya Sports Toto (Vincent Tan)
58. Pacificmas (Foreign, OCBC)	Oriental Holdings (Loh family)
59. Ramatex (Ma Wong Ching, Ma On May, Wong Lang Piow)	Purecircle Ltd. (Foreign)

(*continued*)

Table 2.4 (continued)

2001	*2013*
60. Road Builder (M) Holdings (Chua Hock Chin)	Malaysia Airlines (Government)
61. Hock Hua Bank (Ling Beng Siew)	Gas (M) (Syed Mokhtar Al-Bukhary)
62. Hume Industries (Quek Leng Chan)	Aeon Co (M) (Foreign)
63. Lingkaran Trans Kota Holdings (Eleena Azlan Shah)	Guinness Anchor (Foreign)
64. Fraser and Neave (Foreign)	Sunway (Cheah Fook Ling)
65. MNI Holdings (Government)	Magnum (Chinese)
66. Puncak Niaga Holdings (Rozali Ismail and Shaari Ismail)	Kulim (M) (Government)
67. Hap Seng Consolidated (Lau Gek Poh)	Bursa (M) (Government)
68. Shell Refining (Foreign)	Berjaya Land (Vincent Tan)
69. Ban Hin Lee Bank (Tan Teong Hean and Abdus Salim Cassim)	IGB Reit (Foreign)
70. Unisem (John Chia Sin Tet)	Tan Chong Motor Holdings (Tan family)
71. Hong Leong Industries (Quek Leng Chan)	IGB Corporation (Foreign)
72. Affin Holdings (Government)	IJM Land (Government)
73. Malaysian Resources Corporation (MRCB) (Government)	Malaysia Building Society (Government)
74. Malayan United Industries (MUI) (Khoo Kay Peng)	Pavilion REIT (Foreign)
75. Batu Kawan (Lee family)	LPI Capital (Chooy Kwee Fong and Yap Leng Heng)
76. Public Finance (Teh Hong Piow)	KPJ Healthcare (Government)
77. JT International (Foreign)	Carlsberg Brewery (M) (Foreign)
78. Utama Banking Group (Taib Mahmud family)	Sunway Reit (Cheah Fook Ling)
79. Arab-Malaysian Finance (Azman Hashim)	MSM (M) Holdings (Government)
80. OSK Holdings (Ong Leong Huat)	Top Glove Corporation (Lim Wee Chai)
81. FFM (Kuok family)	Bintulu Port Holdings (Government)
82. Time Engineering (Halim Saad, through Renong)	QL Resources (Chia Family)
83. Kedah Cement Holdings (Foreign)	Dayang Enterprise Holdings (Hasmi Hasnan and Amar Abdul Hamed Sepawi)
84. Guinness Anchor (Foreign)	Mah Sing Group (Leong Hoy Kum)
85. Courts Mammoth (Foreign)	Dutch Lady Milk Industries (Foreign)
86. SP Setia (Liew Kee Sin)	Shangri La Hotels (M) (Robert Kuok)
87. DRB Hicom (Saleh Sulong)	Pos (M) (Syed Mokhtar Al-Bukhary)
88. Tan Chong Motors (Tan family)	Parkson Holdings (William Cheng)

(*continued*)

Table 2.4 (continued)

2001	*2013*
89. BIMB Holdings (Government)	Media Prima (Government)
90. TA Enterprise (Tiah Thee Kian)	Sarawak Oil Palms (Ling family)
91. Bintulu Port Holdings (Government)	IJM Plantations (Government)
92. MK Land Holdings (Mustapha Kamal)	Kossan Rubber Industries (Lim family)
93. Malaysian Plantation (Lim Tiong Chin, Chan Chin Cheung, Wong Kim Lin, Loong Tze Tung, Surin Upatkoon, Tan Toh Hua)	TSH Resources (Kelvin Tan Aik Pen)
94. Genting (M) (Lim family)	UOA Development (Kong Pak Lim)
95. KFC Holdings Malaysia (Ishak Ismail, Abdullah Omar, Izhar Sulaiman, Shamsul Baharain Sulaiman)	Berjaya Corporation (Vincent Tan)
96. Amway (M) Holdings (Foreign)	Capitaland (M) Mall Trust (Foreign)
97. Malaysian Tobacco Company (Foreign)	Keck Seng (M) (Foreign)
98. Jaya Tiasa Holdings (Tiong Hiew King)	Hong Leong Capital (Quek Leng Chan)
99. Cahya Mata Sarawak (Taib Mahmud family)	AirAsia X (Kamarudin Meranun and Tony Fernandes)
100. Tractors Malaysia Holdings (Government)	Cahya Mata Sarawak (Taib Mahmud family)

whether their patrons remained in power. A serious political falling-out occurred between Mahathir and his deputy, Anwar, as the economy spiralled into a recession. Mahathir would later accuse Anwar of trying to undermine his administration.[51] When Anwar was removed from office in September 1998, his business allies lost control of their corporate assets. This was most obvious in the case of the Malaysian Resources Corporation Bhd (MRCB) group, controlled ultimately by an obscure holding company, Realmild Sdn Bhd.[52] The MRCB group, then linked to other top 100 companies in 1997 such as the media-based New Straits Times Press Bhd (NSTP) and Malakoff Bhd, was ultimately controlled by four men, Khalid Ahmad, Ahmad Nazri Abdullah, Abdul Kadir Jasin and Mohd Noor Mutalib. MRCB group also had control of Malaysia's then leading private television network, TV3, another listed enterprise. These four men were prominent journalists, long associated with NSTP. Anwar had helped them institute a management buyout of NSTP as well as eventually obtaining control of MRCB.[53] They lost control of MRCB and the companies associated with this group following Anwar's removal from the political system. MRCB would eventually emerge as a GLC, while MoF Inc. and other GLICs would obtain control of NSTP and TV3.[54]

Other businesspeople connected with Anwar who lost control of their corporate assets included Tong Kooi Ong, the Lim family who owned the Magnum group and Ahmad Sebi Bakar. Commenting on the problems encountered by Anwar's business associates, one foreign report went so far as to list the companies under siege: MRCB, Idris Hydraulic, Multi-Purpose Holdings, Phileo Allied, Rashid Hussain, Abrar Corporation and Hong Leong, even claiming that one of these companies had been taken over by the nephew of reappointed Minister of Finance Daim (see *Business Times* (S) 6 September 2004). In 2001, when Daim fell out of favour with Mahathir, the corporate assets owned by his business allies and proxies were taken over by the GLICs.[55]

Following Daim's departure as Minister of Finance, Mahathir instituted an unprecedented act. Though the sitting Prime Minister, he assumed the office of Minister of Finance, clearly an attempt to consolidate power in the office of the chief executive. This centralization of power was justified on the grounds that it was the Prime Minister's responsibility to stabilize the economy and take all actions necessary to do so, including using the GLICs for this purpose.

In 2003, just before Mahathir stood down as Prime Minister, among the top 100 firms quoted on the stock exchange, the largest privately owned business groups did not have overwhelming control of the corporate sector. There was, in fact, fairly wide dispersal of ownership of corporate equity of the top 100 quoted firms (see Table 2.4). In 2001, the combined wealth of Malaysia's 20 wealthiest businesspeople amounted to RM41.7 billion, only about 10% of the bourse's market capitalization (*Malaysian Business* 2 January 2001). Political feuding among UMNO elites had diminished the volume of wealth concentration in the hands of well-connected individuals. While a few well-connected business groups had attained some international repute during Mahathir's tenure, his attempt to create Bumiputera corporate captains was ultimately little more than a series of business-related controversies (see Appendix 2.1). The GLICs and GLCs re-emerged as key corporate players when they were used to take over companies entangled in these political feuds, financial downturns and business controversies.

Reformer Abdullah (2003–2009): Performance Management of GLICs and GLCs

In October 2003, Abdullah Ahmad Badawi took office as the fifth Prime Minister of Malaysia. Unlike Mahathir, Abdullah had no interest in business—he was seen as a politician with strong religious credentials given his family background and upbringing[56]—and one of his primary aims was to reform the public administration system. Abdullah's policy agenda was markedly dissimilar from Mahathir's, with a focus on nurturing rural industries by modernizing the agriculture sector. This also served as a means to eradicate hard-core rural poverty. Abdullah, however, continued to ratify programmes targeting Bumiputera firms through the BCIC, but he would now place much emphasis on supporting SMEs which then constituted about 98% of all businesses.[57] These goals that Abdullah had for Malaysia were expressed lucidly in the *9th Malaysia Plan, 2006–2010*, where he outlined his agenda to employ the GLCs far more productively, including to support his initiatives to develop Bumiputera SMEs.

Abdullah's extensive range of initiatives to help SMEs included establishing the SME Bank in 2005 to facilitate more productive channelling of financial aid to small firms.[58] He stressed the need to use the vendor system more effectively to link SMEs to MNCs to help small firms gain greater access to both local and foreign markets. The Small and Medium Industries Development Corporation (SMIDEC)[59] was redesignated SME Corporation Malaysia in January 2009, a one-stop agency reporting directly to the Prime Minister though under the jurisdiction of the Ministry of Trade and Industry (MITI). SME Corp is responsible for coordinating policies and implementing programmes to support SMEs in all economic sectors.

Abdullah recognized that reform of the GLICs and GLCs was imperative. In 2005, 57 enterprises listed on the Bursa Malaysia were GLCs, with a market capitalization of RM260 billion, then constituting 36% of the bourse's total capitalization. As one report noted: "Although the market capitalization of the GLCs is equivalent to half the size of the economy, analysts have long been dismayed by their poor return.... GLCs' return to shareholders has trailed behind overall market performance by 21 percent over the last five years" (*Business Times* (S) 15 May 2004).

Abdullah recruited corporate leaders from a new generation of professionally trained Malays to head the GLCs, though this process was initiated by Mahathir when he appointed Nor Mohamed Yakcop as economic advisor in 2001, a role once played by Daim. Nor Mohamed aimed at instilling a more corporate approach in the functioning of what was then viewed as slow-moving government-owned enterprises that were dominating the economy.[60] In May 2004, Abdullah introduced the GLC Transformation Programme, a ten-year endeavour between 2005 and 2015 launched under the Putrajaya Committee on GLC High-Performance, whose implementation was to be led by Khazanah.[61] Even Khazanah was subjected to a major reform. In 2004, a new chief executive, Azman Mokhtar, was appointed while the board of directors was revamped when civil servants were replaced by professionals from the private sector. Azman, an accountant by training with a post-graduate degree from the University of Cambridge, had been employed by Salomon Smith Barney and the Union Bank of Switzerland before launching his own consultancy firm, BinaFikir.[62] Azman had never served in government (*Business Times* (S) 12 May 2004; *The Straits Times* 15 May 2004). To secure the services of professionals from the private sector, those appointed to senior management positions in the GLICs and GLCs would be paid salaries benchmarked against their counterparts in the private sector and offered bonuses and stock options (*Business Times* (S) 12 May 2004). However, this new managerial team would also be subjected to regular assessment, based on key performance indicators (KPIs) determined by the government.

As far as Khazanah was concerned, Abdullah was clear that he wanted this GLIC to "become among the biggest and most dynamic investment firms", while of his reforms he argued that "the concept of close partnership between government and business still forms the foundation of Malaysia Inc., but it is imperative that we shift the basis of this partnership to that of tangible achievement and performance. It is vital that we move away from the culture of the iron rice bowl and of promotion by seniority towards a culture which recognizes and promotes performance" (quoted in *The Straits Times* 15 May 2004). Abdullah went on to add that MoF Inc. would transfer more of its assets to Khazanah to further strengthen the asset base of the latter. The value of the assets then held by Khazanah was reportedly about RM40 billion, far less than total value of assets held by GLICs such as the EPF which amounted to RM200 billion (see *Business Times* (S) 15 May 2004).

The government was also concerned that private markets attributed a discount on value when it came to GLCs listed on the Malaysian bourse. This created a political imperative for the promulgation of a programme to reform these quoted government-owned enterprises. These GLCs were to become high-performing companies, given their prominent presence in the domestic economy. This was the first time such a major coordinated and concerted effort was undertaken to enhance the management and governance of the GLCs.

Under this transformation programme, the management of the GLICs, as well as the top 20 GLCs, or G20,[63] was to be revamped to deliver better financial and operational performance by operating in a more commercial manner rather than as socially oriented enterprises, though the social obligations of these companies were not to be negated. The financial objectives of these reforms included registering higher market capitalization and dividend returns along with a lower debt-to-equity ratio and ensuring larger and more diversified asset ownership. GLICs and GLCs were to become regional champions, invest in new sectors, divest non-core and non-performing assets and collaborate more with the private sector. GLCs that were seen as potential regional champions were CIMB, Malayan Banking, Axiata and IHH Healthcare.[64] GLICs were required to further internationalize themselves and do so far more visibly. For example, Malayan Banking, CIMB and RHB Capital, Malaysia's largest banks, were expected to acquire financial institutions in foreign countries. The government saw these Malaysian banks as institutions that were financially strong enough to acquire foreign rivals (*Business Times* (S) 6 October 2004). These Malaysian banks subsequently acquired major financial institutions in Southeast Asia.

Khazanah had no overseas bureaus in 2004, but went on to establish offices in China, India, Turkey and the United States. A decade later, by July 2015, Khazanah announced that 44% of its investment portfolio constituted foreign assets. PNB set up offices in Japan and the UK, besides having a private equity partnership in New York. EPF's global investments in 2014 accounted for 25% of its total government assets. LTH invested in several real estate opportunities in Saudi Arabia, the UK and Australia. The G20 established revenue-generating operations in 42 countries and increased their overseas share of revenue from 28% to 34% during the transformation programme.[65]

To improve its financial performance, Khazanah divested its non-core or non-performing assets, which included its interests in Proton, Pos Malaysia, TIME dotCom and Westports. PNB divested its stakes in HeiTech Padu and Titan Chemicals. Khazanah invested in new areas such as education (Educity Iskandar), healthcare (IHH Healthcare), creative media (Pinewood Iskandar), leisure and tourism (Kidzania, Legoland and

Puteri Harbour Family Theme Park). GLIC–private sector collaboration was evident in Khazanah's development of the Medini business district in Iskandar Malaysia, a multi-party project, in Teluk Datai in Langkawi (with Shangri-La) and in the Shuaibah Independent Water and Power Project in Saudi Arabia (with Tenaga and Malakoff). EPF was part of the redevelopment of the Battersea Power Station in the UK with Sime Darby and SP Setia, a Chinese-owned company that was taken over by the government. LTAT and LTH worked with several partners to promote entrepreneurship programmes with provisions for an entrepreneur fund. LTH also jointly acquired properties with Amanah Raya Bhd for investment purposes.[66]

According to the *GLC Transformation Report*, prior to 2004, the directors of these enterprises were primarily former bureaucrats, serving members of parliament and regulators who were open to political influence. In the first two years of the programme, 58 board members of the G20 were replaced with professionals and people with experience in the corporate sector.[67] The Malaysian Directors Academy (MINDA) was established in 2006 to train high-performing directors. MINDA formed partnerships with leading institutions such as the International Institute of Management Development (IMD), INSEAD and Harvard University.

Since one aim of the GLC reforms was to create global champions, Abdullah saw through the mega-merger of three huge plantations companies in 2007. This mega-merger of Sime Darby, Golden Hope and Guthrie created one of the largest plantations companies in the world. Sime Darby was retained as the name for the newly merged entity. PNB was the lead GLIC with common shareholdings held either directly or through ASNB in the three companies. There was some controversy over this merger as it was not seen as value accretive (as with most mergers) and that it was not in the interest of market competition.

Under Abdullah, the GLICs functioned under the same framework set by Mahathir but there were very few corporate scandals and conflict-of-interest situations in this period,[68] a trend that was evident under his predecessor (see Appendix 2.1). However, Abdullah served only one term as Prime Minister due to two factors, the first being the debacle of the 2008 general election when the BN lost its two-thirds majority in parliament for the first time since it was formed after the 1969 crisis. UMNO blamed its electoral loss on Abdullah's failure to fulfil the reforms he had pledged to institute when securing the premiership. The second factor was the global financial crisis. A major consequence of this crisis was that the value of company equity on the Malaysian bourse dropped by 40% between July 2008 and February 2009. This crisis wiped out nearly all the share value gains that the GLCs had earned since 2004 (*The Edge* 7 December 2008). The economic contraction resulted in negative gross domestic product (GDP) growth rates, declining export revenues and rising unemployment levels.

Najib's Reforms (2009–2013): The Change That Did Not Occur

When Najib Razak replaced Abdullah as Prime Minister in April 2009, he vowed to usher Malaysia into a new era of "transparency, democracy and the rule of law" (*The Star* 4 April 2009). He went on to introduce a slew of economic, social and educational reform plans that entailed, among other things, creating a new model of development for Malaysia, as he put it, to reinvigorate the economy. These reform plans included the *Government Transformation Programme* (GTP), the *New Economic Model, Parts I and II* (NEM), the *Economic Transformation Programme* (ETP), the *Education Blueprint 2011–2015* and the *Tenth Malaysia Plan, 2010–2015.* These plans were encapsulated under his widely publicized slogan *1Malaysia*, for Najib a catchword that signified that his form of governance and mode of policy planning and implementation would transcend political, economic and social differences based on race and religion. Najib proposed far more reforms than those offered by Abdullah (Funston 2016: 83–106), acknowledging in the process that they were imperative, as the economy was plagued by rent-seeking and cronyism. Najib stressed that political patronage would be minimized as he planned to actively privatize the GLCs. One year after coming to power and following the introduction of these policy reforms, Najib's popularity, according to one poll, increased from a mere 30% to about 70%. Najib's transformation ideas had evidently resonated with a large segment of Malaysians.

By 2010, serious problems within the economy were evident, specifically the poor quality of technological development, high dependence on foreign capital to generate growth and the ineffectiveness of big business to drive industrialization. Between 2000 and 2010, official figures indicated a clear reluctance by domestic private firms to invest in the economy.[69] Najib conceded the need to review the government's longstanding position on ethnic- and business-based affirmative action to halt the recession and draw domestic investments (*The Star* 30 June 2009). Najib's corporate equity deregulation initiative was a clear attempt to send a message to domestic firms that they could invest, without fear, in order to nurture productive and innovative enterprises.

In January 2010, when Najib presented the GTP, his first major public document, it outlined seven National Key Results (NKRAs). One objective of the NKRAs was to improve the performance of the GLCs. To implement these NKRAs, a new unit, the Performance Management and Delivery Unit (Pemandu) was established, comprising well-qualified individuals from the public and private sectors. Pemandu was to ensure "end-to-end delivery", by working with the relevant ministries and bureaucrats to enforce implementation of public policies. Idris Jala, a turn-around expert from the private sector was commissioned to set it up.[70]

However, following reforms of ethnic-based equity ownership regulations in key sectors and among publicly listed firms, protests emerged from UMNO members. Mahathir joined the queue, questioning the wisdom of liberalizing ethnic equity ownership procedures as deregulation would allow for greater foreign presence in a developing economy still in the process of nurturing domestic enterprises. SMEs owned by Bumiputeras had not managed to acquire a meaningful presence in key sectors of the economy, including in manufacturing, despite numerous government initiatives, such as vendor schemes, to enhance their participation in the industrialization process. Following serious criticisms by right-wing groups about this plan to end the use of preferential treatment when distributing government-generated concessions to foster the rise of domestic enterprises, Najib reversed his decision. He then announced that his government would practise "market friendly affirmative action", an issue that was outlined in his *Tenth Malaysia Plan*. The demands of these groups, particularly Persatuan Pribumi Perkasa (Perkasa),[71] were reputedly a reflection of the discontent within UMNO about Najib's proposed policy shift. UMNO members had become accustomed to government patronage through affirmative action that entailed the distribution of government concessions to Bumiputera businesses (Gomez 2012b).

By 2013, this back-pedalling on policies led to growing concerns about the novelty and effectiveness of Najib's reform agenda. Indeed, even in the early days of his premiership, Najib had indicated a desire to be in far more control of major GLCs when he moved to place his close ally as a director of Malaysia's cash-rich oil enterprise, Petronas, which culminated in the departure of its CEO and chairman, Hassan Marican (Lopez 2012: 830–831).[72] Although Najib had promised to check corporate malpractice, business scandals of huge monetary proportions were exposed. These scandals implicated government-controlled companies through which well-connected businesspeople and prominent BN politicians had secured lucrative rents.[73] Major projects were selectively privatized, making it easy for the opposition to disentangle Najib's propaganda from UMNO's reality.[74]

In May 2013, when the 13th general election was held, Najib asked the electorate to use it as a referendum on his policies. However, in the election, the BN fared very badly, even losing the popular vote, but it retained power with a slim majority in parliament. After this general election, it became evident to Najib and the party he led, UMNO, the hegemonic power in BN, that it was imperative for the coalition to retain, if not increase, Bumiputera support in order to remain in power.

In September 2013, about three months after this election, Najib made an important announcement that had major implications on the corporate sector as well as government-owned companies. Najib introduced his Bumiputera Economic Empowerment (BEE) policy. The goals of the BEE were: (a) enable Bumiputera human capital; (b) strengthen Bumiputera equity ownership in the corporate sector; (c) strengthen Bumiputera non-financial assets; (d) enhance Bumiputera entrepreneurship and commerce; and (e) strengthen the service delivery ecosystem.

The significance of this announcement by Najib about the BEE was that it indicated a major change of policy direction in two respects. Firstly, the Prime Minister was clearly espousing the enforcement of affirmative action in business, a policy directive that has been in place since 1971. This was a fundamental policy shift, as he had admitted in 2010 that the government's longstanding support of affirmative action in business was hampering domestic and foreign investments. The second important issue about Najib's BEE policy was his decision to use the GLCs to implement it, particularly through its Vendor Development Programme (VDP), first introduced in the 1980s. Through this programme, the government aimed to tie small firms to the GLCs.

Najib's decision that implementation of the BEE was to be undertaken by the GLICs and GLCs was a cause for concern because he also serves as Minister of Finance, in the ministry ultimately responsible for the functioning of government-owned enterprises. In this regard, it is worth quoting at length how Najib planned to use the GLICs and GLCs to implement the BEE:

> In response to the laments of entrepreneurs who were encountering problems of market access, I will direct all ministries and GLC to strengthen their Bumiputra vendor development systems. The selection of vendors must be

based on merit among Bumiputras. In this manner, Bumiputra entrepreneurs could be capable of becoming strong and progressive. In line with this, I also want the vendor contract and concession periods to be synchronized with the bank loan repayment periods so their projects could run smoothly.

In connection with empowering the Vendor Development Programme or VDP, Petronas must boost its VDP programme, to strengthen its supply chain for the oil and gas sectors. The same goes for Tenaga Nasional in the energy sector, Telekom Malaysia and Axiata in the communication sector, UEM in construction while Sime Darby and Felda Global Ventures for the plantation sector.

With the empowerment of the Bumiputra economy too, I want all Chief Executive Officers in GLCs to fix targets on the participation of Bumiputra including acquisitions awarded to vendors. This should be included in the Key Performance Index for the Chief Executive Officers of the respective companies.

In this regard, I am happy to share that in the oil and gas sector between now and 2017, Petronas is implementing and will carry out several main upstream and downstream projects. Through these projects, we have worked out so that Bumiputra companies would benefit from contracts worth RM20 billion each year for upstream and downstream service work. The shelf life of such facilities is usually about 25 years or more. It is estimated at least 22 critical work scopes would be created to benefit Bumiputra companies.

To tackle the issue of supply chain, the government through GLC and GLIC would develop a group of Bumiputra entrepreneurs who would involve themselves in activities related to manufacturing and industrialization which have potentials and higher value added. In this context, GLC and GLIC would helm efforts to create several Bumiputra consortiums in the sectors involved….

In a move to ensure opportunities for Bumiputra companies to obtain contracts and in preparation to compete in the future, the carve out policy would be expanded to other big projects under the ministry, GLCs and GLICs. This policy was successfully carried out in the MRT projects where 47% or nine billion ringgit were awarded to Bumiputra companies selected on meritocracy. For example, four additional projects which had been identified to take part in the programme are Merdeka Heritage Tower Project, Bukit Bintang City Centre, MATRADE Exhibition Centre and the Sungai Buluh Rubber Research Institute Development programme.

Najib's repeated emphasis on "merit", or "picking winners", among Bumiputeras when dispensing business concessions was probably the most significant difference in his affirmative action policy, compared to the

NEP. A major criticism of business-based affirmative action was that it was based on race, not on merit—a reason for its failure.[75]

These were not the only major changes in Najib's economic plan involving government-owned firms. From 2009, the GLICs and GLCs were deployed to generate growth, while foreign investments were actively courted. The GLICs and their GLCs were encouraged to work extremely closely with state-owned enterprises (SOEs) from China. These ties between Malaysia's GLCs and China's SOEs contributed to unprecedented growth in state–state-based business ventures. Both governments have, however, attempted to incorporate private firms into these government-driven endeavours, a majority of which are infrastructure projects.

For example, in February 2013 the Malaysia-China Kuantan Industrial Park (MCKIP) project was announced, a US$480 million venture by government-owned enterprises from both countries. The total volume of investments in this industrial park on 1,500 acres of land will rise to US$75 billion by 2020. In this project, port services in the city of Kuantan, in Najib's home state of Pahang, are to be expanded and a steel plant, an aluminium processing facility and an oil palm refinery are to be constructed. The MCKIP consortia includes IJM Corp, a GLC, and the Rimbunan Hijau group, owned by the well-connected Sarawak-based Tiong family (*New Straits Times* 6 February 2013). The MCKIP project was one response to an agreement between Malaysia and China, in April 2011, to develop the Qinzhou Industrial Park (QIP) project in Guangxi province, also involving government-owned enterprises from both countries. The QIP, estimated to cost US$838 million, has a massive land base, covering nearly 13,600 acres, and is slated to have a population of 470,000 when completed. Other members of this consortia were Chinese businesses from Malaysia, such as publicly listed SP Setia, which subsequently was taken over by PNB, and Rimbunan Hijau.[76]

The most controversial deal where state–state business relations occurred involved 1MDB, an ailing and deeply debt-ridden GLC directly controlled by MoF Inc. To deal with its massive debts, 1MDB announced in 2015 that it planned to sell 60% of its equity in the 486-acre Bandar Malaysia project, a massive infrastructure development venture located in Kuala Lumpur's golden triangle.[77] 1MDB's majority stake in Bandar Malaysia was sold to China Railway Group, China's largest construction enterprise, and Indah Waterfront Holdings, controlled by Lim Kang Hoo, a Malaysian businessman who has direct and indirect business ties with prominent elites.[78]

Inter-governmental business relations with Singapore increased appreciably under Najib. A piece of land owned by Malaysia's railway company, KTM Bhd, at Tanjong Pagar on the Malaysia–Singapore border was ceded to Singapore in 2010 after a ten-year deadlock on its ownership. The sovereign wealth funds of both countries, Khazanah and Temasek, formed a joint-venture in 2011 to develop the reverted land. Other joint endeavours involving GLCs from both countries included Sime Darby Property Bhd and CapitaLand Ltd., to develop a RM500 million mall in Kuala Lumpur. Ascendas Pte Ltd. linked up with UEM Land Bhd to develop a RM3 billion integrated eco-friendly technology park in Nusajaya, Johor, while FASTrack Autosports Pte Ltd. and UEM Land are to develop the Motorsports City in Nusajaya. A high-speed railway link between Kuala Lumpur and Singapore was mooted, a project linked to Bandar Malaysia and 1MDB (*The Star* 16 March 2013).

The State of Play: GLICs' Architecture Defined

Table 2.5 provides a list of the leading government-linked agencies, at the federal and state levels, that have become part of the Malaysian economy between the 1950s and 2009. This list comprises enterprises created by each of the six Prime Ministers, with a focus on those institutions that had a business dimension or played a key role in developing core sectors of the economy. This list also includes enterprises at the federal and state levels that acted as investment holding agencies.

What is evident in Table 2.5 is that Mahathir's premiership defined the architecture of the GLICs, in terms of their ownership and control structure. By 2003, the GLICs that had been established were of a very specific typology, with five types in evidence: government investment special purpose vehicles (SPV), sovereign wealth funds (SWF), retirement savings funds, special purpose savings funds and unit trust management (see Table 2.6). Through MoF Inc., the only government investment SPV, the federal government can, as mentioned, function like a company. Khazanah is the only SWF, defined as a special-purpose investment fund owned by the federal government and created by it for macroeconomic purposes, that is to hold, manage and administer assets to achieve financial objectives and to employ a set of investment strategies that include investing in foreign financial assets (IWG 2008). MoF Inc. and Khazanah differ in that the latter can invest in foreign assets whereas the former does not, focusing largely on local investments or ownership of private assets. MoF Inc. also largely invests in government-linked enterprises.

Table 2.5 Major public enterprises and trust agencies

Public enterprise	*Year of incorporation*
Federal Land Development Authority (FELDA)	1956
Selangor SEDC	1964
Penang SEDC	1965
Terengganu SEDC	1965
Bank Bumiputra (M) Bhd	1965
Johor SEDC	1966
Federal Land Consolidation and Rehabilitation Authority (FELCRA)	1966
Majlis Amanah Rakyat (MARA, Council of Trust for Indigenous People)	1966
South Kelantan Development Authority (KESEDAR)	1967
Kelantan SEDC	1967
Kedah SEDC	1967
Melaka SEDC	1967
Negeri Sembilan SEDC	1967
Perak SEDC	1967
Bank Pertanian Malaysia Bhd (Agricultural Bank of Malaysia)	1969
Pahang Investment & Industrial Company Ltd	1969
Perbadanan Nasional Bhd (PNS, National Corporation) (formerly known as Pernas)	1969
Lembaga Padi dan Beras Negara (LPN, National Padi and Rice Authority)	1971
Pahang Agricultural Development Authority (PADA)	1971
Pahang Tenggara Development Authority (DARA)	1971
Urban Development Authority (UDA)	1971
Selangor Agricultural Development Authority (SEADA)	1972
Johor Tenggara Development Authority (KEJORA)	1972
Food Industries of Malaysia (FIMA)	1972
Credit Guarantee Corporation	1972
Perlis SEDC	1973
Pahang Trading Company (PTC)	1973
Johor Port Authority (JPA)	1973
Farmers' Organization Authority (FOA)	1973
Terengganu Tengah Regional Development Authority (KETENGAH)	1973
Rubber Industry Smallholders Development Authority (RISDA)	1973
Permodalan Nasional Bhd (PNB, National Equity Corporation)	1978
Heavy Industries Corporation of Malaysia Bhd (HICOM)	1980
Amanah Ikhtiar Malaysia (AIM)	1987

(*continued*)

Table 2.5 (continued)

Public enterprise	*Year of incorporation*
Tabung Ekonomi Kumpulan Usaha Niaga (TEKUN)	1988
Perbadanan Usahawan Nasional Bhd (PUNB)	1991
Multimedia Development Corporation (MDEC)	1996
Syarikat Prasarana Negara Bhd	1998
Malaysian Biotechnology Corporation (MBC)	2005
Pelaburan Hartanah Bhd (PHB)	2006
Malaysian Agriculture Food Corporation (MAFC)	2006
Ekuiti Nasional Bhd (EKUINAS)	2009

Source: Gomez, Satkunasingam and Lee (2015: 107)

Table 2.6 Types of GLICs

<table>
<tr><th></th><th>GLIC</th><th>Type</th><th>Agenda</th><th>Source of funds</th></tr>
<tr><td>1.</td><td>Minister of Finance Incorporated (MoF Inc.)</td><td>Government Investment Special Purpose Vehicle (SPV)</td><td>To increase value and returns of federal government assets</td><td rowspan="2">Government tax and debt funds
Funds can be directly obtained from the debt and equity markets, particularly by Khazanah</td></tr>
<tr><td>2.</td><td>Khazanah Nasional</td><td>Sovereign Wealth Fund (SWF)</td><td>To initiate and implement strategic industries and national initiatives</td></tr>
<tr><td>3.</td><td>Employees Provident Fund (EPF)</td><td rowspan="3">Retirement Savings</td><td>Social safety net—private sector employees</td><td rowspan="5">Funds directly collected from the investing public</td></tr>
<tr><td>4.</td><td>Kumpulan Wang Persaraan (Diperbadankan) (KWAP)</td><td>Social safety net—civil servants</td></tr>
<tr><td>5.</td><td>Lembaga Tabung Angkatan Tentera (LTAT)</td><td>Social safety net—military personnel/ veterans</td></tr>
<tr><td>6.</td><td>Lembaga Tabung Haji (LTH)</td><td>Special Purpose Savings</td><td>Social agenda—savings for hajj pilgrimage</td></tr>
<tr><td>7.</td><td>Permodalan Nasional Bhd (PNB)</td><td>Unit Trust Management</td><td>Social agenda—raise equity ownership of Bumiputeras</td></tr>
</table>

A majority of the GLICs are not directly funded by the government—EPF, KWAP, LTAT, LTH and PNB. These GLICs obtain their funds directly from the investing public in the form of savings. They use these funds to invest and generate returns on them for their investors. MoF Inc. and Khazanah obtain their funds from the government, though both can also raise funds in the debt markets. All GLICs can also raise their own funding by selling down their equity positions on the assets in which they have invested. The GLICs have an important social agenda, along with the required economic agenda of good investment returns. Thus, GLICs are in a situation where they must balance social and economic outcomes for the government. These social obligations include the need for them to help nurture domestic companies, particularly those owned by Bumiputeras. This also means that the government and the companies it owns and controls have to be seen as patient investors, even tolerating losses, as these enterprises evolve into independent corporations with the ability to compete in the national economy as well as globally. By 2013, between them the seven GLICs had ownership of 35 major publicly listed companies (see Table 2.7).

By the end of Mahathir's 22-year administration in 2003, the GLICs' ownership and control structure was set in place. This structure was not how Mahathir had envisioned it. His agenda was to privatize public agencies, part of his Malaysia Inc. vision, which constituted the rise of world-renowned business groups with a reputation for producing brand products. Economic crises, along with serious intra-elite political feuding, contributed to the dismantling of his initially fruitful attempt to create Bumiputera corporate captains, primarily by channelling to them privatized rents along with financial support through GLC-based banks. Before he left office, Mahathir admitted that his policies to develop independent entrepreneurial Bumiputera-owned companies had failed, leading instead to "crutch mentality".[79] Indeed, his long tenure was one that was characterized by bailouts by the GLICs, in many cases because of business controversies that had emerged from his practice of selective patronage (see Appendix 2.1). Mahathir's legacy, in so far as the nexus between government and business was concerned, was the creation of a GLIC ownership and control structure that reflected a government active in the corporate sector, through publicly listed and unquoted GLCs it owned and controlled.

Table 2.7 Public-listed companies owned by the GLICs, 2013

	GLC	*Estimated effective shareholding of GLICs*	*Total estimated ownership percentage by GLICs*
1	Malayan Banking	PNB via ASNB (42.34%) EPF (14.11%) PNB (5.68%) KWAP (1.99%) LTAT (0.61%)	64.73%
2	Tenaga Nasional	Khazanah (32.42%) PNB via ASNB (11.63%) EPF (12.22%) KWAP (0.96%) MoF Inc. via wholly owned Petronas (0.38%) MoF Inc. (golden share)	57.61% with a golden share to MoF Inc.
3	Axiata Group	Khazanah (38.87%) PNB visa ASNB (13.8%) EPF (12.16%) KWAP (1.36%) LTH (1.17%) PNB (0.54%)	67.9%
4	CIMB Group Holdings	Khazanah (28.31%) EPF (16.9%) PNB via ASNB (6.52%) KWAP (3.36%) LTAT (0.33%)	55.42%

(*continued*)

Table 2.7 (continued)

	GLC	*Estimated effective shareholding of GLICs*	*Total estimated ownership percentage by GLICs*
5	Sime Darby	PNB via ASNB (40.66%) EPF (13.59%) PNB (11%) KWAP (2.87%) LTH (1.66%) LTAT (0.3%)	70.08%
6	Petronas Chemicals	MoF Inc. via wholly owned Petronas (64.35%) PNB via ASNB (5.92%) EPF (12.02%) KWAP (2.85%)	85.14%
7	Petronas Gas	MoF Inc. via wholly owned Petronas (60.66%) PNB via ASNB (6.81%) EPF (13.63%) KWAP (5.3%) PNB (0.26%)	86.66%
8	IHH Healthcare	Khazanah via SPV: Pulau Memutik Ventures Sdn Bhd (43.89%) PNB via ASNB (3.05%) EPF (8.74%) PNB (0.32%)	56%

9	Petronas Dagangan	MoF Inc. via wholly owned Petronas (69.86%) PNB via ASNB (7.25%) EPF (6.24%) KWAP (1.09%) PNB (0.44%) Non-GLICs: State Secretary Kedah Inc. (0.19%) Secretary of Penang State Government (0.2%) State Financial Secretary Sarawak (0.2%)	84.88% by GLICs only. Total government ownership is 85.47%
10	MISC	MoF Inc. via wholly owned Petronas (62.67%) PNB via ASNB (8.37%) EPF (8.32%) KWAP (2.13%) LTH (0.99%) PNB (0.48%) MoF Inc. (golden share) Non-GLICs: Pahang State Government (0.46%) State Financial Secretary of Sarawak (1.51%) Penang Development Corporation (1.14%)	82.96% with one golden share to MoF Inc. Total government ownership is 86.07%
11	RHB Capital	EPF (41.34%) PNB via ASNB (8.03%) KWAP (3.78%) LTAT (0.58%)	53.73%
12	Telekom Malaysia	Khazanah (28.73%) PNB via ASNB (19.16%) EPF (8.54%) KWAP (4.49%) LTH (2.29%) PNB (1.6%) MoF Inc. (golden share)	64.81% with one golden share to MoF Inc.

(*continued*)

Table 2.7 (continued)

	GLC	*Estimated effective shareholding of GLICs*	*Total estimated ownership percentage by GLICs*
13	Felda Global Ventures	LTH (7.78%) KWAP (7.27%) EPF (7.05%) PNB via ASNB (6.64%) PNB (1.49%) LTAT (0.55%) MoF Inc. (golden share) Non-GLICs: Chief Minister of Sabah State (1.81%) Sabah State Government via Sabah Development Bank Bhd. and Ekuiti Yakinjaya Sdn Bhd and Sawit Kinabalu Sdn Bhd (3.01%) Pahang State Government (5%) FELDA (21.22%) Felda Asset Holdings Company Sdn Bhd (18.66%)	30.78% with one golden share to MoF Inc. Total government ownership (80.48%)
14	UMW Holdings	PNB via ASNB (49.7%) EPF (16.61%) PNB (4.81%)	71.12%
15	Malaysia Airport	Khazanah (40.22%) PNB via ASNB (14.94%) EPF (12.68%) PNB (1.41%) KWAP (1.11%) LTAT (0.4%) MoF Inc. (golden share) Non-GLICs: State Financial Secretary of Sarawak (0.36%) Chief Minister of Sabah State (0.36%) Penang State Secretary (0.4%) Pahang State Government (0.33%)	70.76% with one golden share to MoF Inc. Total government ownership is 72.21%

16	Gamuda	PNB via ASNB (11.7%) EPF (5.64%) KWAP (3.99%)	21.33%
17	UEM Sunrise	Khazanah via wholly owned UEM Group (66.06%) EPF (4.33%) LTH (2.95%)	73.34%
18	KLCCP Holdings	MoF Inc. via wholly owned Petronas and KLCC Holdings Sdn Bhd (64.68%) MoF Inc. via wholly owned Petronas (10.79%) EPF (3.53%) LTAT (0.12%) PNB (0.19%) PNB via ASNB (7.62%)	86.93%
19	UMW Oil & Gas	PNB via ASNB (8.22%) EPF (6.3%) KWAP (4.36%) PNB (1.08%) LTAT (0.5%) LTH (0.93%) PNB via UMW Holdings Bhd (2.65%) PNB via ASNB and UMW Holdings (27.41%) EPF via UMW Holdings (9.16%)	60.61%

(*continued*)

Table 2.7 (continued)

	GLC	*Estimated effective shareholding of GLICs*	*Total estimated ownership percentage by GLICs*
20	IJM Corp	PNB via ASNB (15.45%) EPF (11.67%) KWAP (7.33%) LTH (5.35%) MoF Inc. (0.61%)	40.41%
21	SP Setia	PNB via ASNB (17.64%) PNB (48.76%) KWAP (6.58%) EPF (5.89%) LTH (3.41%) LTAT (0.28%)	82.56%
22	BIMB Holdings	LTH (54.69%) EPF (9.19%) PNB (5.11%) PNB via ASNB (5.05%) KWAP (2.84%)	76.88%
23	Affin Holdings	LTAT (35.18%) LTAT via Boustead Holdings Bhd (12.14%) EPF (7.89%) KWAP via Boustead Holdings (1.48%) EPF via Boustead Holdings (0.05%)	56.74%
24	Boustead Holdings	LTAT (58.69%) KWAP (7.17%) EPF (0.25%)	66.11%
25	Malaysia Building Society	EPF (64.73%) PNB (3.6%)	68.33%

26	MMHE	LTH (6.15%) PNB via ASNB and MISC Bhd (5.57%) PNB via ASNB (3.27%) EPF (3.1%) EPF via MISC (5.53%) LTAT (1.2%) LTH via MISC (0.66%) PNB via MISC (0.32%) PNB (0.21%) KWAP (0.14%) MoF Inc. via Petronas and MISC (41.68%) KWAP via MISC (1.42%) Non-GLICs: Pahang State Government via MISC (0.31%) State Financial Secretary of Sarawak via MISC (1.00%) Penang Development Corporation via MISC (0.76%)	69.25% by GLICs only Total government ownership is 71.32%
27	Malaysia Airlines	Khazanah (69.37%) PNB via ASNB (1.66%) EPF (0.12%) MoF Inc. (golden share) Non-GLICs: Chief Minister of Sabah State Government (0.19%) State Financial Secretary Sarawak (0.27%) Sabah State Government via Warisan Harta Sabah Sdn Bhd (0.3%)	71.15% with one golden share to MoF Inc. Total government ownership is 71.91%
28	Kulim Malaysia	KWAP (8.1%) EPF (4.6%) LTAT (0.24%) PNB via ASNB (0.39%) Non-GLICs: Johor Corp (Johor state-owned corporation) (54.88%) Johor Corp via Waqaf An-Nur Corp (4.92%)	13.33% by GLICs only Total government ownership is 73.13%

(*continued*)

Table 2.7 (continued)

	GLC	*Estimated effective shareholding of GLICs*	*Total estimated ownership percentage by GLICs*
29	Bursa Malaysia	MoF Inc. (16.18%) MoF Inc. via Capital Market Development Fund (5.64%) EPF (8.5%) PNB via ASNB (4.27%) KWAP (3.34%)	37.93%
30	KPJ Healthcare	EPF (12.75%) LTH (10.39%) KWAP (2.04%) Non-GLICs: Johor Corp (Johor state-owned corporation) (37.74%) Johor Corp via Waqaf An-Nur Corp (7.14%)	25.18% by GLICs only Total government ownership is 70.06%
31	IJM Land	EPF (5.77%) KWAP (1.69%) PNB via ASNB (3.6%) EPF via IJM Corp (7.43%) KWAP via IJM Corp (4.67%) PNB via ASNB and IJM Corp (9.83%) LTH via IJM Corp (3.4%) MoF Inc. via IJM Corp (0.39%)	36.78%

32	MSM Malaysia	PNB via ASNB (12.68%) EPF (6.03%) LTH via Felda Global Ventures Bhd and Felda Global Ventures Sugar Sdn Bhd (3.97%) KWAP via Felda Global Ventures and Felda Global Ventures Sugar (3.71%) EPF via Felda Global Ventures and Felda Global V entures Sugar (3.6%) PNB via ASNB, Felda Global Ventures and Felda Global Ventures Sugar (3.39%) KWAP (2.6%) PNB via Felda Global Ventures and Felda Global Ventures Sugar (0.76%) LTAT (0.24%) LTH (0.05%) LTAT via Felda Global Ventures and Felda Global Ventures Sugar (0.28%) Non-GLICs: Chief Minister of Sabah State via Felda Global Ventures and Felda Global Ventures Sugar (0.9%) Sabah State Government via Sabah Development Bank Bhd and Ekuiti Yakinjaya Sdn Bhd and Sawit Kinabalu Sdn Bhd via Felda Global Ventures and Felda Global Ventures Sugar (1.54%) Pahang State Government via Felda Global Ventures and Felda Global Ventures Sugar (2.55%) FELDA via Felda Global Ventures and Felda Global Ventures Sugar (10.82%) Felda Asset Holdings Company Sdn Bhd via Felda Global Ventures and Felda Global Ventures Sugar (9.52%)	37.3% by GLICs only Total government ownership is 62.64%

(*continued*)

Table 2.7 (continued)

	GLC	*Estimated effective shareholding of GLICs*	*Total estimated ownership percentage by GLICs*
33	Bintulu Port Holdings	LTH (2.65%) MoF Inc. via wholly owned Petronas (28.52%) MoF Inc. (golden share) PNB via ASNB (7.061%) KWAP (9.079%) EPF (3.843%) EPF via MISC Bhd (0.19%) KWAP via MISC (0.04%) PNB via MISC (0.011%) PNB via ASNB and MISC (0.19%) LTH via MISC (0.023%) MoF Inc. via wholly owned Petronas and MISC (1.4%) Non-GLICs: State Financial Secretary Sarawak (26.674%) State Financial Secretary Sarawak via Equisar Sdn Bhd and Equisar Assets Sdn Bhd (13.043%) Pahang State Government via MISC (0.011%) State Financial Secretary of Sarawak via MISC (0.035%) Penang Development Corporation via MISC (0.026%)	53.007% with one golden share to MoF Inc. Total government ownership is 92.8%
34	Media Prima	MoF Inc. via Amanah Raya Bhd and Gabungan Kasturi Sdn Bhd (11.14%) EPF (16.78%) PNB via ASNB (4.93%) KWAP (2.48%)	35.33%

35	IJM Plantations	EPF (15.26%) PNB via ASNB (0.74%) KWAP (0.19%) PNB via ASNB and IJM Corp (8.51%) KWAP via IJM Corp (4.04%) EPF via IJM Corp (6.43%) LTH via IJM Corp: (2.95%) MoF Inc. via IJM Corp: (0.34%) Non-GLICs: Sabah State Government via Desa Plus Sdn Bhd (4.62%)	38.46% by GLICs only Total government ownership is 43.08%

Abdullah was well aware of the problems of a GLIC-GLC system that had a major presence in the economy but was poorly managed and a tool for the practice of patronage. He professionalized the management of the GLICs and GLCs to get these enterprises to operate in a more competitive manner, moving away from the personalized form of capitalism that Mahathir had initiated and institutionalized. What is evident in Table 1.2 and Appendix 2.1 was the more limited involvement of the GLICs in controversial business deals or to institute bailouts during Abdullah's tenure. The one situation when a bailout occurred involved the use of EPF to deal with the large volume of unpaid loans that had been channelled to students to pursue tertiary education.

Najib's early policy pronouncements indicated his desire to continue the work Abdullah had put in place and his intent to privatize GLCs to reduce government participation in the economy. This agenda began to change, specifically when he had to deal with the results of a general election which indicated that he would face difficulties keeping the BN in power. Over time, the mode of operation of the GLICs and GLCs became akin to the personalized nature of government/political–business ties instituted by Mahathir, seen particularly in the case of the business deals involving some of these firms and 1MDB. Najib's mode of ownership and control of the GLICs and the GLCs under their control is the subject of the next chapter.

Appendix 2.1 History of GLIC-Linked Controversies

All the GLICs have been involved in national controversies, including asset-shifting between them, bailouts of well-connected companies, loan or investment provisions to government-related assets considered sub-standard, as well as allegations of abuse of funds for vested interests. This non-exhaustive table lists notable controversies involving the GLICs in Malaysian history.

GLICs—Controversial Corporate Actions

No.	*GLIC*	*Notable controversies*	*Remarks*
1.	Minister of Finance Incorporated (MoF Inc.)	**Malaysia Airlines** • Sold 15% stake in MAS to western investors without the knowledge of its Chairman in 1986. In 1988, Bank Negara became MAS's largest stakeholder after taking over shares held by MoF Inc. (*The Star* 13 September 1988)	Asset shifting of GLC equity between MoF Inc., foreign investors and Bank Negara
		MISC Bhd • MoF Inc.'s shares in MISC were transferred to Bank Negara (*New Straits Times* 30 April 1998)	Another example of asset shifting to Bank Negara by MoF Inc.
		Perwaja Steel • Rescued financially burdened Perwaja Steel, a Japan-Malaysia joint-venture (*Business Times* 23 January 1991)	Bailout of a government-to-government (G-to-G) project
		Bakun Dam • MoF Inc. took over in 1997 the controversial Bakun Dam project from well-connected Ekran Bhd, owned by Ting Pek Khiing (*Business Times* 21 November 1997)	Seen to acquire assets deemed controversial
		1Malaysia Development Bhd (1MDB) • In 2009, 1MDB was established following the federalization and renaming of Terengganu Investment Authority (TIA). The government aimed to use 1MDB as a sovereign wealth fund for all states, instead of just one state, Terengganu (*Malaysiakini* 6 August 2009)	1MDB is wholly owned by MoF Inc. with a unique funding and asset acquisition model, via debt and the use of government guarantees. Its future listing was supposed to recapitalize assets and create value; this did not happen. MoF Inc. took over its assets when it encountered financial difficulty
		Proton • MoF Inc. provided Proton a RM1.25 billion soft loan due to poor cash flow. Barely four years prior to this, Proton had been privatized (*Malaysiakini* 7 June 2016)	Provision of soft loans to Proton, privatized to well-connected Syed Mokhtar Al-Bukhary

(*continued*)

(continued)

No.	*GLIC*	*Notable controversies*	*Remarks*
2.	Permodalan Nasional Bhd (PNB)	**Pernas**	
		• Rescued Pernas in 1995 as it had difficulties servicing loans, with a reported price tag of RM900 million (*The Sun* 21 February 1995)	Seen as a bailout by the government
		Asian Currency Crisis, 1997	
		• After this crisis, PNB was allegedly used to support share prices and bailout financially strapped companies and financial institutions (*New Straits Times* 18 February 1999)	PNB served as a means to save firms during the crisis
		Bank Bumiputra	
		• In 1984, Petronas had to rescue Bank Bumiputra, in which PNB then had the largest stake, from bad loans made to Hong Kong-based property speculators (*The Star* 22 September 1984)	A bailout of PNB by Petronas
		Golden Handshake dispute	
		• PNB gives "golden handshakes" to its retiring or resigning chief executive officers (CEOs), sometimes up to 20% of the paid-up capital of the companies under its control. It is not known how long this phenomenon has been going on and whether it is still being practised (*Malaysiakini* 24 August 2004)	Unusual reward practices by management
		SP Setia	
		• SP Setia, one of Malaysia's leading property developers, was bought over by PNB (*Reuters* 28 April 2014)	A takeover of a high-performing Chinese-owned company that many viewed as unnecessary
		Menara Warisan	
		• Strong criticisms against the construction of Menara Warisan/Menara KL118 (*Asia Times* 3 November 2010). The project is still riddled with controversies (*Malay Mail* 10 August 2013)	A mega-project wholly owned by PNB to construct the tallest building in Malaysia

3.	Khazanah Nasional	**Asian Currency Crisis, 1997** • Khazanah obtained a RM2 billion loan from EPF, a move criticized by its contributors (*Business Times* 27 March 1998) • Loans were made to Danaharta, an asset management company the government established in 1998 to ring-fence poor quality debts and remove them from the books of financial institutions (e.g., borrowed RM1.3 billion from EPF and Khazanah) (Lai 2012: 239) • Invested RM4 billion to rescue UMNO-linked Renong/UEM (Lai 2012: 239) • Rescued UMNO-linked Time Engineering (RM5.2 billion worth of debt) (Lai 2012: 239) • Bank Bumiputra received a capital injection from Khazanah worth RM1.1 billion in 1998 after recording a net loss of RM1.4 billion that year. Due to this "bailout", Khazanah had an 18% stake with the rest belonging to MoF Inc. (*The Star* 19 September 1998)	Played a hand in the bailout of distressed firms by taking over and restructuring them
		Proton • Poor Proton economic performance and failed Proton–Volkswagen negotiations due to fear of political fallout (Lai 2012: 247–248)	Became a shareholder of Proton and tried to restructure the business due to its poor business performance
		Pos Malaysia • Khazanah divested its entire 32% stake in Pos Malaysia, turning it into a wholly privatized entity which worried the 15,000-strong union as they were in a midst of a pay-hike negotiation (*Malaysiakini* 7 April 2010)	Divestment of a government asset, the postal service, to the well-connected Syed Mokhtar
		MAS-AirAsia Swap • Failed AirAsia-MAS share swap (*Wall Street Journal* 9 August 2011; *The Star* 7 September 2013)	Tried to restructure MAS by swapping shares with AirAsia. Attempt failed and was cited as anti-competitive. AirAsia and MAS were charged in court under new anti-competitive laws
		Malaysian Agrifood Corporation Bhd (MAFC) • Huge losses in agriculture sectors (totalling RM202 million in 2010 and 2011) (*The Ant Daily* 7 November 2013)	MAFC was to help the government boost the food supply chain and make the sector modern, vibrant and dynamic

(*continued*)

(continued)

No.	*GLIC*	*Notable controversies*	*Remarks*
4.	Employees Provident Fund (EPF)	**Bad Investments and Loans**	There are alleged inefficiencies in investments and loans provided by EPF. Seen to be giving unsecured loans to GLCs
		• According to *Auditor General Report 2010*, EPF approved loans worth RM55.1 billion not backed by government guarantees (*Malaysiakini* 28 October 2011)	
		Perwaja Steel	EPF gave loans to a non-profitable company that was over-leveraged
		• In 1996, EPF gave Perwaja a RM500 million loan even though it owed a bank RM10 billion and had a total loss of RM3 billion (*Malaysiakini* 17 March 2002)	
		Time Engineering	Loan provision and IPO subscription in a struggling UMNO-owned asset
		• In 1996, EPF approved a short-term loan of RM500 million at an interest of 9% to Time Telecommunications Holdings, an arm of UMNO-linked Time Engineering (*Malaysiakini* 28 March 2001)	
		• In 2001, EPF spent RM269 million on the 81.6 million unsubscribed public portion of the initial public offering (IPO) of TIME dotCom shares at RM3.30 when the share was hovering between RM1.96 to RM2.10; eventually suffered a loss of over RM100 million (*Malaysiakini* 16 March 2001)	
		STAR LRT	Loan given to a loss-making public transportation asset. Lost equity value in its investment in this company
		• EPF gave STAR LRT (public transportation light rail transit) more than RM600 million in loans, even when it was operating at a loss, resulting in the fund's equity stake of RM135 million being subsequently written off. Its share of the loss amounted to RM96 million in 1999 (*Malaysiakini* 25 July 2001)	
		Bakun Dam Hydroelectric Project	Loan given to a controversial public utility project
		• EPF used to finance the controversial Bakun Dam project (RM5.75 billion in loans given by EPF and KWAP combined) (*Malaysiakini* 25 February 2001)	
		PTPTN (Higher Education Loan)	Loan given to the national higher education fund corporation which had collection problems
		• PTPTN was forced to borrow RM2 billion from EPF due to a debt amounting to RM7 billion (*Malaysiakini* 21 February 2005)	

		RHB Bank • Bought RHB Bank which had links to Taib Mahmud (his son was then the chairperson) (*Malaysiakini* 28 May 2007) • Scrapped proposed merger of RHB Capital (41%), CIMB (14.5%) and MBSB (65%); possible tussle between MoF Inc. and EPF in the proposed merger (*The Star* 21 October 2014).	Acquired a politically connected bank. Was opposed to a mega-bank merger that was proposed
		Federal Territories Housing Scheme • RM1.5 billion taken from EPF to fund a housing scheme implemented by Federal Territories Minister despite not consulting the EPF board of employees representative[a]	Used to fund a housing scheme for the federal territories without full board consultation
		FELDA and FELDA Global Ventures • Felda took RM6 billion loan from EPF as its reserves had been depleting since 2004 (*Bernama* 30 June 2011) • As of 2013, EPF and KWAP have suffered a combined paper loss of RM75 million from their purchase of Felda Global Venture Holding shares (*Free Malaysia Today* 11 January 2013)	Provided loans to another statutory body, FELDA, due to its depleting funds. Lost money in investments in this listed GLC
		Pembinaan PFI • EPF provided RM20 billion loan to Pembinaan PFI, a GLC plagued by transparency issues and debt ridden (*Kinibiz* 19 November 2014)	Provision of a huge loan to an unknown debt-ridden GLC
5.	Lembaga Tabung Angkatan Tentera (LTAT)	**PSC-Naval Dockyard Sdn. Bhd.** • LTAT took over PSC-Naval Dockyard as it was unable to deliver its RM24.3 billion contract, then Malaysia's biggest (*Malaysiakini* 12 April 2005)	Acquired a well-connected defence-related company and its contract
		Scorpene deal • In 2007, Perimekar, jointly owned by LTAT, Boustead Holdings and KS Ombak, were involved in a controversial defence acquisition deal (*Malaysiakini* 27 April 2007) • Lodin Wok Kamaruddin's Perimekar allegedly received a RM500 million commission for the Scorpene submarine deal; he resigned after the deal was reached in 2010 (*Free Malaysia Today* 1 June 2011)	Huge commissions for a defence deal paid by the government to its related company

(*continued*)

(continued)

No.	*GLIC*	*Notable controversies*	*Remarks*
		1MDB • In 2010, LTAT reached a deal with 1MDB to serve as a contractor in the redevelopment of the Sg. Besi Airport (*Malaysiakini* 10 June 2010) • 1MDB reportedly owed Perbadanan Perwira Hartanah Malaysia RM396.41 million in September 2015. This debt caused LTAT to delay gratuity payments to non-pensionable veteran soldiers (*Malaysiakini* 4 April 2016)	Received a contract from 1MDB. 1MDB owes LTAT money which allegedly caused delays in gratuity payments to veteran soldiers
		Automatic Enforcement System (AES) • LTAT acquired a 50% stake in Irat Properties Sdn Bhd, responsible for the automated traffic enforcement system (AES) operations considered a failure in financial terms as well as in operational planning (*Malaysiakini* 7 March 2015)	Acquired shares in a company that was ridden with implementation and financial problems
		Awan Megah and Astacanggih • Deepak Jaikishan dropped a lawsuit against Raja Ropiaah and her company Awan Megah (a Boustead subsidiary) over a botched land deal and failed development of a defence research centre after Boustead Holdings acquired an 80% stake in Astacanggih Sdn Bhd, his company, for RM30 million (*Free Malaysia Today* 8 January 2013) • Raja Ropiaah, a Selangor Wanita UMNO Chief, was apparently awarded a RM100 million privatization deal to develop a defence research centre called Pusat Pengajian Pertahanan Nasional (Puspahanas). Boustead proceeded to pay RM130 million to Awan Megah to acquire the 223 acres of land though ownership was not in its possession. (*Free Malaysia Today* 8 January 2013)	Shows a complicated land deal involving a politician and a controversial businessman where an LTAT-controlled GLC was involved
6.	Lembaga Tabung Haji (LTH)	**Outsourced Fund Management** • In 2002, Tabung Haji lost almost RM200 million through a fund management company which used investment money on forex (*Malaysiakini* 18 March 2002)	Indicates weak monitoring by LTH's management of its funds

		Negative Reserves • Opposition claimed LTH's financial reserves were in the negative (LTH's reserve deficit at end of 2015 was expected to hit RM3.195 billion) based on a Bank Negara letter to Tabung Haji. As a result, Tabung Haji would not have enough money to pay all contributors if they were to withdraw their savings immediately (*Malay Mail* 11 February 2016)	Indication of potentially weak financial management on LTH's part
		FELDA Global Ventures • As the third-largest stakeholder in Felda Global Ventures, LTH's shares only yielded an income of RM7.6 million over four years since it was listed, with a purchase price of RM1.3 billion (*The Star* 16 February 2016)	Poor returns on investment in a controversial government-linked asset
		TH Heavy Engineering (THHE) LTH's subsidiary, THHE, suffered huge loss. LTH allegedly wrote a corporate guarantee of US$228 million to THHE (*The Edge* 4 July 2016)	Guarantee given was huge and materially very risky financially to LTH
		Tun Razak Exchange (1MDB Project) • LTH purchased two land plots at Tun Razak Exchange, one for RM194 million (RM2,860 psf), and the other for RM578 million (RM3,900 psf), 43 times the original price paid by 1MDB in 2012, which had acquired it from the government at RM74.2 psf (*Astro Awani* 8 May 2015). This news caused the average amount deposited in LTH for May 2015 to drop to RM40 million, compared to the RM71 million monthly average from January to April 2015 (*Malay Mail* 20 May 2015). To quell public fear, its chairperson announced that "the land it purchased from 1MDB would be immediately resold to give the public peace of mind" (*Malaysiakini* 19 July 2015). The land was not sold	Public anxiety over LTH being used to acquire 1MDB assets at a high price
		Bandar Malaysia (1MDB Project) • LTH bought RM920.8 million worth of Bandar Malaysia Islamic bonds (*The Sun Daily* 12 May 2015)	LTH invested in this 1MDB-related project
7.	Kumpulan Wang Persaraan (Diperbadankan) (KWAP)	**Funding and Change of Board Composition** • KWAP obtained RM2.28 billion additional funds from the government, allegedly to cover pension and benefits (*Free Malaysia Today* 23 March 2016)	Government injected money to fund KWAP operations

(*continued*)

(continued)

No.	GLIC	Notable controversies	Remarks
		Time Engineering • In 2001, KWAP and EPF bailed out Halim Saad's Time Engineering and TIME dotCom by teaming up with Danaharta and buying 76% of TIME dotCom's IPO of RM1.88 billion to obtain a 17.2% stake in the company. Both GLICs incurred a total paper loss of RM310 million, after a share price plunge (Rodan 2004: 122)	Losses due to a bailout of struggling well-connected firms
		Malaysia Airlines • In 2001, KWAP bought RM1.8 billion worth of MAS shares owned by Tajudin Ramli through Naluri Bhd (*Malaysiakini* 8 January 2001) • KWAP bought sukuk bonds from poor-performing MAS in 2011; considered a bailout (*Free Malaysia Today* 16 June 2012)	Bought corporate bonds from loss-making GLC, MAS
		FELDA Global Ventures • In 2013, EPF and KWAP suffered a combined paper loss of RM75 million from their purchase of Felda Global Venture Holding shares (*Free Malaysia Today* 11 January 2013)	Lost money in investments in the listed GLC, Felda Global Ventures
		F&B Nutrition Sdn. Bhd. Acquisition • Acquired value of F&B Nutrition was 22 times its 2015 earnings (*The Star* 18 April 2016)	Controversial asset acquisition
		SRC International Sdn. Bhd. • 1MDB subsidiary transferred to MoF Inc. • Najib approved a RM4 billion loan to SRC International from KWAP in 2011 (*Malay Mail* 25 March 2015)	Gave a loan to a GLC linked to 1MDB
		Tun Razak Exchange (1MDB Project) • KWAP bought a piece of land in Tun Razak Exchange at 30 times more than its cost (*Malaysiakini* 11 May 2015)	Bought 1MDB assets at a high value
		1MDB • KWAP invested RM1.4 billion in 1MDB and its subsidiaries as of March 2015 (*The Star* 19 May 2015)	Invested heavily in scandal-ridden 1MDB

[a]https://www.therocket.com.my/en/the-epf-housing-illusion/

Notes

1. Although the Malay Reservation Act of 1913 and the Land Enforcement Act of 1917 were enforced to protect Malay peasant land from being taken over by non-Malays, the implementation of this legislation led to the ghettoization of Malay peasants in these "reserves" (Hing 1983).
2. RIDA had been registering heavy financial losses due to bad planning, the poor capacity of its staff to implement the objectives of this agency and political interference. Its name was changed to MARA to give RIDA "a new face, a new set-up and a new life" (Gale 1981: 44–56).
3. UDA was corporatized as UDA Holdings Sdn Bhd in 1996 and listed in 1999. Khazanah acquired 50% of UDA Holdings' equity in 2004 from MoF Inc. and took it private in 2007. In 2009, Khazanah returned UDA Holdings to MoF Inc.
4. These features of MoF Inc. were highlighted in 2011 during a legal suit by former Pos Malaysia Bhd chairman Adam Kadir against the Minister of Finance and the government (see *The Star* 30 April 2011).
5. MoF Inc. acquired a 23.6% stake in KUB from Danaharta. The single largest shareholder in KUB then was Hassan Harun, its executive chairman, who owned 28% of its equity (*Business Times* (S) 28 March 2005). Wong (2011: 416–418) disclosed that KUB was mired in "poor management" and debt following the 1997 crisis, but it was saved by its huge 30% stake in Sime Bank. This bank, also mired in debt, was saved following a takeover and it was renamed RHB Bank. KUB's stake in RHB Bank fell to about 15% when the bank's equity was sold to improve the cooperative's ailing financial standing (Wong 2011: 416). See Chap. 3 for a history of RHB Bank.
6. This scheme was, however, only for civil servants serving in the Federated Malay States, then constituting just four of the 11 states in the Malayan peninsula.
7. The scheme was revised through the Pensions Act 1980.
8. The trust fund that was created to assist, but not administer, public pension that was situated under the Accountant General.
9. Since the life expectancy of Malaysians was increasing and the government's pension commitments were expected to grow, the retirement age of civil servants was increased in 2001 from 55 to 56, before increasing further to 58 in 2008. In 2012, the retirement age was increased to 60 (Tolos et al. 2014; Pensions Act; Minimum Retirement Age Act).
10. *KWAP Annual Report 2013.*
11. *KWAP Annual Report 2013.*
12. About half of KWAP's investments are in fixed income, roughly a quarter in domestic equities, while around 6% are in international equities and assets (*The Star* 28 May 2016).
13. Prior to this, there was a pension-like scheme for workers in only certain sectors of the economy, such as mining and plantations (Mohamed 1995).

14. *EPF Annual Report 2013.*
15. EPF tied up with Taliworks Bhd to acquire stakes in the Cheras-Kajang Highway and the New North Klang Straits Bypass, as well as a waste management company, SWM Environment Holdings which has a 21-year concession to provide solid waste collection services and public cleansing management in three states, Negeri Sembilan, Malacca and Johor.
16. EPF's first venture with the Goodman Group, a Sydney-based commercial property company, was in 2012. EPF created this joint-venture to participate in the development of industrial properties in Australia run by Goodman. In 2013, EPF, along with Goodman, made a foray into the German market. Meanwhile, Goodman was hoping that its ties with EPF would allow it to secure access to projects in the Klang valley, where Kuala Lumpur is situated, and in the rapidly developing Iskandar region in Johor (*The Australian* 17 February 2015).
17. In 2015, an amendment to the act required all officers to contribute to LTAT as well (*LTAT Annual Report 2015*).
18. Pharmaniaga, initially an investment holding company, became a health-based enterprise after acquiring several pharmaceutical firms in 1998. Its principal activities are manufacturing generic pharmaceuticals, supplying medical products and services and equipping hospitals. Since 1998, Pharmaniaga has enjoyed government concessions such as a 15-year contract to supply medical drugs to government hospitals and clinics. In 2009, the government awarded Pharmaniaga a similar ten-year contract. Boustead acquired Pharmaniaga from UEM Group in 2010 (*Pharmaniaga Annual Report 2016*).
19. LTAT owns three specific corporations that serve the needs of its members. Perbadanan Perwira Niaga Malaysia (Pernama), established in 1983, operates a network of retail stores in army camps nationwide. Some of Pernama's products have a duty-free price. Perbadanan Perwira Harta Malaysia (PPHM), established in 1984, acts on behalf of LTAT in the acquisition, possession, rental, development and sale of property. Perbadanan Hal Ehwal Bekas Angkatan Tentera (Perhebat), established in 1994, offers retired and retiring armed personnel training and retraining programmes, to prepare them for a second career. This information was obtained from LTAT's *2013 Annual Report.*
20. *LTH Annual Report 2013.*
21. LTH's investments abroad include TH Trust Australia, LTH Property Holdings Ltd., TH Alam Holdings Inc. and LTH Property Investment Inc.
22. Syed Anwar, in Nor Mohamed (2016: 56–61), recounts these events when he was incorporated into LTH by the government to revamp the fund. Syed Anwar himself states that the establishment of this panel was a "fundamental doctrine that I hope is still very much in effect today" (quoted in Nor Mohamed 2016: 60).

23. While EPF and KWAP are under the jurisdiction of the Minister of Finance, LTAT and LTH report to the Minister of Defence and Islamic Affairs respectively. However, LTAT and LTH require approval from the Minister of Finance for specific investment decisions. The ownership and control patterns of these institutions through the Ministry of Finance are dealt with in depth in the next two chapters.
24. The source of this information was PUNB's website. See also Nor Mohamed (2016: 179–184), where Mohd Nasir Ahmad, who was appointed the CEO of PUNB in 2001, provides an account of its activities.
25. Partly for this reason, Pernas encountered a serious crisis in 1995 and had to be bailed out by PNB.
26. From January 1991, the price of these units was left to the market. ASN shareholders had to bear the risks of transacting their shares at market prices, although there was little possibility of much depreciation in the unit price since ASNB and PNB had interests in Malaysia's most lucrative corporate stock. However, since ASNB's assets primarily comprised quoted companies, the fate of the local bourse as a whole affected the value of ASN units.
27. *Permodalan Nasional Berhad Corporate Profile, 2012.*
28. This figure included shares owned by Bumiputera individuals as trust-based government agencies were then responsible for acquiring corporate assets on behalf of this community, as stipulated under the NEP.
29. Among Mahathir's authored books, apart from *The Malay Dilemma* that was once banned by the government, are *Guidelines for Small-scale Bumiputera Businessmen*. On becoming Prime Minister, the businessman in him promised to end waste and inefficiency in government. His first slogan was "Clean, Efficient, Trustworthy".
30. Kumpulan FIMA, a food processing enterprise, was incorporated in 1972 and substantially owned by MoF Inc. Mahathir, then a senator, was appointed a director of this GLC and its subsidiaries Malaysian Can Company and Ayam FIMA. Mahathir remained a director of Kumpulan FIMA until his appointment as Prime Minister (Gomez 1990: 32–33).
31. In 1991, the government introduced a privatization master plan.
32. Jesudason (1989), Gomez (1990, 1994, 1999), Gomez and Jomo (1997), Searle (1999), Sloane (1999) and Wain (2009) review the rise of well-connected companies during Mahathir's long tenure.
33. Chapter 3 provides a historical review of ownership of the financial sector.
34. For a discussion on the role of the government, through GLCs, to fill in what was seen as entrepreneurial gaps in the economy, see Shirley and Nellis (1991).
35. In the production of the national car, the government deliberately bypassed domestic Chinese expertise in car assembly and sales. In HICOM's tie-up with Mitsubishi to produce these cars, the Japanese held a controlling interest. Mitsubishi channelled outdated technology into the Malaysian car project (Leutert and Sudhoff 1999).

36. Gomez (1999) provides a comprehensive assessment of the NEP's impact on Chinese businesses. His case studies of Chinese enterprises reveal the different methods used by their owners to develop their firms during the NEP's implementation.
37. In 1998, Mahathir authorized the release of a list of the recipients of privatized concessions. See: http://ww1.utusan.com.my/utusan/info.asp?y=1998&dt=0621&sec=Umno&pg=um_02.htm. Some of these businessmen are in this list. For a case study of companies owned by Francis Yeoh, Vincent Tan, Ting Pek Khiing and Ananda Krishan, see Gomez and Jomo (1997) and Gomez (1999).
38. See Gomez (1999: 114–115) for an account of the controversy surrounding the privatization of Sports Toto.
39. Magnum Corp, then owned by the Lim family, had been incorporated in 1966 as Empat Nombor Ekor Bhd. As Table 2.2 indicates, by 1971 it had emerged as a large enterprise.
40. Mahathir was responsible for reconstituting another GLIC during his tenure—KWAP in 1991, two years before Khazanah was established.
41. To be precise, MoF Inc. owns all but one share in Khazanah. The remaining share is owned by the Federal Lands Commissioner.
42. The South–South Cooperation programme was an attempt by Mahathir to encourage developing economies in Asia, Africa and Latin America to work together far more closely to reduce their dependence on industrialized countries of the West for investments and trade to ensure economic growth (Ahmad Faiz 2005).
43. This project to manufacture and distribute car-related products in Beijing comprised Japan's Mitsubishi Corp as well as three Chinese state-owned enterprises, the China North Industrial Group, China Aerospace Corp and Aviation Industries of China (*The Straits Times* 10 June 1994).
44. Mohamad Sheriff, an economist by training, had been in public service for 31 years (*Business Times* (S) 21 June 1994).
45. A comparison of the top companies in 1997, in Table 2.3, and in 2001, in Table 2.4, provides a clear indication of the fall of businessmen who had emerged rapidly as corporate captains during the 1990s.
46. By 2012, Proton was under the control of Khazanah which sold its stake in the car-maker to the well-connected Syed Mokhtar Al-Bukhary (*The Star* 12 January 2012).
47. Sime Bank was originally known as United Malayan Banking Corporation (UMBC), an enterprise created by Chang Ming Thien in 1960. See Chap. 3 for a brief history of this bank.
48. This issue of the decline of Chinese enterprises is dealt with in Chap. 4 of this volume.
49. For a review of the early history of Chinese-owned banks, as well as Public Bank, see Gomez (1999: 75–83).

50. For a case study of T. Ananda Krishnan's corporate ventures, see Gomez and Jomo (1997: 159–165).
51. When Anwar's allies accused Mahathir of corruption, collusion and nepotism, Mahathir released a list of privatized projects awarded by the government. UMNO members in this list included Anwar's relatives and close allies. Interestingly, too, GLICs were recipients of privatized rents, including MoF Inc., PNB, LTAT, EPF and LTH. This list of the beneficiaries of privatized projects is available at: http://ww1.utusan.com.my/utusan/info.asp?y=1998&dt=0621&sec=Umno&pg=um_02.htm
52. Anwar would argue that Realmild was a company acting in trust for UMNO and thus ultimately controlled by Mahathir (see *Business Times* (S) 30 November 1998). Anwar has consistently maintained this view when queried about his links with Realmild and MRCB.
53. For details about the management buyout of NSTP and the emergence of the MRCB group, see Gomez and Jomo (1997: 68–69).
54. Further details about this transfer of control of MRCB and NSTP to the GLICs are provided in Chap. 3.
55. For the reasons behind Daim's removal as Finance Minister, see Gomez (2001): in the *Far Eastern Economic Review* article entitled "Why Mahathir Axed Daim".
56. Both Abdullah's father and paternal grandfather, Ahmad and Abdullah Fahim, had held the office of mufti of Penang (Wong 2016).
57. The government defines a small company as one with a sales turnover of between RM250,000 and RM10 million or between five and 50 full-time employees. A medium-scale company is one with a sales turnover of RM10-RM25 million or between 51 and 150 full-time employees. The 2005 census of the corporate sector revealed that SMEs constituted about 99.2% of all business establishments. SMEs then employed 5.6 million workers and contributed about 32% of real GDP.
58. SME Bank was the outcome of the merger of two financial-based development institutions, Bank Pembangunan and Bank Industri & Teknologi. See Chap. 3 for a discussion on SME Bank.
59. The government had established SMIDEC in 1996 to encourage Bumiputera involvement in the industrial sector.
60. See Chap. 4 for an in-depth discussion on the GLC reforms introduced by Nor Mohamed Yakcop.
61. Khazanah, whose mandate involved nurturing and guiding the GLCs, was deeply involved in preparing the GLC Transformation Programme and introducing changes in the management of these enterprises (*Khazanah Annual Report 2013*).
62. BinaFikir was credited with the successful restructuring of Malaysia Airlines after it introduced and implemented in 2002 what it called the Widespread Asset Unbundling (WAU) scheme (Wong 2011: 432–434).

63. The G20 now comprises 17 GLCs, an outcome of mergers among the plantations based enterprises. As of June 2015, the G20 were Affin Holdings, BIMB Holdings, Boustead, CIMB, MAS, Malayan Banking, MBSB, MRCB, Sime Darby, Telekom Malaysia, Tenaga Nasional, UEM, CCM, Malaysia Airports, TH Plantations, UMW and Axiata.
64. See Chap. 3 for a history of these quoted firms.
65. See the *GLC Transformation Programme Graduation Report* for details about these foreign investments by the GLICs and GLCs.
66. Amanah Raya was formerly the Department of Public Trustee and Official Administrator. It went through a corporatization exercise in 1995. It is now a wholly owned government company, with shares held by MoF Inc. More details about this company is provided in Chap. 3.
67. Some notable CEO appointments during the first two years after this programme was introduced were Sabri Ahmad (Golden Hope), Abdul Wahab Maskan (Guthrie), Ahmad Zubir Murshid (Sime Darby), Wahid Omar (Telekom), Che Khalib Noh (Tenaga), Ahmad Pardas Senin (UEM), Idris Jala (MAS), Syed Zainal Abidin (Proton) and Nazir Razak (CIMB). See Chap. 4 for details about the appointment of these professionals as members of the management teams of the GLICs and GLCs.
68. There were, however, serious allegations of cronyism and patronage involving his family members. Abdullah's son, Kamaluddin, had an interest in Scomi Group, a public-listed global service provider in the oil and gas industry that had been privy to government rents. His son-in-law, Khairy Jamaluddin, at a young age, became a shareholder of a quoted investment firm, ECM Libra, with equity holdings amounting to millions of ringgit. Abdullah's brother, Ibrahim, owned a food-based enterprise that had secured a lucrative contract from Malaysia Airlines. For a discussion about these controversies from Abdullah's perspective, see Wong (2016).
69. See the *Tenth Malaysia Plan* (Chart 2.2): 38.
70. Idris had served Shell for 21 years before being identified by the government in 2005 to serve as the CEO of the ailing national airline, MAS. Within two years, he turned this loss-making enterprise into a profitable venture. In 2009, Idris was appointed as a senator and given ministerial status when he was asked to lead Pemandu. Under Idris' leadership, Pemandu was, within half a decade, listed in 2014 as one of the top 20 government innovation teams in the world (*The Star* 2 July 2014). Idris himself was listed by Bloomberg as one of the top 50 policy-makers in the world (see *The Star* 9 September 2014). For an insightful assessment of Pemandu activities, see Barber (2016).
71. Perkasa was one Malay group that was particularly vocal that the government reconsider its intent to cease the policy of affirmative action. Mahathir was the patron of Perkasa, an organization led by a politician who had once been a UMNO member.
72. Hassan Marican's departure from Petronas was linked to his reluctance to appoint Najib's political aide, Omar Mustapha, as a member of the oil

corporation's board of directors. Petronas, though a statutory body under the Petroleum Development Act (PDA), was also incorporated as a company in 1974, giving this GLC a dual identity. Petronas' other unique feature as a GLC is that it falls directly under the control of the Prime Minister, although the company is owned by MoF Inc., which is under the jurisdiction of the Minister of Finance. See Lopez (2012) for a detailed account of Petronas' history and the controversy involving Hassan Marican's departure from this company.

73. These mega-million ringgit scandals involved the Port Klang Free Zone (PKFZ) and National Feedlot Corporation (NFC), enterprises in which the government had a majority stake. The NFC scandal centred around the husband of UMNO's women's wing chief Shahrizat Jalil. His company had allegedly received a RM250 million contract from the Ministry of Agriculture to breed cattle even though it did not have any experience in this industry. See Vighneswaran and Gomez (2014) for an account of this scandal. The PKFZ controversy involved the award of a contract, without an open tender, to a well-connected company to design, construct and finance a trade zone in Port Klang, in the state of Selangor. The RM2.5 billion PKFZ scandal involved senior leadership of UMNO's leading partner in the BN, the Malaysian Chinese Association (MCA), and Sarawakian businessman-turned-politician Tiong King Sing. Lee and Lee (2012) provide an in-depth analysis of the PKFZ scandal.
74. George Kent Bhd, a firm owned by Najib's ally Tan Kay Hock, was awarded the RM1 billion Ampang Line LRT extension project (*Focus* 18 May 2013). Syed Mokhtar Al-Bukhary had received privatized projects such as Penang Port and Proton Holdings. Syed Mokhtar has interests in numerous other sectors including gas distribution, rice and sugar trade, power production, water treatment, banking and education. Najib's closest ally, Jho Low, is associated with the controversial 1MDB, a GLC under the Prime Minister's direct control (*Focus* 4 May 2013).
75. For an in-depth assessment of affirmative action through the NEP, see Gomez and Saravanamuttu (2013).
76. For details on these joint-ventures, see Gomez et al. 2016b.
77. See Chap. 1 for further details about the Bandar Malaysia project.
78. Lim was ranked by *Forbes* in 2015 as Malaysia's 27th richest person with assets worth US$650 million (*Forbes Asia* 24 February 2016). He has an interest in four public-listed companies: Iskandar Waterfront City, Ekovest, Knusford and PLS Plantations. Ekovest's shareholders include Haris Onn Hussein, the brother of the Minister of Defence, Hishammuddin Hussein. The son of the Sultan of Johor, Tunku Ismail Sultan Ibrahim, is the chairman of Knusford whose Managing Director is Ahmad Zaki Zahid, once closely associated with Prime Minister Abdullah.
79. See Mahathir's speech entitled "The New Malay Dilemma", delivered at the Harvard Club of Malaysia dinner on 27 July 2002.

CHAPTER 3

GLICs and Corporate Ownership

GLICs as Business Groups

Business groups, where much of the country's equity-based wealth has been concentrated, have long been a part of corporate Malaysia.[1] In the colonial and immediate post-colonial periods, foreign firms, particularly those owned by the UK, which dominated the economy, adopted this ownership mechanism. Malaysia's largest Chinese-owned enterprises have similarly held corporate equity through well-interlocked companies within business groups (Gomez 1999).[2] A feature of business groups is their extremely diversified pattern of growth, a common corporate strategy since the colonial period. Chinese immigrants ventured into any field of business that held the prospect of high returns. Businesspeople from other ethnic groups and the GLCs replicated this pattern of enterprise development well into the 2010s, as business groups and their pyramid-like ownership structure can function as a major control device of the firms they own.[3]

The complex ownership network map of the GLICs is outlined in Fig. 3.1. This map illustrates the corporate ownership links of the GLICs, highlighting their shareholdings of the 35 GLCs among Bursa Malaysia's top 100 firms.[4] MoF Inc., at the apex of this corporate structure, is the key enterprise in control of the firms linked to the government. MoF Inc. has majority ownership of the government's leading company-based GLICs, Khazanah and PNB, as well as Petronas, an important corporate player given its dominant presence in the oil and gas sector, and Amanah Raya Bhd, a major trustee company.

E.T. Gomez et al., *Minister of Finance Incorporated*,
DOI 10.1007/978-981-10-4897-5_3

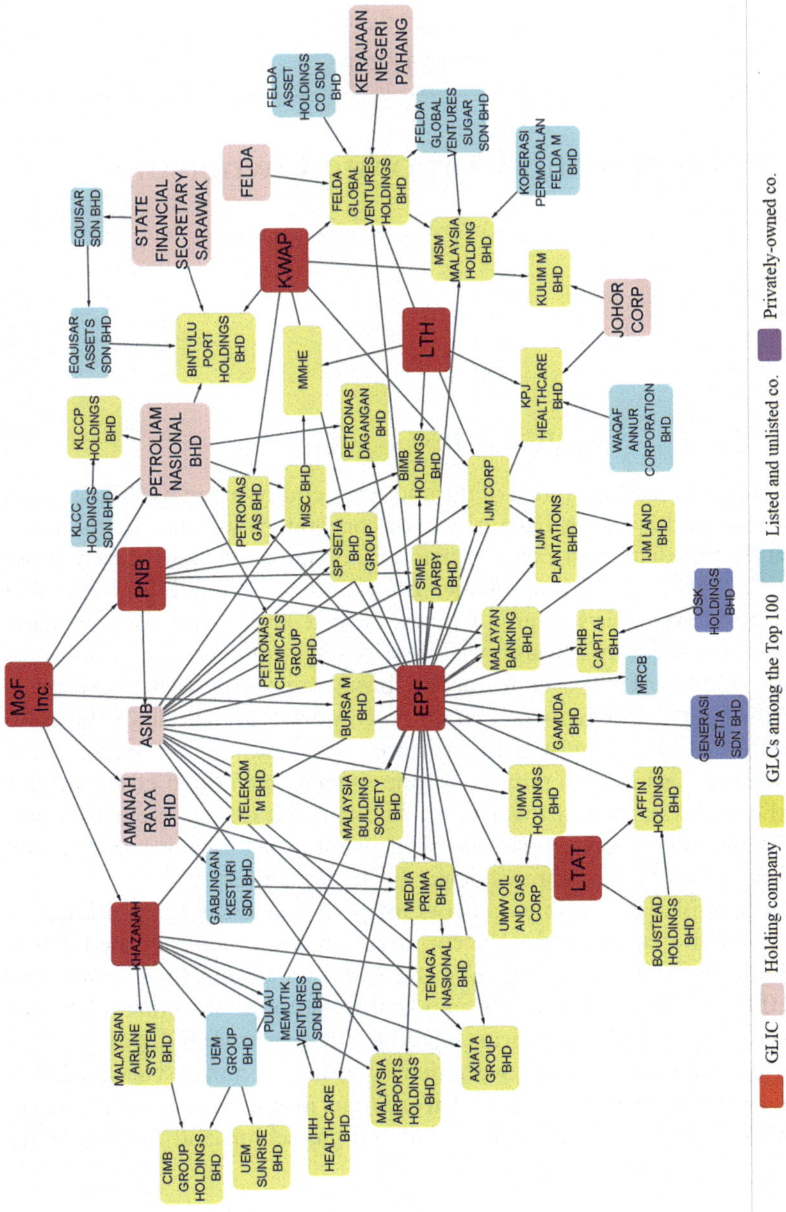

Fig. 3.1 Substantial share ownership network of GLICs, 2013

Khazanah has a number of interesting features. Firstly, it has majority ownership of GLCs situated in the utilities, services, banking and property development sectors. Secondly, Khazanah has ownership of all the utilities, Tenaga, Axiata and Telekom, and both transportation companies, MAS and MAHB. Thirdly, Khazanah owns the largest number of companies in which MoF Inc. has a golden share, and four are from these two sectors.

MoF Inc. has just one share in PNB, which functions as a golden share. PNB is the majority shareholder of the greatest number of GLCs, held primarily through ASNB and this unit trust agency's various shareholding schemes. PNB owns a majority interest in the largest enterprises, in terms of market capitalization, in core sectors—the financial sector (Malayan Banking), plantations (Sime Darby) and property development and construction (Gamuda). In the oil and gas sector, it has a majority interest in the UMW group.[5] Importantly, too, PNB's interests in companies in the property development and construction sector are through the takeover of these enterprises, such as SP Setia.[6]

EPF, LTAT, LTH and KWAP, the savings-based GLICs, have a controlling stake in fewer companies than Khazanah and PNB. EPF has a majority interest in two financial institutions, RHB Capital and MBSB, as well as Media Prima which controls major print, television and radio media outlets.[7] LTAT owns two quoted GLCs, one in the plantations sector, the well-diversified Boustead, which has an interest in Affin Holdings, the majority stakeholder of Affin Bank. LTH owns one company in the finance sector, BIMB, which in turn owns Bank Islam. KWAP does not have a controlling stake in any of the 35 GLCs, although it has a direct interest in all but seven of these companies. In only 11 of these GLCs does KWAP hold more than 5% of the equity.

Figure 3.1 further reveals that the GLICs use obscure private companies to hold substantial shareholdings of important GLCs, such as the media giant Media Prima, through Amanah Raya's wholly owned Gabungan Kesturi Sdn Bhd. Other unlisted companies have an interest in GLCs. For example, Khazanah's wholly owned UEM Group and Pulau Memutik Ventures Sdn Bhd have shares in UEM Sunrise and IHH Healthcare respectively. MoF Inc.'s wholly owned Petronas has ownership of KLCC Holdings Sdn Bhd, a substantial shareholder of KLCCP Holdings. Felda Global Ventures Holdings' (FGV) wholly owned Felda Global Ventures Sugar Sdn Bhd has shares in MSM Malaysia Holdings.[8] There are private companies, owned by individuals, which have an interest in quoted GLCs, for example, Generasi Setia (M) Sdn Bhd.[9]

Among these privately held companies is Amanah Raya, established in 1921 as the Department of Public Trustee and Official Administrator to provide trust, legacy management and will services. Its name change occurred after it was corporatized. Amanah Raya is 99.99% owned by MoF Inc., while the remaining equity is owned by the Federal Commissioner of Lands. The Chairman of Amanah Raya is Sabbaruddin Chik, a former UMNO leader who has served as a federal minister.[10] Amanah Raya has eight subsidiaries which focus on three areas: capital markets, property management and trust management (*Business Times* (S) 1 February 2006).

Investment holding companies owned by state governments in the Malaysian federation figure as substantial shareholders of leading publicly listed GLCs. For example, the State Financial Secretary of Sarawak, Johor Corp and Kerajaan Negeri Pahang are shareholders of Bintulu Port Holdings, KPJ Healthcare and FGV respectively. Two state-level GLICs have ownership of companies in the top 100: Johor Corp and the State Financial Secretary of Sarawak. Johor Corp owns a plantations enterprise, Kulim, and the healthcare services-based KPJ Healthcare. Johor Corp's ownership of Kulim was a result of a takeover, while KPJ Healthcare was incorporated and developed by this state-level holding company. The Sarawak state government owns a services-based company, Bintulu Port Holdings, which has three major subsidiaries. It also owns shares in Petronas Dagangan, MAHB and MISC. Other state-level governments have an equity interest in these 35 companies, though not substantially. Penang state has shares in Petronas Dagangan and MAHB; Sabah in IJM Plantations, MAS, FGV and MAHB; Pahang in FGV, MAHB and MISC; and Kedah in Petronas Dagangan.

Interestingly, as in the case of the property development and construction firms, many GLCs listed in Fig. 3.1 were established by private individuals. Among Malaysia's largest financial institutions owned by the GLICs, most of them were not incorporated by the government, except for CIMB—though even this statement has to be qualified.[11] CIMB's roots can be traced to a Sarawak-based family-owned bank, the Bian Chiang Bank, renamed Bank of Commerce when it was acquired in 1979 by UMNO's holding company, Fleet Holdings Sdn Bhd (Gomez 1990: 54–55). This bank was later merged with Bank Bumiputra, leading to the emergence of the CIMB Group. The shipping-based MISC, though founded by the government in 1968, was developed by Robert Kuok, Malaysia's wealthiest entrepreneur (Gomez 1999: 40). When MAS and Bank Bumiputra were incorporated by the government, Kuok served as a director of these firms. Other publicly listed GLCs established by the government were the utilities companies and those in the oil and gas sector. KLCCP Holdings was developed by the government. FGV was established by FELDA, a government statutory body, and KPJ Healthcare was established by the Johor state government.

Ownership of GLCs in Key Economic Sectors

The economic sectors in which the seven GLICs collectively have a large stake are banking, utilities, plantations, property development and construction, and media. The corporate structures of publicly listed GLCs indicate that different direct and indirect ownership methods have been adopted by these GLICs. The corporate structures of the leading companies in each of these sectors focus only on drawing attention to the direct and indirect ownership patterns of the GLICs and the quoted GLCs that fall under their domain. These figures do not provide an in-depth view on the corporate ownership patterns of the publicly listed GLCs, many of which themselves function as major business groups.[12]

Acquisitions in the Property Development and Construction Sector

Figures 3.2, 3.3, 3.4, 3.5, 3.6 and 3.7 outline the corporate structures of the leading GLCs in in the property development and construction sector, UEM Sunrise, Gamuda, SP Setia, the highly diversified IJM group and the Petronas-linked KLCCP Holdings—all ultimately under the domain of MoF Inc. While the corporate structures of the IJM group and KLCCP Holdings are particularly complex in nature, those of UEM Sunrise, Gamuda and SP Setia are not. IJM, Sunrise, Gamuda and SP Setia were once Chinese-owned firms.

UEM Sunrise was the outcome of a merger in 2010 between two major enterprises, UEM (of the UEM Group) and Sunrise, owned by prominent businessman Tong Kooi Ong.[13] Following this merger, UEM Sunrise emerged as one of Malaysia's leading property developers with expertise in the area of township development as well as high-rise residential and commercial development projects. Tong, Danny Tan Chee Sing and Allan Tam, the key players in Sunrise, are no longer listed as directors of UEM Sunrise. UEM Group, a highly diversified enterprise, has majority ownership of another quoted company, UEM Edgenta, formerly known as the Faber Group, and deeply involved in the hotel sector. UEM and Faber Group were owned by UMNO during the 1980s and 1990s (Gomez 1990).

Fig. 3.2 Ownership pattern of UEM sunrise, 2013

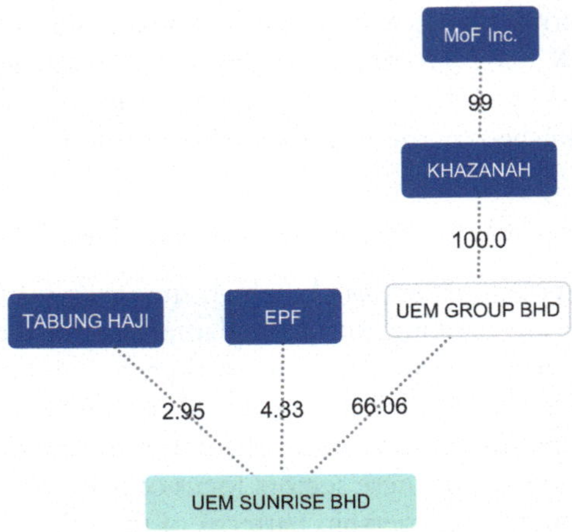

Four GLICs have a direct and indirect interest in UEM Sunrise, although Khazanah clearly has a majority interest in the company through UEM Group (see Fig. 3.2). Khazanah wholly owns UEM Group, which in turn has a massive 66.1% interest in UEM Sunrise. Two other GLICs, Tabung Haji and EPF, have a combined 7.28% interest in UEM Sunrise.

Gamuda, established in 1967 by Koon Yew Yin and his partners, was listed on the main board in 1992.[14] Gamuda was a subsidiary of Mudajaya, a company acquired by publicly listed IGB Bhd to form IJM. Gamuda was sold to Lin Yun Ling in 1975 (*Free Malaysia Today* 2 October 2015). By 2013, Gamuda was seen as the largest construction and engineering enterprise in Malaysia, with a market capitalization of RM11 billion. Gamuda was responsible for the construction of three major expressways, the Shah Alam Expressway, the SPRINT highway and the Lebuhraya Damansara Puchong highway. Lin fell off Gamuda's list of substantial shareholders in 2008. His equity interest in Gamuda in 2013 stood at 2.97%.[15]

As in the case of UEM Sunrise, Gamuda is directly owned by three GLICs and indirectly by MoF Inc. (see Fig. 3.3). These three GLICs, PNB (11.7% through ASNB), EPF (5.64%) and KWAP (3.99%), collectively own about 21.3% of Gamuda's equity. There are no GLIC directors on Gamuda's board of directors. One director-cum-shareholder is Eleena Azlan Shah, a member of the Perak royal house.[16] Lin was on the board, as Group Managing Director, in 2013. Gamuda has a 45% interest in Lingkaran Trans Kota Holdings Bhd (LITRAK), a highway concessionaire publicly listed on the main board and ranked 102 by market capitalization.

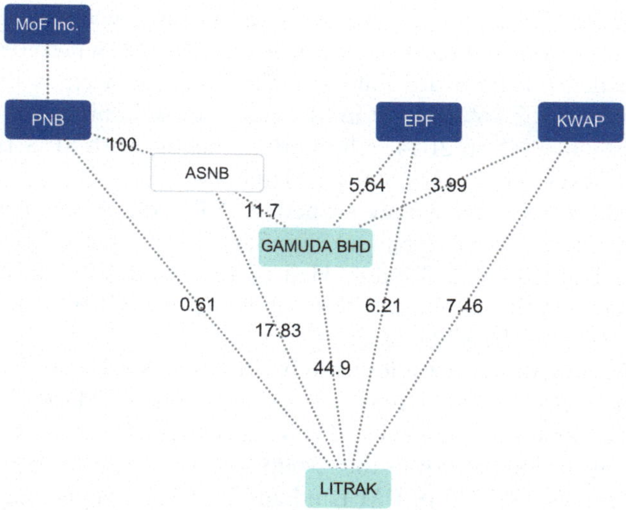

Fig. 3.3 Ownership pattern of Gamuda group, 2013

The GLICs have not always sustained a substantial shareholding of Gamuda's equity. When quoted on the bourse in 1992, Eleena was appointed to Gamuda's board. Eleena emerged as Gamuda's largest shareholder in 1999 and remained so until 2004. In 2005, EPF acquired a larger stake in the company. In 2008, PNB emerged as a substantial shareholder in Gamuda, through ASNB, when Lin fell off the list.

SP Setia, developed by Liew Kee Sin and Voon Tin Yow in 1974, acquired a sound reputation through well-managed domestic property development projects (*The Edge* 8 April 2013). In 1990, Liew and Voon, both then in their early 30s and colleagues at a property development company, ventured into business by acquiring Syarikat Kemajuan Jerai Sdn Bhd, which owned 225 acres of land in Ampang, close to the city of Kuala Lumpur. In the mid-1990s, when Syarikat Kemajuan Jerai was acquired by SP Setia through a share swap basis, Liew and Voon became shareholders and directors of SP Setia (*Kinibiz* 23 September 2014).

SP Setia went on to undertake projects in Vietnam, Singapore, Australia, China and London. In 2011, PNB emerged as SP Setia's largest shareholder with a stakeholding of just under 33%. PNB then increased its shareholding, triggering a mandatory general offer that led eventually to SP Setia's takeover. However, within a year, EcoWorld Development Bhd appeared in the property development sector with former top executives of SP Setia and Liew's son on its board of directors (*Kinibiz* 23 September 2014). Liew remained on the board following the PNB takeover, as President/CEO, with only a 2.76% interest in SP Setia. Liew sold his entire equity in the company to PNB in 2014, relinquishing his ties with SP Setia to join EcoWorld Development (*The Star* 22 March 2014).

PNB, along with its wholly owned ASNB, collectively has a massive 66.4% interest in SP Setia (see Fig. 3.4). Four other GLICs, KWAP (6.58%), LTAT (0.28%), Tabung Haji (3.41%) and EPF (5.89%) have equity interest in the company. Khazanah is the only GLIC that does not have an interest in the SP Setia Group.

The IJM conglomerate was founded by Tan Chin Nam—also the founder and owner of IGB—who attained a standing as one of Malaysia's leading property developers by the 1990s. IJM has an extremely complex interlocking stock ownership pattern as this group has an interest in three publicly listed companies, IJM Corp, IJM Land and IJM Plantations (see Figs. 3.5 and 3.6). Yap Lim Sen initiated the idea of developing a strong construction arm in IGB by merging IGB Construction with two firms, Jurutama Sdn Bhd and Mudajaya Sdn Bhd.[17] Solidstate Sdn Bhd was the result of the acquisition of Mudajaya and Jurutama by IGB, acquired via a share swap

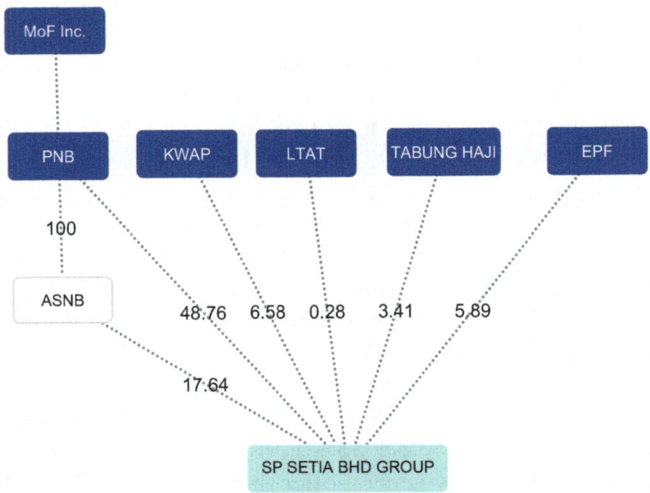

Fig. 3.4 Ownership pattern of SP Setia group, 2013

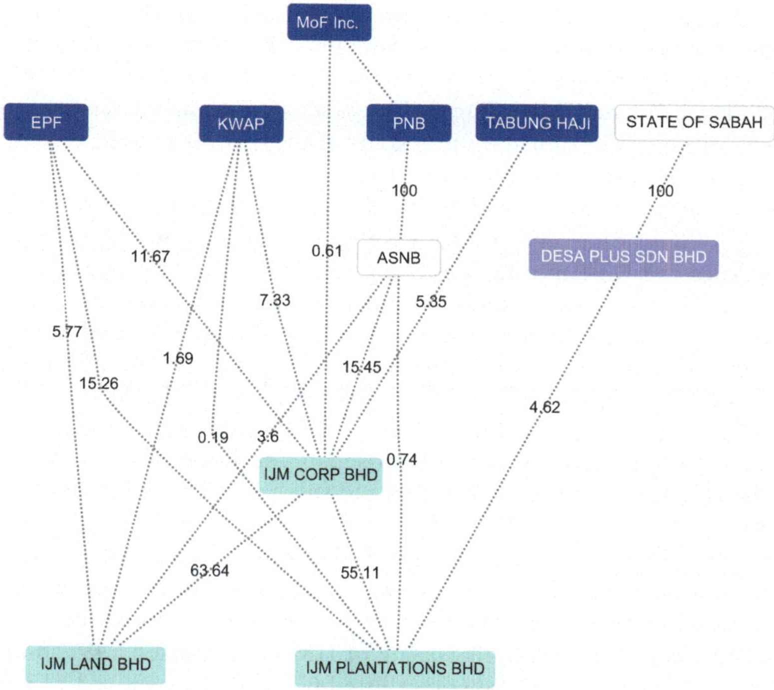

Fig. 3.5 Ownership pattern of IJM group (IJM Corp, IJM Land & IJM Plantations), 2013

in 1983.[18] In 1984, it underwent a name change, to IJM Engineering and Construction Sdn Bhd, and then to IJM Corporation Bhd in 1989.

IJM Corp has grown to be bigger than IGB, with the former's market capitalization more than double that of the latter in 2013. IJM Corp's operations run across Malaysia, China, Vietnam, Australia, Singapore and London, with 240 companies under it. Though once under Chinese ownership, five GLICs—MoF Inc., PNB, EPF, LTH and KWAP—have collectively secured a majority interest in companies in the IJM Corp group. IJM Corp is one of two companies in which MoF Inc. has a direct stake, although it owns just a minor interest of 0.61%. IJM Corp is a substantial shareholder of IJM Land and IJM Plantations, with a 63.6% and 55.1% stake respectively. There are no interlocking of shareholdings and directorships between IJM Corp and IGB. This could be attributed to the shift in ownership of IJM Corp.

The Sabah state government has a 4.62% stake in IJM Plantations through a private firm, Desa Plus Sdn Bhd. In 1985, IJM Plantations entered a project to develop estates in Sabah. Since then, its land bank in Sabah has increased, expanding to Indonesia. The company regards itself as a "boutique" oil palm agribusiness in Sabah. IJM Plantations was listed on the Bursa's main board in July 2003.

IJM Land was established in 1989 and was formerly known as RB Land Holdings Bhd. This company is the result of a merger between IJM Properties and RB Land. Besides being one of the largest property developers in Malaysia, with projects in different parts of the country, it ventured into property development in China.[19] Although EPF and PNB are among the largest equity shareholders of companies in the IJM group, there are no GLIC directors on the board of directors of IJM Corp or its subsidiaries. One of the key players in the IJM group, before the takeover of these companies by GLICs, was Krishnan Tan Boon Seng; he remains on the IJM Corp's board of directors and still has an equity interest in the company.

In the IJM Corp Group, the use of the pyramid structure is particularly pronounced (see Fig. 3.6). This structure shows the companies under the control of IJM Corp that are listed on the Bursa, though below the top 100. Scomi Group is an associate of IJM Corp, ranked 249, and is a substantial shareholder of two other listed GLCs that are ranked 115 and 500 respectively. IJM Corp has shares in Kumpulan Europlus Bhd,[20] ranked 219, which in turn has a stake in Trinity Corporation Bhd,[21] ranked 360. These companies are involved in various sectors. Scomi Energy Services

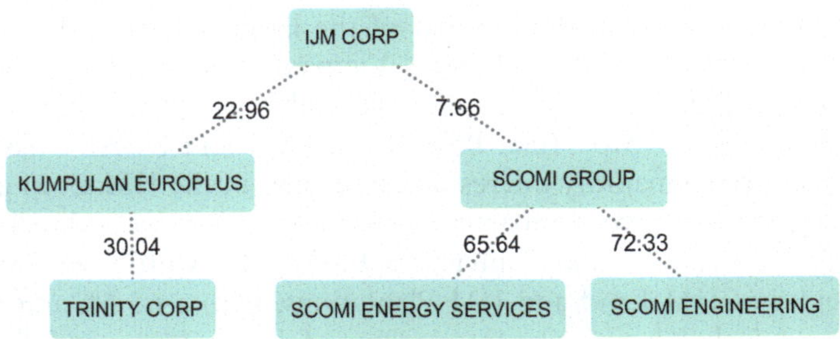

Fig. 3.6 IJM Corp—business group and pyramid structure

Bhd is a service provider in the oil and gas, and coal industries, while Scomi Engineering Bhd provides services in public transport solutions.

This review of the involvement of major GLCs in property development and construction highlights one crucial issue: the growing presence of the government in this sector. In spite of Najib's call for the divestment of GLCs through privatization soon after he became Prime Minister in 2009, during his administration the GLICs have been particularly focused on infrastructure development, seen in the takeover of Sunrise. Other Chinese-owned construction companies such as Gamuda and SP Setia have come under PNB.

Four GLICs have an interest in KLCCP Holdings, which in turn owns Suria KLCC, the owner of the mammoth Petronas Twin Towers in the heart of Kuala Lumpur (see Fig. 3.7). MoF Inc. has a majority interest in KLCCP Holdings through wholly owned Petronas, which has a direct and indirect

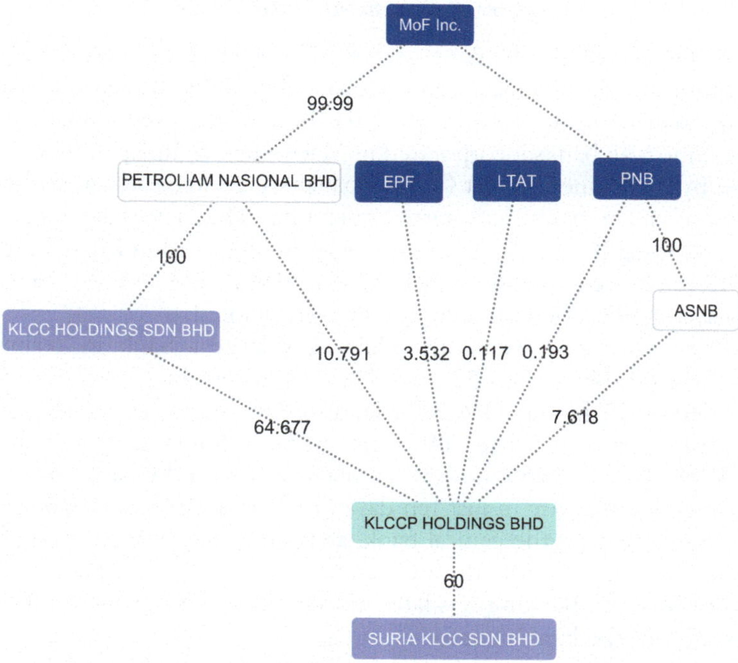

Fig. 3.7 Ownership pattern of KLCCP holdings group, 2013

share in this listed firm through KLCC Holdings Sdn Bhd, totalling 75.5%. Despite MoF Inc.'s dominant shareholding of KLCCP, three other GLICs have a stake in the company, albeit a nominal interest each. PNB appears as the second largest GLIC shareholder, through ASNB, with a total 7.81% interest. However, none of the directors is a GLIC director as well. One director stands out on the KLCCP board, Augustus Ralph Marshall, a close business associate of the extremely well-connected T. Ananda Krishnan.[22]

The Petronas Twin Towers was part of the development of the Multimedia Super Corridor, a zone for information and multimedia technology that stretched from the Kuala Lumpur International Airport to Kuala Lumpur City Center. Then Prime Minister Mahathir Mohamad would later claim that the twin towers symbolized the "advancement and zest of a nation".[23] The idea of the Kuala Lumpur City Center and the towers reputedly originated from Ananda Krishnan, who was closely associated with Mahathir (*BBC News* 30 October 2003).

Capture of Financial Institutions

A brief history of the banking sector is instructive to understand the implications of the significant equity ownership shifts that have occurred among financial institutions in Malaysia. Besides the predominantly UK banks, almost all banks incorporated in Malaya before Independence were owned by the Chinese. Most Chinese banks were established about half a century after UK banks had started operating. The first Malay bank, the Malay National Banking Corporation, was incorporated in Kuala Lumpur in 1947 but ceased operations in 1952 (Lim 1967: 233). Of the 26 banks in Malaya in 1959, only six were locally incorporated.

Malayan Banking, currently Malaysia's largest bank in terms of assets, was established on 31 May 1960 by Khoo Teck Puat and publicly listed on 17 January 1962.[24] Malayan Banking expanded so rapidly that within five years it had 109 branches, both domestically and abroad (Gill 1985: 19). In 1966, however, a massive run on the bank wiped out 40% of its deposit base in just ten days (Yoshihara 1988: 204–205).[25] In 1967, Bank Negara, the central bank, stepped in to restructure Malayan Banking, bringing it under its direct control later that year. Majority ownership of Malayan Banking was later transferred to PNB, which still owns almost 55% of the bank's equity.

Bank Bumiputra (now part of the CIMB Group, Malaysia's third-largest bank) was incorporated in 1966 to serve as the flagship of Malay capital. Although Bank Bumiputra's incorporation was viewed as an attempt to break Chinese and foreign domination of the banking sector (Snodgrass: 1980: 53), among the bank's original directors who played a key role in its development was the Malaysian magnate, Robert Kuok. Another central figure in Bank Bumiputra's management was Kuok's close ally Khoo Kay Peng, who went on to build MUI Bank (which evolved into Hong Leong Bank after its takeover by Quek Leng Chan's Hong Leong group) (Gomez 1999: 34–35). By the early 1980s, Bank Bumiputra was under the control of PNB, which divested its stake in the bank to Petronas in 1984 following a major scandal, the BMF affair.[26] Following the 1997 currency crisis, Bank Bumiputra was again mired in controversy as it was deeply burdened with hefty non-performing losses, held primarily by well-connected businessmen. In 1998, Bank Bumiputra declared a massive loss and required a capital injection of RM750 million to stay afloat. The government also bought over the bank's non-performing loans (Gomez 2002: 102–103). Bank Bumiputra was eventually merged with Bank of Commerce and became part of the CIMB group, which then emerged as the country's second-largest bank with RM65 billion in assets. At that point, the merged enterprise's biggest shareholders were MoF Inc. and Khazanah (*Business Times* (S) 9 February 1999).

United Malayan Banking Corporation (UMBC), now RHB Bank, Malaysia's third-largest bank was established by Chang Ming Thien in 1959. Following a run on the bank in 1976, he lost 30% of its equity to government-owned Pernas. In 1981, Chang relinquished his remaining majority stake in UMBC to Multi-Purpose Holdings Bhd (MPHB), then the holding company of the Malaysian Chinese Association (MCA), UMNO's leading partner in the Barisan Nasional (BN) coalition. In 1984, MPHB exchanged its interest in UMBC for a majority interest in the Malaysian French Bank, owned by Daim Zainuddin, then the soon to be appointed Minister of Finance. In 1986, Daim sold his stake in UMBC to Pernas, allegedly at an inflated price, an incident that came to be known as the "UMBC scandal" (Gomez 1990: 41–42). Pernas channelled ownership of UMBC to Datuk Keramat Holdings Bhd, a publicly listed company ultimately controlled by Mohamed Noor Yusof, who had served as Mahathir's political secretary. UMBC was subsequently enmeshed in numerous allegations of corruption and was sold in 1995 to a GLC, Sime Darby, and renamed Sime Bank (Gomez and Jomo 1997: 59).[27] After the 1997 crisis, when it was revealed that Sime Bank was laden with huge non-performing loans, it was taken over by Rashid Hussain, a well-connected businessman who renamed it RHB Bank. Following a falling-out between Rashid and Mahathir, ownership of the bank was shifted to family members of the then Chief Minister of Sarawak, Taib Mahmud, who later divested this equity to EPF who now is the bank's majority shareholder. This brief history of RHB Bank reflects the way ownership of a major bank was passed between government bodies and well-connected businessmen, usually at the expense of the former to benefit the latter, before coming under the control of a financially well-endowed GLIC.

United Asian Bank Bhd (UAB), controlled by banks in India, came perilously close to receivership in 1986, and Bank Negara stepped in, injecting almost RM363 million to revive it. Bank Negara later made known its intention to divest its 74% stake in UAB for cash if an acceptable bid was made (*Malaysian Business* 1 October 1990). In September 1990, UAB and the UMNO-linked Bank of Commerce (BCB), then the ninth-largest bank, announced their merger through a share swap. Renong Bhd, then under UMNO control through Halim Saad, a businessman closely associated with party treasurer Daim, had a 64% stake in BCB through two subsidiaries.[28] The UAB–BCB merger made the new concern—the name Bank of Commerce was retained—the fifth-largest bank in the country. Bank of Commerce would subsequently evolve into CIMB, following its merger with Bank Bumiputra, by then an enterprise persistently bailed out by the government.

In 1999, eight of the top ten local banks, once primarily dominated by Chinese and foreign interests, were brought under the control of Bumiputera and government companies. The two exceptions were publicly listed Public Bank, then the fourth-largest bank, and Southern Bank, the tenth largest, both under Chinese control. This consolidation exercise occurred when the government announced its desire to merge Malaysia's 58 financial institutions into six anchor banks. The government's justification for this consolidation exercise was that far too many financial institutions were serving a population of around 24 million. Under this consolidation plan, banks owned by prominent Malays who were not closely associated with then Minister of Finance Daim did not receive anchor bank status even though their owners had much banking expertise and had developed their enterprises with relatively little government assistance. In this exercise, the most dynamic banks were brought under direct or indirect control of the government and influential politicians, in particular Daim.[29] Of the six anchor bank groups, the Daim-linked Multi-Purpose Bank grouping had the largest number of financial institutions,[30] which would have given the enlarged enterprise a significant national presence.[31] What is significant about this consolidation is the loss of Chinese-owned banks, many of which were catering to SMEs.

The proposed consolidation exercise upset the Chinese, as the merger of their most enterprising banks diminished their presence in this sector. With a general election then impending, and since Mahathir was aware that UMNO needed non-Malay, especially Chinese, support to secure a strong presence in parliament, the number of anchor banks was increased from six to ten and included several better-run and thriving institutions (see Table 3.1). This decision reportedly sparked a rift between Mahathir and Daim.[32]

Table 3.1 Consolidation in 1999—anchor banks and partners

Anchor bank	*Merger partners*	*New owner*
Malayan Banking	Mayban Finance, Aseambankers Malaysia, PhileoAllied Bank, Pacific Bank, Sime Finance Bank, Kewangan Bersatu	Malaysian government
Bumiputra-Commerce	Bumiputra-Commerce Finance, Commerce International Merchant Bankers	Malaysian government
RHB Bank	RHB Sakura Merchant Bankers, Delta Finance, Interfinance	Rashid Hussain
Public Bank	Public Finance, Hock Hua Bank, Advance Finance, Sime Merchant Bankers	Teh Hong Piow
Arab-Malaysian Bank	Wah Tat Bank, Hock Hua Bank, Inter Finance, Advance Finance, Sime Merchant Bank	Azman Hashim
Hong Leong Bank	Hong Leong Finance, Wah Tat Bank, Credit Corporation Malaysia	Quek Leng Chan
Perwira Affin Bank	Affin Finance, Perwira Affin Merchant Bankers, BSN Commercial Bank, BSN Finance, BSN Merchant Bank	Malaysian government
Multi-Purpose Bank	International Bank Malaysia, Sabah Bank, MBf Finance, Bolton Finance, Sabah Finance, Bumiputra Merchant Bankers, Amanah Merchant Bank	Daim's allies
Southern Bank[a]	Ban Hin Lee Bank, Cempaka Finance, United Merchant Finance, Perdana Finance, Perdana Merchant Bankers	Tan Teong Hean
EON Bank	EON Finance, Oriental Bank, City Finance, Malaysian International Merchant Bankers, Perkasa Finance	Malaysian government

Source: Gomez (2005: 234–235)

[a]Southern Bank was taken over by CIMB in 2006

This forced consolidation exercise indicated that the Prime Minister could radically change ownership and control patterns in key sectors of the economy and that other arms of the government and public institutions had become subservient to the executive. It also revealed the impact that concentration of political power can have on property rights. Majority ownership of a company meant nothing when a strong state was determined to push through corporate restructuring.

By 2013, there were only nine banks and the GLICs were key players in terms of ownership of these financial institutions (see Table 3.2). Malayan Banking remains under the control of PNB. Khazanah owns the third largest bank, CIMB, while LTAT owns Affin Bank. Other banks controlled by GLICs include RHB Bank and Bank Islam. Table 3.2 further illustrates the rise of foreign ownership of privately owned banks, with the well-connected Azman Hashim sharing control of AmBank with Australia-based ANZ, while Alliance Bank, once under the control of Daim, is now owned by the Singapore's leading GLIC, Temasek.

Figures 3.8, 3.9, 3.10, 3.11 and 3.12 outline the ownership patterns of Malaysia's leading banks through the GLICs. Figure 3.8 indicates that MoF Inc. has ultimate ownership of Malayan Banking through PNB, along with three other GLICs.[33] While PNB has significant ownership of this bank with 48% equity, three other GLICs—EPF, KWAP, and LTAT—collectively

Table 3.2 Ownership structure of key commercial banks, 2013

Name	*Major shareholder*	*Status*	*GLIC ownership*	*Percentage ownership*
Affin Bank	LTAT	GLC	LTAT	35.18
Alliance Bank	Temasek	Privately owned	EPF	13.97
AmBank (M)	ANZ/Azman Hashim	Privately owned	EPF	11.81
CIMB Bank	Khazanah	GLC	Khazanah	28.31
Hong Leong Bank	Quek family	Privately owned	EPF	1.68
Malayan Banking	PNB	GLC	PNB	48.02
Public Bank	Teh Hong Piow	Privately owned	EPF	13.2
RHB Bank	EPF	GLC	EPF	41.34
Bank Islam	LTH	GLC	LTH	54.69

Source: Gomez et al. (2015: 117)

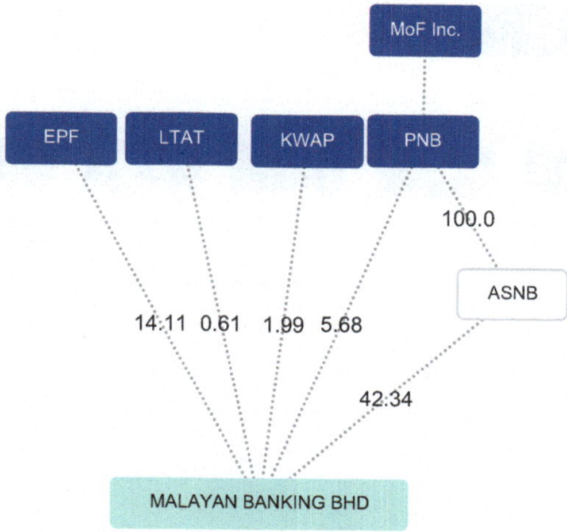

Fig. 3.8 Ownership pattern of Malayan Banking, 2013

hold another 17% stake. In CIMB, MoF Inc. again has an interest through Khazanah and PNB (through ASNB), which collectively own about 35% of this financial institution's equity (see Fig. 3.9). EPF holds another 17% interest, while KWAP and LTAT each hold a small stake. Figure 3.10 indicates the highly convoluted ownership pattern of Affin Holdings, which owns Affin Bank. Three GLICs have direct and indirect interests in Affin Holdings, but it is ultimately controlled by LTAT, which is under the jurisdiction of the Minister of Defence as well as Lodin Wok Kamaruddin, a close associate of Prime Minister Najib. Figure 3.11 indicates that RHB Bank is controlled by five GLICs, though majority ownership lies with EPF.

BIMB was established in 1983, the outcome of a concerted effort by LTH, Pertubuhan Kebajikan Islam Malaysia (PERKIM[34]) and the National Steering Committee for Islamic Bank to create an institution to serve the financial needs of Malaysia's Muslim population. BIMB later extended its services to non-Muslims. It was the first shariah-based banking institution in Malaysia and in Southeast Asia. BIMB went on to create a network of 145 branches across the country, a feat that contributed to according Malaysia recognition as a global leading player in Islamic banking. BIMB was responsible for pioneering Malaysia's attempt to present itself as "one of the world's major Islamic financial hubs".[35]

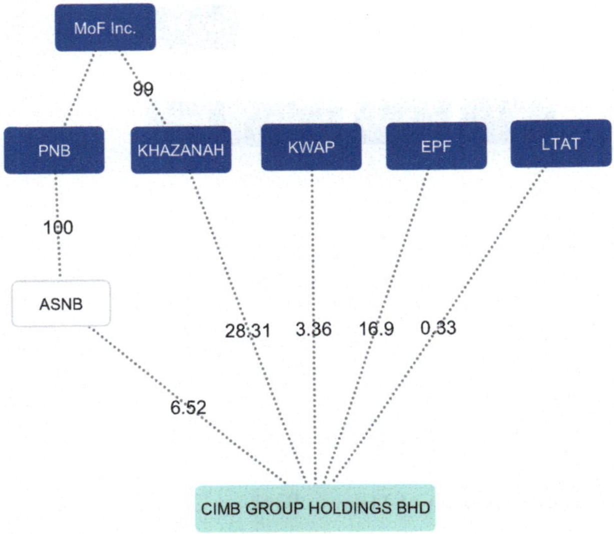

Fig. 3.9 Ownership pattern of CIMB group holdings, 2013

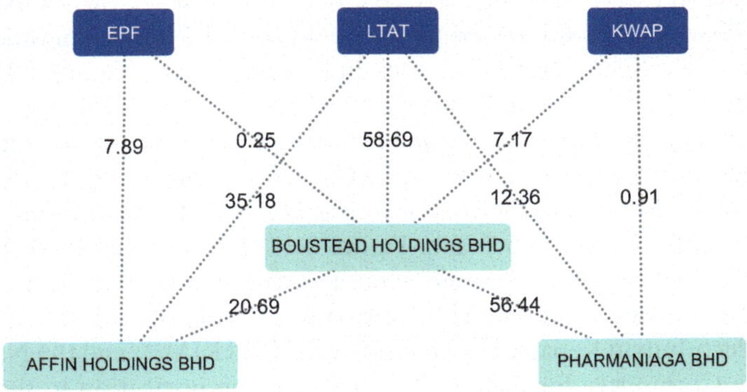

Fig. 3.10 Ownership pattern of Affin holdings, 2013

Figure 3.12 shows the ownership structure for BIMB Holdings. Five GLICs have direct and indirect ownership. LTH is the largest shareholder with ownership of almost 55% of the shares. MoF Inc. has indirect ownership through PNB, which has a total of 10.16% of the bank's equity, directly and through ASNB. EPF has a substantial 9.19% interest, but KWAP has nominal 2.84% stake.

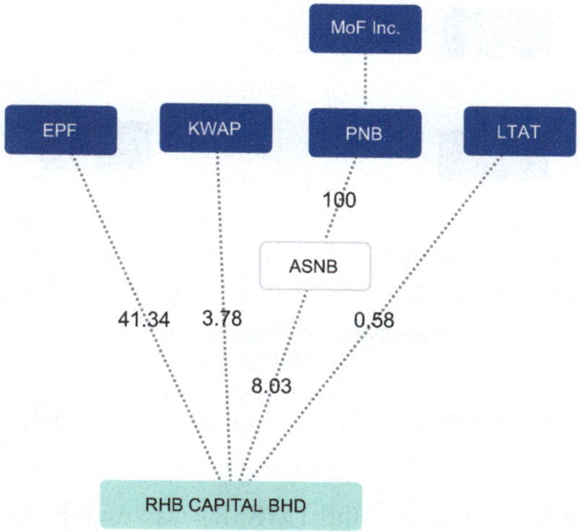

Fig. 3.11 Ownership pattern of RHB capital, 2013

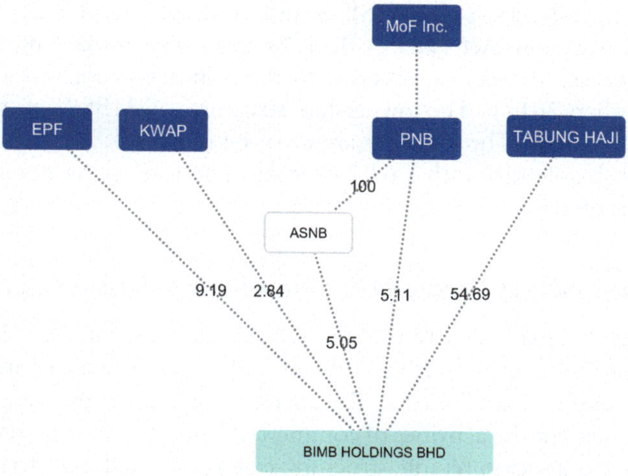

Fig. 3.12 Ownership pattern of BIMB holdings—Bank Islam, 2013

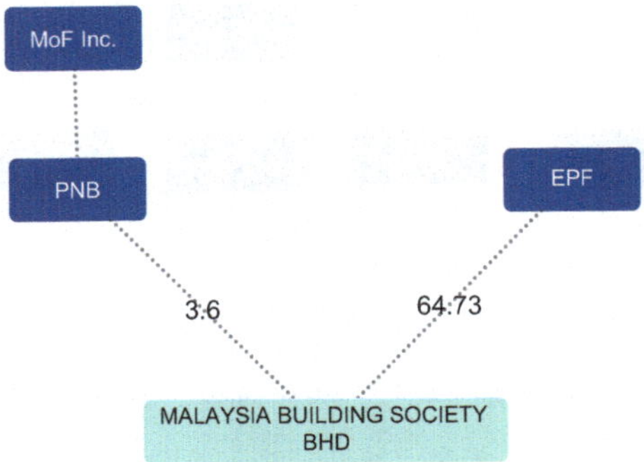

Fig. 3.13 Ownership pattern—Malaysia Building Society (MBSB), 2013

Malaysian Building Society Bhd (MBSB) was established in 1950 and publicly listed in 1963. Deemed an "exempt finance company" in 1972 by the Ministry of Finance, this status enabled it to "undertake a financing business in the absence of a banking licence".[36] MBSB was initially involved in property financing, but emerged as a financial provider for a wide range of products and services.[37] MBSB is not subjected to the Banking and Financial Institutions Act 1989 or Bank Negara's responsible lending guidelines. However, MBSB is answerable to the Ministry of Finance (*The Edge* 22 November 2012). The ownership structure of MBSB, as shown in Fig. 3.13, is simple. Three GLICs are involved in MBSB, although EPF is a substantial shareholder with a 64.73% stake. The total government interest in MBSB is 68.33%.

Ownership of Development Financial Institutions (DFIs)

Development Financial Institutions (DFIs) are a small but important segment of the financial sector. DFIs are policy-based financial institutions that have roles that are linked to the government's development objectives. DFIs complement the activities of commercial banks but they target strategic sectors such as agriculture, infrastructure, export-oriented industries, capital-intensive and high-technology companies and SMEs. In 2005, the total assets and loans of DFIs accounted for only 5% of the entire financial system.[38]

When the Development Financial Institutions Act was enacted in 2002, the six institutions bound by this legislation were Bank Pembangunan & Infrastruktur Malaysia, Bank Industri & Teknologi Malaysia, Malaysia

Export Credit Insurance (MECIB), Export-Import Bank of Malaysia (EXIM Bank), Bank Kerjasama Rakyat Malaysia and Bank Simpanan Nasional (BSN). Following a rationalization exercise between Bank Pembangunan & Infrastruktur and Bank Industri & Teknologi in 2005, SME Bank was established as a wholly owned subsidiary of Bank Pembangunan Malaysia.[39] EXIM Bank and MECIB merged that same year.[40] The Association of Development Financial Institutions of Malaysia (ADFIM) now has 19 members.[41] This study focuses only on the six prescribed DFIs (see Table 3.3).

Malaysian Industrial Development Finance (MIDF), incorporated in 1960, was the country's first DFI. Its purpose was to promote the development of the domestic manufacturing industry through the provision of medium- and long-term loans, primarily to acquire fixed assets, in order to diversify the economy which was then over-reliant on natural resources such as rubber and tin. In 2006, MIDF expressed its ambition to become a leading financial services provider in three areas: investment banking, asset management and development finance. To achieve that goal, in 2003 MIDF merged with Amanah Capital Partners, acquired Utama Merchant Bank and established its investment bank, MIDF Investment. MIDF now has many subsidiaries in specialized activities.[42]

Other major DFIs have a clear sectoral slant. Agrobank focuses on the agricultural sector, Bank Pembangunan promotes Bumiputera participation in commerce and industry, Bank Industri assists the development of the industrial and manufacturing sectors and EXIM Bank supports international trade and export-oriented industries. Bank Simpanan Nasional provides microfinancing, while Bank Rakyat helps develop cooperatives and SME Bank aims to nurture SMEs. Since established SMEs can secure financial aid from commercial banks, DFIs were incorporated to help small fledgling enterprises. Before SME Bank was created, DFIs that played this role were Bank Pembangunan and Credit Guarantee Corporation (CGC).[43]

Table 3.4 and Fig. 3.14 indicate that there is a centralized structure governing the major DFIs. Five of the six major DFIs are owned directly or indirectly by MoF Inc. The only exception is Bank Rakyat, which falls under the Ministry in charge of cooperatives, as required by the Bank Kerjasama Rakyat Malaysia Berhad Act 1978, and Bank Simpanan Nasional, which is a statutory body under the control of the Ministry of Finance.

Following the 1997 currency crisis, there were calls for the development of a sturdier financial system. One recommendation in Bank Negara's Financial Sector Masterplan (2001) was the formulation of a comprehensive regulatory and supervisory framework to facilitate the development

Table 3.3 List of DFIs

Development Financial Institutions prescribed under DFIA 2002
Agrobank
Bank Pembangunan
Bank Rakyat
Bank Simpanan Nasional
Export-Import Bank
SME Bank
Development Financial Institutions not prescribed under DFIA 2002
Borneo Development Corporation (Sabah)[a]
Borneo Development Corporation (Sarawak)[a]
Credit Guarantee Corporation
Malaysian Industrial Development Finance
Sabah Credit Corporation
Sabah Development Bank
Lembaga Tabung Haji[b]
Entrepreneur Development Organizations
Amanah Ikhtiar Malaysia
Johor Corporation
Majlis Amanah Rakyat
Malaysian Technology Development Corp
Perbadanan Nasional Bhd
Perbadanan Usahawan Nasional Bhd
TEKUN Nasional

Source: Association of Development Financial Institutions of Malaysia

[a]Both Borneo Development Corporations do not appear in Bank Negara's list of non-prescribed DFIs
[b]Lembaga Tabung Haji is not a member of ADFIM, but is listed as a non-prescribed DFI by Bank Negara

of DFIs. Thus, in 2002, the Development Financial Institutions Act was passed. The Act binds the six prescribed DFIs to perform their mandated socioeconomic functions.[44] Furthermore, the DFIs were required to submit regular statements of corporate intent, planned activities, implementation strategies and performance targets. A minimum capital requirement was introduced to ensure the financial soundness of DFIs.[45]

The 1997 crisis revealed that the DFIs were well run. While government-owned commercial banks were adversely affected by the crisis, the DFIs survived unscathed. During the crisis, the DFIs and the GLICs showed that sound governance was evident among government-owned institutions. The GLICs, in fact, had to bailout numerous ailing enterprises, including private banks. Another indication of the DFIs' professional management was that there was little evidence of any abuse of them since their establishment. The only major scandal involving a DFI occurred in 1975 when

Table 3.4 Role and year of establishment of major DFIs

DFI	*Year*	*Owner*	*Sector focus*
Malaysian Industrial Development Finance[a]	1960	PNB	Local manufacturing
Agrobank	1969	MoF Inc.[b]	Agriculture
Bank Pembangunan	1973	MoF Inc.	Infrastructure, Maritime, Technology, Oil and Gas
Bank Rakyat	1954 (1978)[c]	Ministry of Domestic Trade, Cooperatives and Consumerism[d]	Cooperatives
Bank Simpanan Nasional	1974	Ministry of Finance	Small savers
EXIM Bank	1995	MoF Inc.	Export-oriented industries
SME Bank	2005	Bank Pembangunan	SMEs

[a]MIDF is not prescribed under the Development Financial Institutions Act 2002

[b]Agrobank acts according to policies promulgated by the Ministry of Agriculture but is owned by MoF Inc.

[c]Bank Rakyat has existed since 1954 under different names, as Bank Agong and later Bank Kerjasama. After the enactment of the Bank Kerjasama Rakyat Malaysia Berhad Act in 1978, this bank obtained permission to offer loans to non-members and companies. Prior to that, Bank Rakyat was a cooperative bank. This Act placed Bank Rakyat under the purview of the ministry in charge of cooperative development. See: http://www.kpdnkk.gov.my/index.php/en/mdtcc/agency/bank-kerjasama-rakyat-malaysia

[d]Except for a brief period after the 2009 cabinet restructuring when Bank Rakyat was placed under the authority of the Ministry of Finance, it has always been owned by the ministry in charge of cooperatives such as the Ministry of Land and Cooperative Development and Ministry of Entrepreneurs and Cooperative Development. See: http://www.bankrakyat.com.my/legasi

then UMNO Chief Minister of Selangor, Harun Idris, misappropriated funds from Bank Rakyat. Harun was found guilty of corruption and sent to gaol (*The Star* 15 June 2016).

Ownership of the leading banks serves as a key mechanism to control how the corporate sector functions and how companies develop. While equity ownership of the banking sector was once widely spread, with banks under the control of a number of private businesses, both domestic and foreign, ownership of this sector has now undergone considerable change, with the one key actor, the government, having a huge interest in commercial and development-based financial institutions.

Following the consolidation of the banks, which drastically reduced the number of these institutions, it became easier for the government to control the financial sector. Crucially, too, Malaysia's GLC-based banks, Malayan Banking, CIMB, RHB Bank, BIMB, Affin Bank and MBSB,

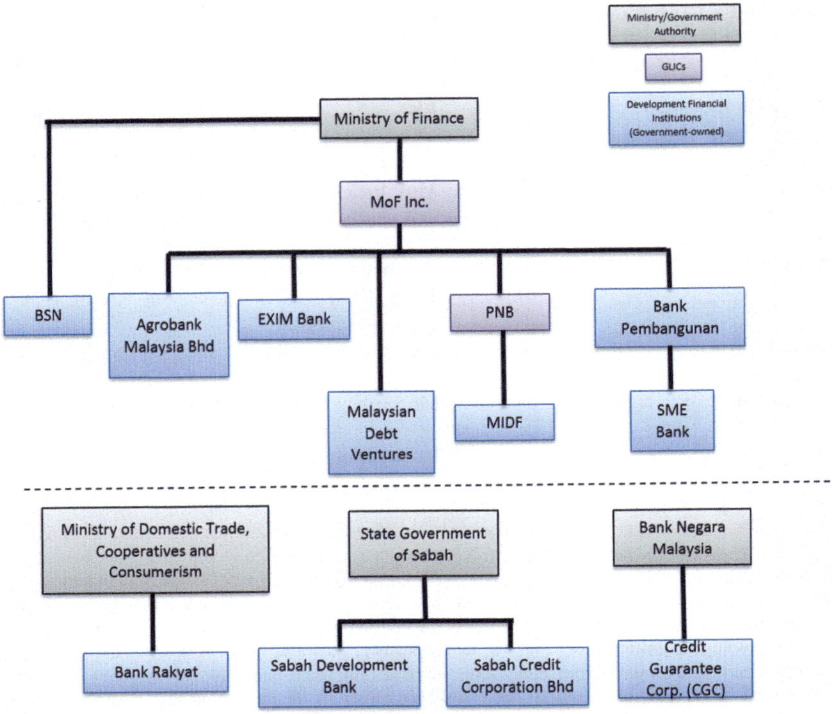

Fig. 3.14 Ownership and control of Development Financial Institutions (DFIs)

collectively own a huge number of subsidiaries. In fact, Malayan Banking, the country's leading financial institution, has the largest number of companies under its control when compared with other listed GLCs, including the giant conglomerate, Sime Darby (see Appendix 4.1). This means that ownership of these banks also allows the government to exert control over the subsidiaries and associate companies of these financial institutions. This is not necessarily a bad thing for the economy, perhaps best seen in the case of the well-managed DFIs. However, history also shows that government ownership of the banking sector has led to a number of major corporate scandals.

Controlling the Media Sector

Another major issue in the context of Malaysia and a review of enterprises owned by the government is ownership of the media. The GLICs' ownership of the media sector is primarily through publicly listed Media Prima (see Fig. 3.15). The Media Prima group controls major newspapers and TV networks such as the *New Straits Times*, *Berita Harian*, TV3, NTV7, 8TV and TV9. Some of these media companies were once directly owned by UMNO, specifically the New Straits Times Press (NSTP) and Sistem Televisyen Malaysia (STM), which operates TV3. These media companies are now under the direct and indirect ownership of three GLICs, all ultimately under the control of MoF Inc. (see Fig. 3.15). Other mainstream media still owned by political parties are *Utusan Malaysia*, which is directly owned by UMNO, and *The Star* which is owned by the MCA.

In the early 1970s, ownership of the NSTP group was secured by UMNO's holding company, Fleet Group Sdn Bhd, controlled by the party's then treasurer, Tengku Razaleigh Hamzah. When Daim was appointed UMNO's treasurer in the 1980s, he took control of the media sector.[46] In the early 1990s, the allies of Anwar, then the Deputy President of UMNO, obtained control of NSTP through a private firm, Realmild Sdn Bhd, whose owners were four senior NSTP executives, Abdul Kadir Jasin, Khalid Ahmad, Mohd Noor Mutalib and Ahmad Nazri Abdullah. Realmild then also had control of TV3, Malaysia's first private television station, incorporated in 1983. These media-related companies were by then under the control of another quoted company, Malaysian Resources Corporation Bhd (MRCB), controlled by Realmild. In 1998, after Mahathir expelled Anwar from UMNO, the four NSTP executives lost control of Realmild and MRCB and their influence over the major media outlets, the *New Straits Times*, *Berita Harian*, the *Malay Mail* and TV3.

Realmild was taken over by Abdul Rahman Maidin, a businessman linked to Daim, who was recalled as Minister of Finance to replace Anwar. Mahathir needed control over the media to stifle dissent from within UMNO, given Anwar's considerable grassroots support. In 2001, when Daim resigned as minister without revealing his reasons for leaving government, Rahman Maidin lost control of Realmild and MRCB. Abdullah Ahmad, closely linked to Mahathir, was appointed editor-in-chief of the *New Straits Times*.

In 2000, the MRCB-NSTP-TV3 group was reputedly mired in debts amounting to RM4 billion (Wong 2011: 382). Mahathir, on the feedback of his economic advisor, Nor Mohamed Yakcop, agreed to the appointment

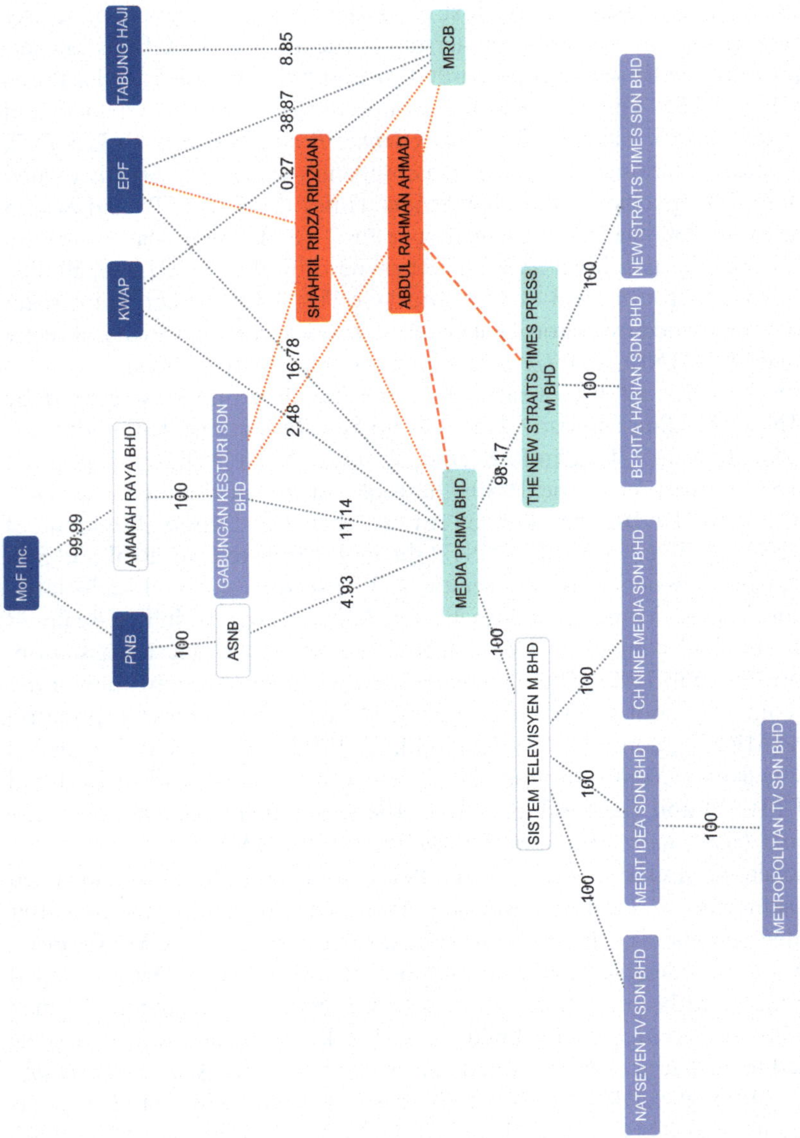

Fig. 3.15 Ownership pattern of Media Prima group, 2013

of two of the latter's protégés, Shahril Ridza Ridzuan and Abdul Rahman Ahmad as directors of MRCB. Their assignment was to turn-around the MRCB group. The activities of the group were divided into two components. MRCB was responsible for its construction and property development activities, particularly its role in developing KL Sentral, a huge infrastructure project in Kuala Lumpur (Wong 2011: 391–395). Profitune Bhd, wholly owned by MRCB, was renamed Media Prima and took over MRCB's equity interests in NSTP and TV3.

The Chairman of MRCB when it was being restructured was Syed Anwar Jamalullail, younger brother of the Raja of the state of Perlis. According to Syed Anwar, Nor Mohamed had asked him to take over the chairmanship of MRCB and help Shahril and Rahman revamp MRCB as well as NSTP and TV3.[47] Under Syed Anwar's control, the huge debts of Realmild, the largest shareholder of MRCB, were substantially trimmed while the ailing NSTP and TV3 were successfully turned around. The transfer of MRCB's equity from Abdul Rahman Maidin to Syed Anwar was apparently ordered by Mahathir (see *Malay Mail* 29 October 2013).

In August 2003, when Media Prima was demerged from the MRCB, the latter lost effective equity interest in the former. In 2004, Amanah Raya, through its wholly owned and obscure two-Ringgit company, Gabungan Kesturi Sdn Bhd, became the largest shareholder of Media Prima. By then, Syed Anwar was no longer on the board of directors.[48] Abdul Mutalib Mohamed Razak replaced Syed Anwar as Chairman in 2004. In 2006, EPF became the largest shareholder of Media Prima. Gabungan Kesturi was its second largest shareholder. By 2013, most media companies had come under the control of Media Prima, in turn controlled by Gabungan Kesturi, and ultimately under the control of MoF Inc. EPF is Media Prima's most substantial shareholder, with a 16.78% interest.

By 2013, the directors of Gabungan Kesturi were Shahril, who is on the boards of EPF and Media Prima, and Abdul Rahman, who was formerly on the boards of Media Prima and NSTP. Shahril and Abdul Rahman had served as directors of MRCB, in August 2001, as Executive Director and Chief Executive Officer respectively.[49]

Major Owners of the Plantations Sector

The plantations-based GLCs, Sime Darby, FGV, Boustead, Kulim and IJM Plantations, are enterprises with huge land banks (see Table 3.5). Figures 3.16, 3.17 and 3.18 illustrate the extensive ownership the GLICs over the plantations sector through these companies.

Table 3.5 Largest plantations-based companies in Malaysia by hectares owned, 2013

Company	*Land banks (ha)*
Sime Darby	**858,879**
IOI Corp	217,918
Kuala Lumpur Kepong (KLK)	250,000
Felda Global Ventures (FGV)	**446,656**
Genting Plantations (formerly known as Asiatic Development)	228,300
United Plantations	59,484
Kulim	**91,644**
Boustead	**82,900**
IJM Plantations	**80,958**

Notes: The GLCs are in bold. United Plantations is foreign-owned, while the others are family firms

Sources: Company annual reports and http://www.sustainablepalmoil.org/

A block shareholding ownership trend, seen in other quoted GLCs, is evident among the plantations-based companies. MoF Inc. owns PNB, which, along with four other GLICs, has ownership of one of the world's largest plantation companies, Sime Darby, which had massive land assets of 858,879 ha in 2013, an outcome of its merger with two major plantations-based GLCs, Guthrie Corp and Golden Hope, and a market capitalization approaching RM60 billion.[50] All but one GLIC, Khazanah, had an interest in Sime Darby (see Fig. 3.16). These GLICs collectively had a 70% stake in Sime Darby.

Sime Darby, founded in 1910 and a global player in agribusiness, operates in 26 countries through more than 500 subsidiaries. Though the largest plantations business group in Malaysia in terms of market capitalization, Sime Darby also has a major interest in four other sectors: motors, property development, industrial, energy and utilities.

As Fig. 3.16 indicates, one Sime Darby subsidiary is Eastern & Oriental Bhd (E&O),[51] a quoted property development and construction company. Sime Darby bought 30% of E&O in August 2011. This 30% equity was then collectively owned by Terry Tham Ka Hon, the once well-connected Wan Azmi Wan Hamzah and GK Goh Holdings Ltd., a Singaporean company.[52] However, Tham retained a 5% stake in E&O. In July 2013, Sime Darby had 32% of E&O's equity. Yet, in 2014, Tham began increasing his interest in E&O by acquiring shares in this company from Sime Darby. In 2016, following another disposal of E&O equity by Sime Darby to Tham, he secured a 21% stake in the company. Sime Darby's equity interest in E&O was reduced to 12.2% (*The Star* 7 June 2016).

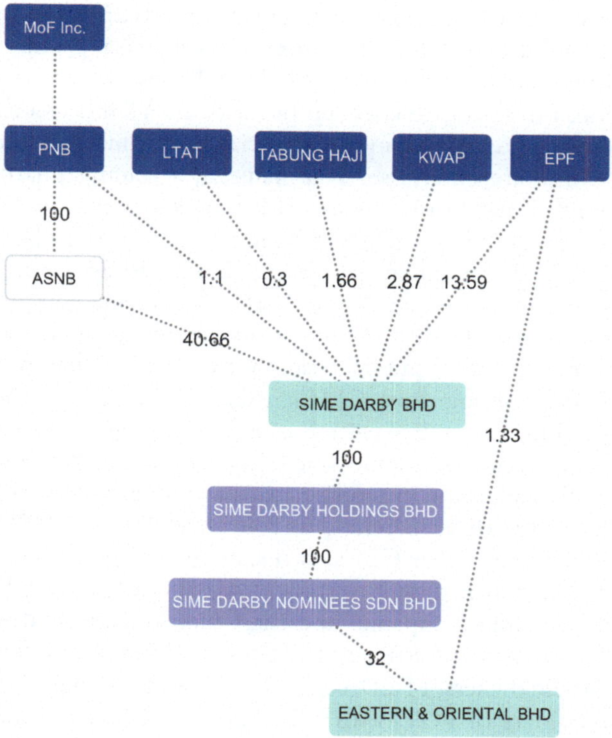

Fig. 3.16 Ownership pattern of Sime Darby group, 2013

Boustead, founded by Edward Boustead in 1828 in Singapore, began trading rubber in 1911. Boustead has since been subjected to a series of acquisitions and consolidations. Publicly listed in 1961, it became a wholly owned Malaysian enterprise in 1976. By the mid-2010s, Boustead had 95 subsidiaries involved in six sectors: plantations, property, banking and finance, pharmaceuticals, trading and heavy industries.

The corporate structure of Boustead Holdings is shown in Fig. 3.10, as part of Affin Holdings. It indicates that this GLC has a vastly different ownership pattern, with far fewer GLICs as shareholders. However, Boustead's flow of ownership control is straightforward and similar to that of Sime Darby. One GLIC, LTAT, has a huge 58.7% interest in Boustead, clearly the key player in terms of decision-making within this group. While

KWAP owns 7.2% of Boustead, EPF has a mere 0.25%, the only other GLICs with an interest in this plantations-cum-financial group.

While Boustead is not as huge as Sime Darby in terms of market capitalization, through its ownership ties with LTAT it is associated with Affin Holdings, a key player in the financial sector, making it an equally important corporate enterprise. Pharmaniaga, a leading pharmaceutical company, ranked 164th in terms of market capitalization, is a subsidiary of Boustead, which has a 56.44% stake in this enterprise. Pharmaniaga's other substantial shareholders include LTAT, with 12.36% shares.

FGV's corporate structure in Fig. 3.18 is extremely complex, compared to that of Sime Darby and Boustead, involving interlocking stock ownership ties with other publicly listed GLCs. FGV's shareholdings are widely dispersed among most GLICs, except MoF Inc. and Khazanah. FGV's ownership and control pattern is unique among plantation companies as each of the others has only one GLIC as a major shareholder. FGV is also the only plantation enterprise that has one golden share, held by MoF Inc. The five GLIC shareholders collectively have a 30.78% interest in FGV. Unlike most other GLCs, two state governments have an interest in FGV. The Sabah state government has about 5% of FGV's equity, through two holding companies and the Chief Minister State of Sabah, while the Pahang state government has a direct 5% interest in the company. Apart from these owners, FELDA and Felda Asset Holdings Company are major shareholders of FGV, with a 21.22% and 18.66% equity interest respectively. FELDA is situated under the Prime Minister's Department.

FELDA's endeavour to develop rural areas by relocating the poor to landholdings where rubber and palm oil were to be produced was extremely successful. From 1994, FELDA stopped receiving government funding as it had developed the ability to generate its own income. FELDA subsequently established a number of corporate entities to complete the value chain for its core activities. These ventures included Permodalan FELDA, a cooperative, FELDA Investment Corporation and FGV.

FGV initially operated as the commercial arm of FELDA. In June 2012, after FGV was listed on the Bursa's main board, it emerged as the world's largest crude palm oil producer and the second largest Malaysian palm oil refiner. FGV also owns a majority 51% interest in publicly listed MSM Malaysia Holdings Bhd, whose primary business is the production, marketing and sale of refined sugar products. Before its takeover by FGV, MSM was in the stable of companies associated with Robert Kuok. Apart from FGV's indirect majority interest in MSM, five GLICs—LTAT, EPF,

KWAP, PNB and LTH—collectively hold another 21.6% interest in this prominent sugar production enterprise. Koperasi Permodalan Felda owns 20% of MSM's equity.

There are reasons for FGV's complex ownership pattern. It is linked to the transition made by the group, with its move towards becoming a more corporate-based enterprise that was intent on developing many businesses. The listing of FGV, and the effort to attain maximum value from the company, was a marked shift as previously it was an enterprise with a socially driven agenda. FGV's deep roots in its socially driven past makes it unique, as the government still has an obligation to ensure the well-being of the settlers. FELDA's link to politics has further complicated the structure of this enterprise. The settlers constitute a huge segment of the electorate in 54 parliamentary constituencies. In 2013, 48 of these 54 constituencies were won by the ruling BN coalition (*The Edge* 6 February 2017).

Since the FELDA project served as a model for other countries intent on redistributing land to the poor to productively cultivate cash crops, the government wanted to push the brand abroad, a mechanism to allow FGV to emerge as a global agribusiness.[53] With the capital available to FGV after its listing, the company's growth was to create a sentiment of pride among the settlers. In addition, FGV's listing proved financially lucrative for them, at least in the short run. Settlers would each get RM15,000 and they would collectively own 37% of FGV's equity. These monetary and equity benefits accruing to the 1.2 million settlers nationally had political significance leading up to the 2013 General Election.

Some members of the cooperative objected to the manner of the listing of FGV, even obtaining an interim court injunction on this matter. To proceed with FGV's listing, FELDA created a wholly owned company, Felda Asset Holdings Company (FAHC), prior to the IPO. Since FAHC's incorporation required two founding shareholders, Isa Samad and Omar Salim, a director in FGV, were listed, though they did not own the company. This was a special purpose vehicle (SPV) to pursue FGV's listing. Isa was formerly Chief Minister of the state of Negeri Sembilan and had long served as a senior UMNO leader. Omar Salim is a long-time civil servant in the Prime Minister's Office and is now head of the Felda Regulatory Unit, reporting directly to the Prime Minister (*Kinibiz* 10 March 2015). Isa went on to be Chairman of FELDA.[54]

The IPO was very successful, raising US$3.1 billion. This was the second-largest listing in the world, after Facebook Inc., and Asia's largest

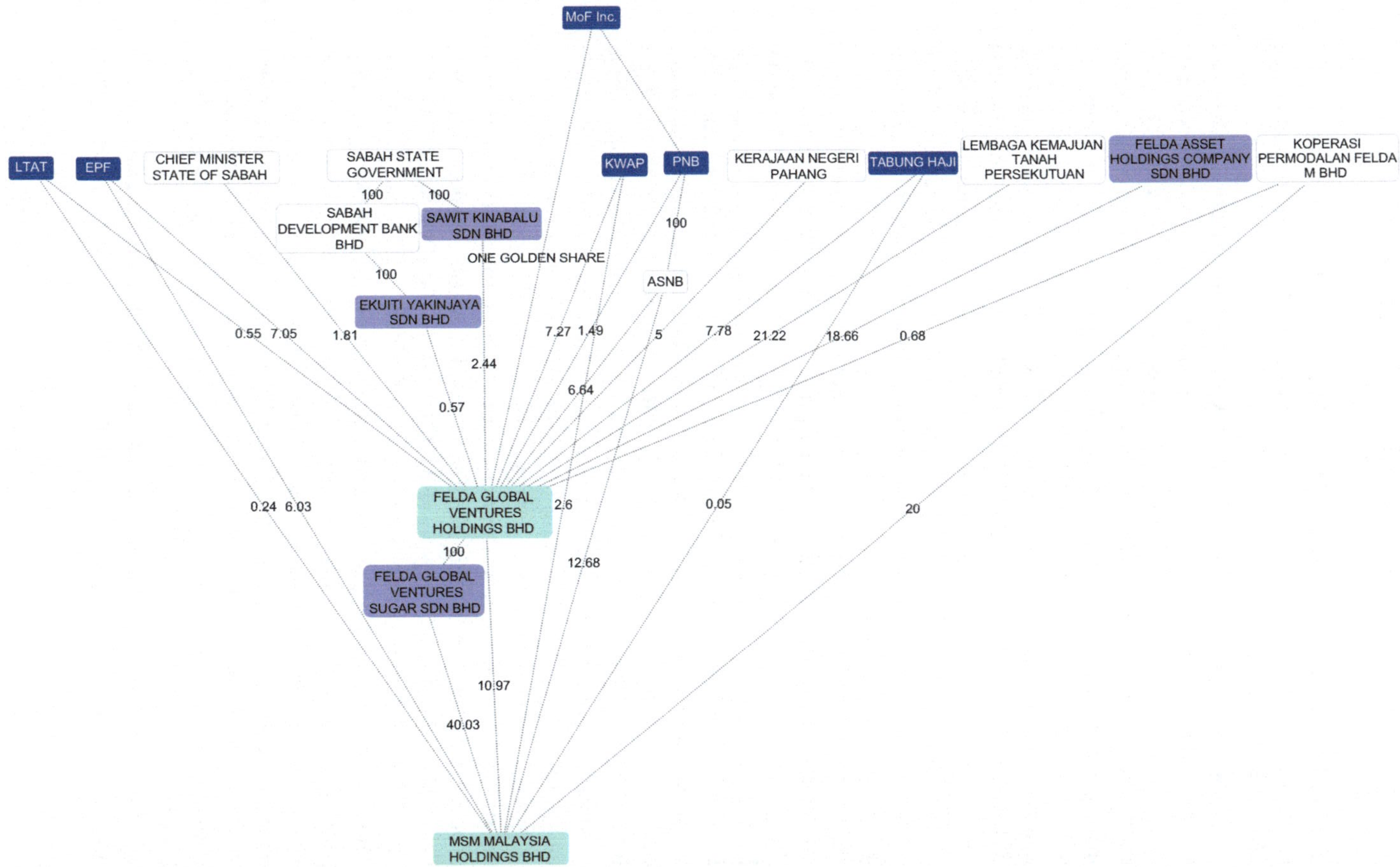

Fig. 3.17 Ownership pattern of FGV group, 2013

listing that year. FGV used the proceeds from the IPO for acquisitions, many of which were not productive. After the FGV listing, FELDA created Felda Investment Corporation (FIC), which has been marred by several scandals, such as the sturgeon-rearing scandal (*Malay Mail* 24 January 2017). The Malaysian Anti-Corruption Commission (MACC) subsequently detained five high-level FELDA officials for corruption amounting to approximately RM44.3 million (*The Edge* 6 February 2017). FELDA later diversified into other sectors, such as nutraceuticals, with the setting up of Felda Wellness Corporation. This company was also involved in a scandal that led to the loss of substantial funds (*Malay Mail* 24 January 2017).

Kulim Malaysia was incorporated as Kulim Rubber Plantations Ltd. in 1933 in the UK. In 1947, the company started to operate a rubber plantation in the state of Johor. The Johor State Economic Development Corporation, now known as Johor Corp, became a shareholder in 1976. While Johor Corp has a 54.88% direct stake in Kulim, Waqaf An-Nur Corporation has an additional 5%.[55] With only 20 subsidiaries, Kulim's core ventures are in the plantations, oil and gas and agro-food sectors.

Figure 3.18 delineates Kulim's corporate structure. Four GLICs collectively own only 13.3% of shares in Kulim. These shareholdings do not represent a high level of control over the company's decision-making process. Interestingly enough, Kulim has greater land assets than Boustead. Kulim had 91,644 ha, just less than 10% of the land assets owned by

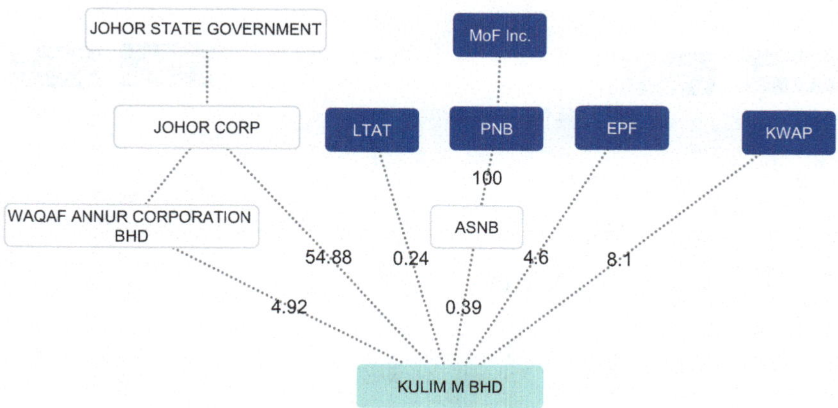

Fig. 3.18 Ownership pattern of Kulim (Malaysia), 2013

Sime Darby. Boustead's land assets were only 82,900 ha, indicating that its major corporate interests are in other sectors of the economy.

Dominant Presence in the Utilities

Figures 3.19, 3.20 and 3.21 illustrate the corporate structures of Tenaga Nasional, the power distribution giant, Axiata, and its related company, Telekom Malaysia. All these major utilities were partially privatized following their listing on the Malaysian bourse. MoF Inc. sits at the top of the hierarchy of all three utility-based GLCs. These three figures further indicate that MoF Inc. has ultimate ownership of these GLCs, though through different GLICs.

Tenaga was established by the government in 1990, an outcome of the corporatized National Electricity Board (NEB). In the late 1980s, NEB was privatized, ostensibly because its operations were based on its access to huge amounts of loans and it needed a major revamp to face growing demand for power as the economy rapidly industrialized. NEB was privatized by Mahathir, despite internal opposition. Tenaga is now the largest electricity utility in Malaysia, with assets amounting to RM110 billion.[56]

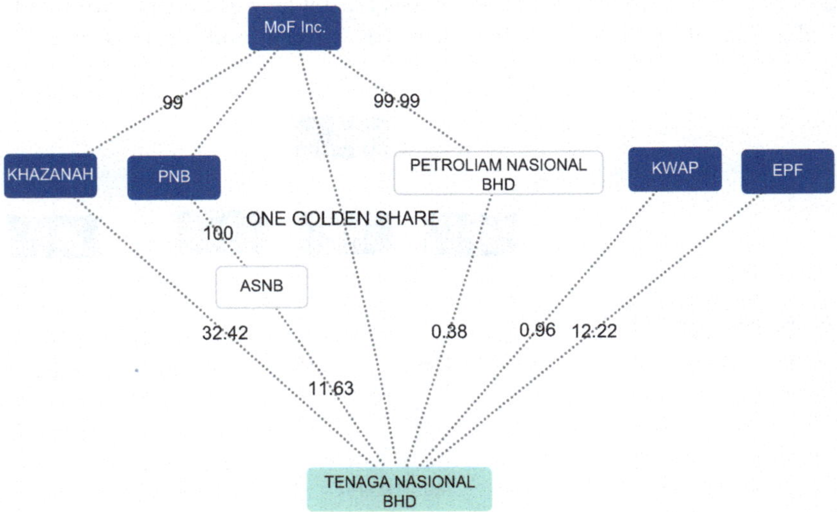

Fig. 3.19 Ownership pattern of Tenaga Nasional, 2013

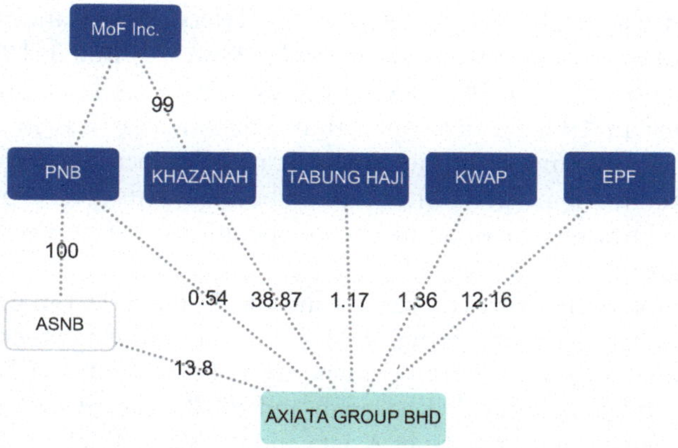

Fig. 3.20 Ownership pattern of Axiata group, 2013

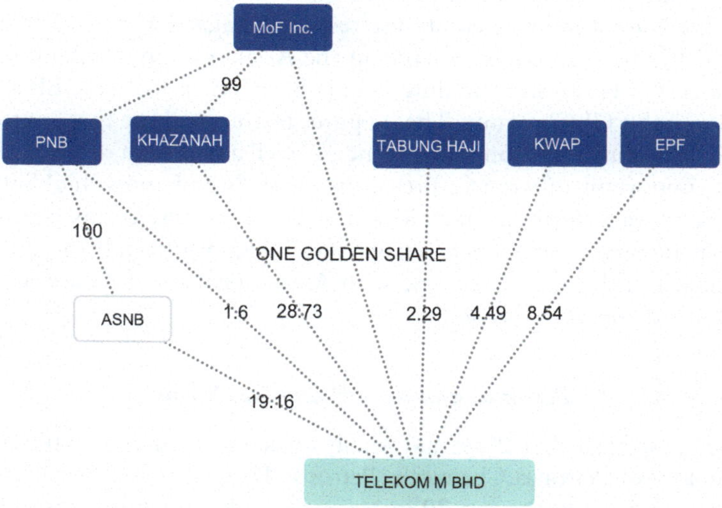

Fig. 3.21 Ownership pattern of Telekom Malaysia, 2013

Telekom was established in 1946 as the Telecommunications Department of Malaya. Corporatized as Syarikat Telekom (M) Bhd in 1987, it was listed on the bourse in 1990.[57] Axiata was established as Telekom Malaysia International in 1992, a division within Telekom that was in charge of international investments and its domestic mobile operator, Celcom.[58] In 2008, Axiata was demerged from Telekom because of its diverse businesses, one in fixed lines and the other in mobile operations. Axiata was then listed on the bourse.[59]

The corporate structures of Tenaga and the Axiata-Telekom group indicate very similar ownership patterns. MoF Inc. has indirect ownership of all three companies through its direct ownership of Khazanah and PNB, both ultimately under its control. Khazanah and PNB collectively have a 44% interest in Tenaga, a 53% stake in Axiata and 49.5% of Telekom's equity.

The block shareholding pattern adopted by the GLICs is evident in the corporate structures of these three GLCs. In Tenaga, apart from Khazanah and PNB, the other major shareholder is EPF with a 12.22% interest. KWAP and Petronas are the other government-linked shareholders. MoF Inc.'s total indirect equity interest in Tenaga is a massive 57.61%. Five GLICs have an equity interest in the Axiata Group, totalling 67.9% of this GLC's entire shareholding. Similarly, in Telekom, five GLICs own 64.81% of this GLC's equity. These figures further indicate that control of the GLCs is directly through MoF Inc., as well as through other GLICs.

Yet, important differences prevail in these three figures, highlighting the diverse ways through which MoF Inc. controls these companies. MoF Inc. has further control over Tenaga and Telekom through the use of a golden share; this is not the case with Axiata, probably because it is the result of a demerger exercise.

Petronas and the Oil and Gas Sector

Petronas, established in 1974, and wholly owned by MoF Inc., is the largest shareholder of Petronas Chemicals, Petronas Dagangan and Petronas Gas, which were listed in the top 20 in terms of market capitalization in 2013 (see Fig. 3.22). Together, these three firms have 40 companies under them, more than half as subsidiaries. The three companies account for almost 8% of the bourse's total market capitalization, with approximately RM135 billion.

EPF, KWAP and PNB, through ASNB, have a stake in these companies as well. The interests of these GLICs in these three companies are greatest in Petronas Gas (26%), followed by Petronas Chemicals Group (20.8%)

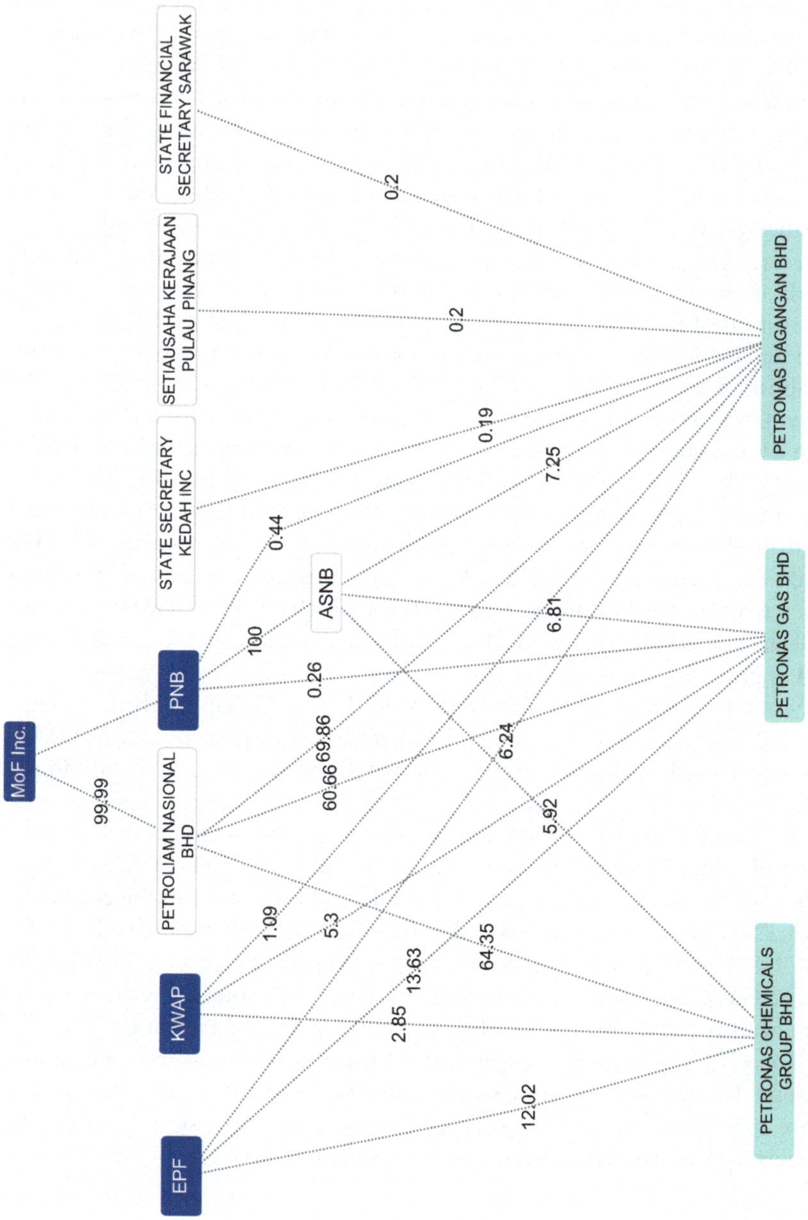

Fig. 3.22 Ownership pattern of Petronas group (Petronas Chemicals, Petronas Gas and Petronas Dagangan), 2013

and Petronas Dagangan (15.02%). However, Petronas is the largest equity shareholder of Petronas Dagangan, also the only one in the group that is owned by three state governments, Kedah, Penang and Sarawak.

Petronas Chemicals, an integrated chemicals producer, is involved in the manufacturing and export of a wide range of chemical products to over 30 countries.[60] Petronas Dagangan, incorporated in 1982 as the marketing arm of Petronas, delivers products and services in four businesses: retail, commercial, liquidified petroleum gas and lubricants. Petronas Dagangan has become Malaysia's largest petroleum retail network with over 100 stations across the country.[61] Petronas Gas was incorporated in 1983, initially a wholly owned subsidiary of Petronas.[62]

The UMW group commenced operations as an automotive repair shop, established by Chia Yee Soh in 1917 as United Motor Works. UMW's ascendancy in the corporate sector began when it secured the distributorship of Toyota motor vehicles in Malaysia, through its subsidiary, UMW Toyota Motor Sdn Bhd. This franchising was secured by Chia Yee Soh's son, Eric Chia, the primary person who transformed this company into a multi-million dollar business group. However, Chia lost control of UMW when the company was badly affected by a serious recession. UMW was taken over by PNB in the mid-1980s (Gomez 1999: 138). UMW is now a well-diversified group, involved in automotive, equipment, manufacturing and engineering, and oil and gas.

Six of seven GLICs are involved in the UMW Group, with the exception of Khazanah (see Fig. 3.23). PNB is the major shareholder in UMW Holdings, with a 54.51% stake. The total volume of UMW Holdings' equity held by all the GLICs is 71.12%. UMW Holdings is a substantial 55.15% shareholder of UMW Oil & Gas Corp Bhd, which provides drilling and oilfield services for the oil and gas industry in Malaysia as well as other Southeast Asian countries.[63] Five GLICs have a stake in the company, with PNB having the most at 9.3%, followed by EPF and KWAP. LTAT and LTH each own less than 1% of the company's equity. The UMW Oil & Gas Corp equity held directly by the GLICs total 21.39%, which is significantly lower, by almost 50%, than that in UMW Holdings.

The GLCs in the oil and gas sector clearly function as major business groups. Interestingly, in spite of the importance of this sector, the golden share approach is not used here, probably because of the significant equity ownership that the GLICs have over these companies.

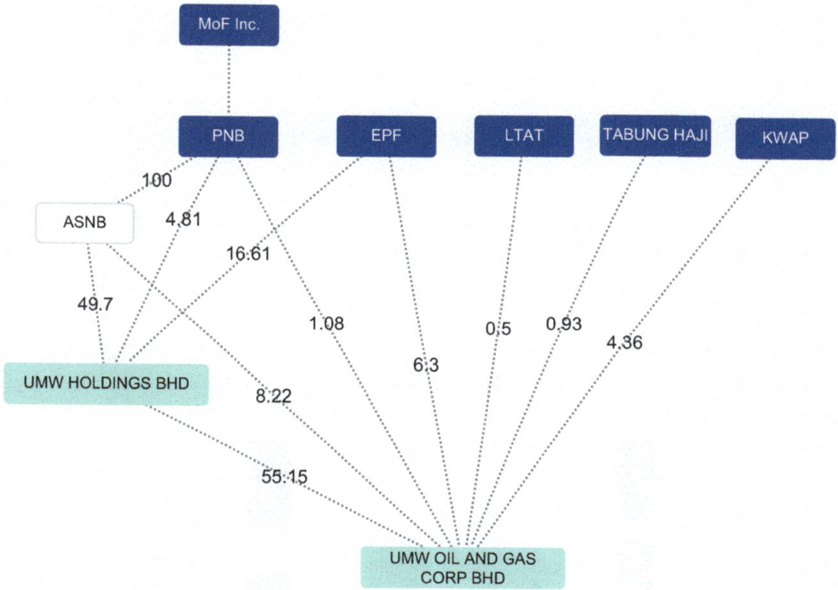

Fig. 3.23 Ownership pattern of UMW Holdings group

GLICs in Healthcare and Services

Table 3.6 provides a profile of the GLCs in the top 100 in the healthcare and services sectors. While numerous GLCs in this study have come under government control through takeovers or mergers, one such enterprise in the healthcare sector is IHH Healthcare. However, another major enterprise in this sector is Kumpulan Perubatan Johor (KPJ), one of the largest private healthcare chains in Malaysia, under the majority ownership of Johor Corp, a statutory body and a state-owned investment company that was established in 1968 (see Table 3.6). Johor Corp ventured into healthcare in 1979 when it established the Johor Specialist Hospital (Chan 2010). KPJ Healthcare is one of very few publicly listed GLCs established by a state government.

IHH—originally Integrated Healthcare Holdings—is an investment holding company. Khazanah is the largest shareholder of IHH, through ownership of a private company, Pulau Memutik Ventures Sdn Bhd. IHH Healthcare is the result of a merger between Singapore's Parkway and

Table 3.6 Ownership pattern in the healthcare and services sectors, 2013

Sector	*Company*	*GLIC ownership structure*
Healthcare	KPJ Healthcare	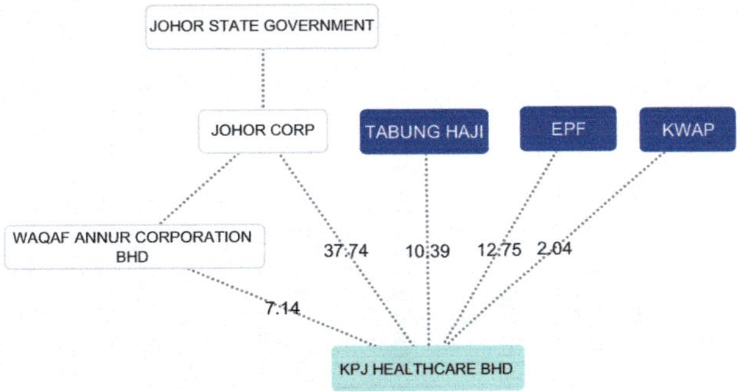
	IHH Healthcare	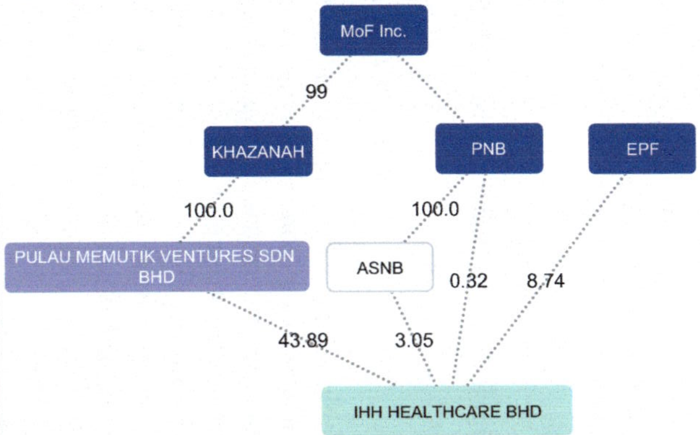

Services	MAS	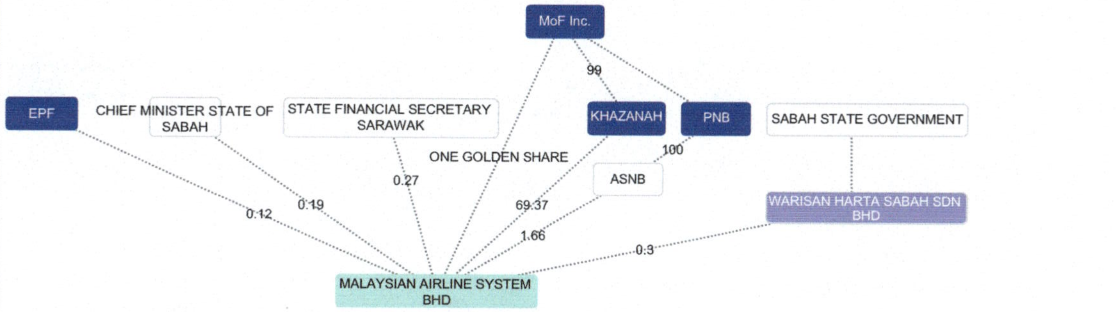
	MAHB	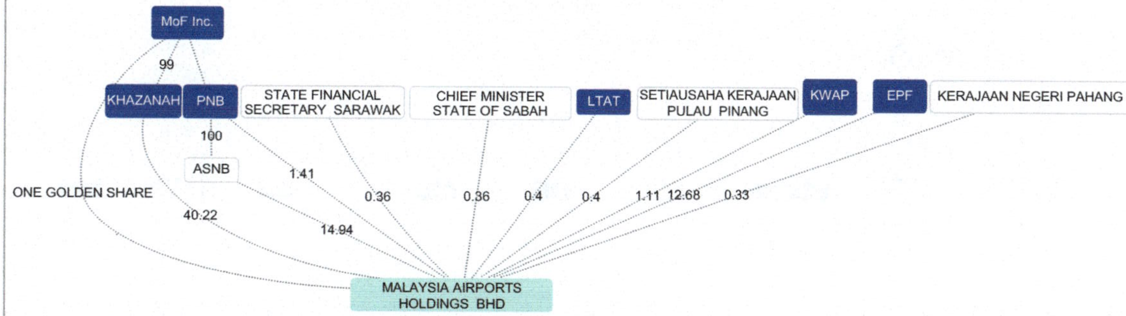

(*continued*)

Table 3.6 (continued)

Sector	*Company*	*GLIC ownership structure*
	MISC	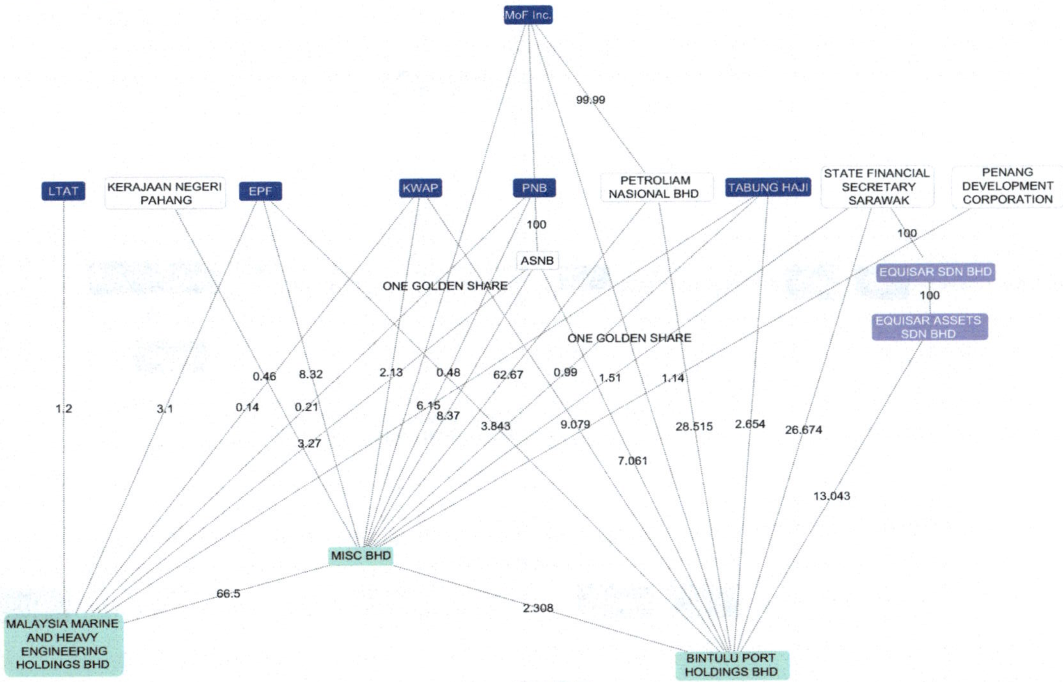

	Bursa Malaysia	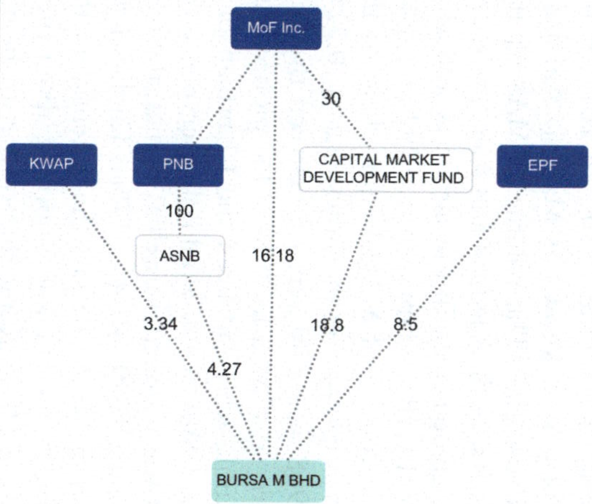

Malaysia's Pantai. Following this merger, IHH emerged as Asia's largest private hospital and healthcare service provider, with a number of major hospitals under its ownership. IHH reportedly also became the second-largest healthcare provider in the world following this merger (*Forbes Asia* 14 February 2017). The company has a presence in a number of countries in Asia and the Middle East. Concurrently publicly listed in 2012 in Malaysia and Singapore, its major assets in these two countries are the Pantai and Parkway medical enterprises respectively. Other major hospitals under the IHH Healthcare group are Gleneagles and Mount Elizabeth (*Financial Times* 3 July 2012). IHH also owns the International Medical University Malaysia (IMU).[64] Khazanah liquidated some of its equity holdings in IHH in June 2016, part of its exercise to reduce its interests in quoted companies in response to a government directive to boost liquidity on the Bursa (*The Star* 2 June 2016).

MAS, known as Malaysian Airline System until 2015, was established in 1973. It was the outcome of the closure of Malayan-Singapore Airlines whose roots can be traced back to the 1940s. In 2015, it underwent a rebranding exercise and is now known as Malaysia Airlines Bhd and it is wholly owned by Khazanah.[65] The volume of MAS equity held by government-related agencies, both at federal and state levels, amounts to 71.91%. MoF Inc. has a golden share in this airline as well as Malaysian Airports Holdings Bhd (MAHB), established in 1992 and listed on the main board in 1999. The volume of MAHB equity held by the GLICs totalled 72.21%, with Khazanah having the largest stake (40.22%).

MISC, founded in 1968 as a joint-venture between the government and private entrepreneurs, was listed in 1987. One pioneering member of MISC was Robert Kuok, who had been the Chairman of Malayan-Singapore Airlines in the 1960s. Kuok would also serve as a director of Bank Bumiputra when it was founded, as well as Pernas, the trust agency established in 1969 (Gomez 1999: 40–41). When Kuok was invited by the government to establish MISC, he saw the potential in the project and invested his own funds. Since he knew nothing about the industry, Kuok invited Frank Tsao, a Hong Kong ship-owner, to help him with the venture. Tsao then invested in the MISC project too, while other investors included LTH. Kuok and Tsao eventually divested their interests in MISC (Gomez 1990: 45–47). In 1997, Petronas acquired almost 30% of MISC's equity and in 1998,[66] following the Asian currency crisis, MISC acquired Konsortium Perkapalan Bhd's assets, owned by Mirzan Mahathir,[67] a controversial deal that was seen as a bailout (*Wall*

Street Journal 1 May 1998). MISC has an interest in two other quoted enterprises, Malaysia Marine & Heavy Engineering Holdings (MMHE) and Bintulu Port Holdings. MoF Inc. has a golden share in MISC and Bintulu Port Holdings as well as its subsidiary, Bintulu Port Sdn Bhd. The key player in this group is Petronas, which owns MISC and in turn MMHE. The Sarawak state government owns Bintulu Port Holdings.

In January 2004, the Kuala Lumpur Stock Exchange (KLSE) was demutualized to become the exchange holding company known as Kuala Lumpur Stock Exchange Bhd (KLSE Bhd) and the stock exchange business of KLSE was transferred to a new wholly owned subsidiary known as Malaysia Securities Exchange Bhd (MSEB). Later that year, MSEB became known as Bursa Malaysia Bhd and it was listed in 2005. Bursa Malaysia is one of the very few publicly listed companies in which MoF Inc. has a direct interest.[68]

Conclusion

There are significant variations in the ownership patterns of the GLCs by the GLICs. Three types of ownership pattern are in evidence (see Table 3.7). In ownership pattern 1, GLCs are owned directly by the GLICs. Twenty-three GLCs have this form of ownership: all three utilities; all five banks and MBSB; the media-based Media Prima; half the number of property development and construction GLCs, Gamuda, SP Setia and IJM Corp; three of those in services, MAS, MAHB and Bursa; two plantations-based GLCs, Boustead and Sime Darby; and the O&G-based UMW Holdings. However, within this ownership pattern, there are variations such as equity ownership of a GLC by two or more GLICs. In addition, some GLCs are subsidiaries of other GLCs. For example, IJM Land and IJM Plantations are subsidiaries of IJM Corp; UMW Oil & Gas is owned by UMW Holdings, as MMHE is by MISC. The use of this ownership pattern is particularly the case in the media sector, where the government uses one GLC, Media Prima, as a holding company to control a vast number of enterprises in print, television and radio broadcasting.

Ownership pattern 2 is GLIC ownership of a GLC through wholly owned private companies, as seen in eight cases. Of these eight GLCs, five of them are owned by MoF Inc. through Petronas, these being Petronas Chemicals, Petronas Gas, Petronas Dagangan, MISC and KLCCP Holdings.[69] Khazanah's ownership of IHH Healthcare is through the wholly owned Pulau Memutik Ventures, while its ownership of UEM

Table 3.7 Key features of the 35 publicly listed GLCs

Sector	*General ownership features*	*Company*	*Owner*	*Method of ownership*
Utilities	Khazanah is the largest direct shareholder of the three utilities MoF Inc.'s control of this sector is through its golden shares in Tenaga and Telekom LTAT has no equity interest in these three GLCs. All other GLICs have at least a direct minority interest	Tenaga Axiata Telekom	Khazanah Khazanah Khazanah	Direct Direct Direct
Plantations	PNB is the largest direct shareholder of the largest enterprise, Sime Darby, with an interest also in IJM Plantations, making it a key player in this sector The use of the golden share is limited, employed only in FGV by MoF Inc. Khazanah does not own shares in these six GLCs, while all the other GLICs have at least a direct minority interest MoF Inc. is not in the ownership structure of Boustead, controlled by LTAT. MoF Inc. does not appear as a direct or indirect shareholder of any company owned by LTAT, suggesting that this GLIC has a semblance of independence from the Ministry of Finance In FGV, among the GLICs, PNB has the largest shareholding	Sime Darby Boustead FGV Kulim (M) IJM Plantations MSM	PNB LTAT FELDA Johor Corp PNB FELDA	Direct Direct Direct Direct IJM Corp Felda Global Ventures Sugar
Construction & Property Development	None of the companies owned by the GLICs was incorporated by the government, with the exception of KLCCP. The infrastructure KLCCP owns, the Petronas twin towers, was constructed by a private enterprise PNB is the largest shareholder of the largest number of companies, with no equity interest only in UEM Sunrise. PNB uses ownership pattern 1 in all these GLCs MoF Inc. has an indirect stake in KLCCP. Ownership pattern 2 is used by MoF Inc. as well as Khazanah in its interest in UEM Sunrise The golden share is not employed in these six companies Gamuda is the only GLC in which the GLICs collectively own less than 30% of the equity	UEM Sunrise Gamuda SP Setia IJM Corp KLCCP Holdings IJM Land	Khazanah PNB PNB PNB MoF Inc. PNB	UEM Group Direct Direct Direct Petronas IJM Corp

Petronas and O&G	MoF Inc. has a huge interest in this sector through its equity holdings in three major GLCs held by Petronas MoF Inc. uses ownership pattern 3 in three GLCs, while PNB uses ownership pattern 1 in two GLCs Both Petronas and UMW Holdings function as major business groups Khazanah does not have any shares in these five GLCs, while all the other GLICs have at least a direct minority interest No golden share is employed in these five GLCs	Petronas Chemicals	MoF Inc.	Petronas
		Petronas Gas	MoF Inc.	Petronas
		Petronas Dagangan	MoF Inc.	Petronas
		UMW Holdings	PNB	Direct
		UMW Oil and Gas	PNB	UMW Holdings
Banking	Direct ownership, that is, pattern 1, is used by all the GLICs that have an interest in the banks No GLIC dominates the sector, although only EPF has ownership of two financial institutions, RHB Capital and MBSB Only KWAP does not own a bank No golden share is employed in these six banks	Malayan Banking	PNB	Direct
		CIMB	Khazanah	Direct
		Affin	LTAT	Direct
		RHB Capital	EPF	Direct
		BIMB Holdings	LTH	Direct
		MBSB	EPF	Direct
Healthcare	LTAT does not have any equity interest in these two GLCs, while all other GLICs, with the exception of MoF Inc., have at least a direct minority interest. LTAT, however, has its own interests in the healthcare sector through Pharmaniaga, a GLC that is not among the top 100 No GLIC dominates this sector The golden share is not used in these two GLCs despite their important role in health services	KPJ Healthcare	Johor Corp	Direct
		IHH Healthcare	Khazanah	Pulau Memutik Ventures

(*continued*)

Table 3.7 (continued)

Sector	*General ownership features*	*Company*	*Owner*	*Method of ownership*
Services	The golden share is used frequently by MoF Inc., except in the case of MMHE and Bursa	Malaysian Airline System	Khazanah	Direct
	MoF Inc. and Khazanah have a significant presence in terms of equity ownership	Malaysia Airports	Khazanah	Direct
	The involvement of state governments is obvious	MISC	MoF Inc.	Petronas
		MMHE	MoF Inc.	MISC
		Bintulu Port Holdings	State Financial Secretary Sarawak	Direct
		Bursa	MoF Inc.	Direct
Media	EPF's ownership of the sector is through a holding company MoF Inc. has substantial indirect equity ownership via Amanah Raya's wholly owned subsidiary Gabungan Kesturi. No golden share in this GLC	Media Prima	EPF	Direct

Sunrise is through the wholly owned UEM Group. Among companies with this pattern of ownership, there is the added feature of a private company being used by a GLC to own another quoted company. For example, FGV's ownership of MSM is through its wholly owned Felda Global Ventures Sugar.

Finally, ownership pattern 3 is GLC ownership by government entities that are not one of the seven GLICs. Three government entities function as the largest shareholder of four of the 35 GLCs. They are Johor Corp, the State Financial Secretary of Sarawak and FELDA. The first two are state-level holding companies, while FELDA is a federal-level statutory body. Johor Corp has ownership of the plantations-based Kulim (M) and the healthcare GLC, KPJ. The State Financial Secretary of Sarawak has ownership of Bintulu Port Holdings, while FELDA has ownership of FGV.

These corporate holding features, as well as other important ownership traits of these 35 GLCs, when reviewed from the perspective of their involvement in different economic sectors, are listed in Table 3.7. In property development and construction, the GLICs were not responsible for the incorporation and development of any of these companies, apart from KLCCP Holdings. These firms were taken over by the GLICs. In the financial sector, after the banking consolidation in 1999, a number of the remaining ten banks came under direct GLIC ownership and that of well-connected companies. By 2013, five of the nine domestic banks were under GLIC ownership. In the plantations sector, many of these GLCs were once foreign owned, then nationalized as part of the government's Malaysianization initiative. The GLCs in the utilities sector are monopolies. In the oil and gas sector, the government has significant involvement through MoF Inc.'s privately owned Petronas.

These findings indicate that though a majority of the 35 GLCs were not created and developed by the government, a large number of them are now owned directly by the GLICs, or indirectly via private limited vehicles. Direct ownership by GLICs allows them to realize the outcomes of their investments. It also allows them to be directly involved in decision-making as majority shareholders. Importantly too, through the GLICs, with possible the exception of LTAT-linked firms, MoF Inc. has de facto oversight and interest in these quoted GLCs.

This GLIC-GLC ownership structure, with MoF Inc. at the apex, points to the strategy that it employs to control these enterprises. In most cases, MoF Inc. has indirect ownership or control of GLCs through GLICs, and to a lesser degree through the use of golden shares, though this is used largely in the utilities and services sectors. The nature of the control mechanisms available to the government through its equity interests in this GLIC-GLC network is the subject under review in the next chapter.

Notes

1. See, for example, the studies by Puthucheary (1960), Lim (1981), Sieh-Lee (1982), Tan (1982), Mehmet (1986), Jesudason (1989), Searle (1999), Sloane (1999) and Gomez (1999, 2006).
2. Chinese enterprises functioning as business groups include Malaysia's leading quoted firms, the Genting, Hong Leong, Berjaya, Kuala Lumpur-Kepong, Lion and MUI groups. In Gomez's (1999) assessment of the rise of these enterprises as business groups, he traces why they chose to hold their corporate equity in this manner.
3. Chapter 4 provides an in-depth discussion of the control mechanisms employed by GLICs, including that of business groups, holding companies and pyramids.
4. See Table 2.7 for a detailed breakdown of the GLICs' ownership patterns of these 35 GLCs.
5. The highly diversified UMW group is primarily known for its involvement in the automotive sector, though it is also involved in the oil and gas industry as well as in manufacturing.
6. A detailed account of the government's takeover of these companies is provided below.
7. EPF is also the largest shareholder of MRCB. See below for an in-depth discussion of Media Prima.
8. Wholly owned private companies used by the Sabah state government are Desa Plus Sdn Bhd, to hold its equity in IJM Corp, while Ekuiti Yakinjaya Sdn Bhd and Sawit Kinabalu Sdn Bhd have an interest in FGV, and Warisan Harta Sabah Sdn Bhd in MAS. These private companies do not appear in Fig. 3.1 as they are not substantial shareholders of the GLCs.
9. Eleena Azlan Shah owns Generasi Setia, which has a 5.11% stake in Gamuda. More information is provided below about Eleena Azlan Shah.
10. Sabbaruddin Chik is the current Chairman of Amanah Raya, appointed in 2016. In 2013, the Chairman was Dusuki Ahmad.
11. BIMB Holdings and MBSB are two financial institutions established by the government. A profile of both institutions is provided below.
12. The next stage to be undertaken in this series of studies of the corporate empire of the government will focus on the quoted and unlisted companies controlled by these publicly listed GLCs.
13. Tong Kooi Ong earned a reputation as a dynamic entrepreneur in the early 1990s when he rapidly built the PhileoAllied Bank as a major financial

institution. He was reputedly closely associated with then Minister of Finance and Deputy Prime Minister Anwar Ibrahim. Tong lost control of this bank following a bank consolidation exercise in 1999. His loss of his interest in the bank was apparently due to his ties with Anwar, who was ousted from government in 1998 (Gomez 2001). Tong subsequently emerged as a prominent corporate figure in the property development sector, through Sunrise, which came under the control of the UEM group. Tong owns a business-based weekly newspaper, *The Edge*.

14. Gamuda: http://archive.gamuda.com.my/timeline.html.
15. Gamuda's annual reports, 2007–2013.
16. Eleena Azlan Shah is the sister of the Sultan of the state of Perak.
17. Yap Lim Sen is one of the IJM founders from IGB and the latter's former chairman.
18. "The Founding Fathers, 30 years on", IJM Corporation: http://www.ijm.com/web/download/ijmStory_3.pdf. and "Corporate History", IJM Corporation: http://www.ijm.com/web/aboutUs/corpHistory.aspx.
19. Source: http://www.sovaholdings.com/index.php/english/About-Us/About-IJM-Land-Berhad.
20. Kumpulan Europlus is now known as WCE Holdings Bhd. WCE stands for West Coast Expressway. The company was responsible for constructing and maintaining this expressway from Banting in the state of Selangor to Taiping in Perak.
21. Trinity Corp is now known as Talam Transform Bhd. The company was debt-ridden, having been badly affected by the 1997 currency crisis. Many of its debts were due to joint-ventures it went into with government-linked institutions in Selangor such as Permodalan Negeri Selangor, Kumpulan Darul Ehsan and Yayasan Pendidikan Selangor.
22. Ananda emerged in the 1990s as the second richest person in Malaysia, with ownership of two major enterprises, the satellite television operator, Astro, and the telecommunications-based Maxis, products of the privatization policy. For an in-depth analysis of Ananda's rise in the corporate sector, see Gomez and Jomo (1997: 159–65).
23. See http://www.petronastwintowers.com.my/about#petronas_TwinTowers.
24. Khoo, a prominent tycoon, was the son of a wealthy Singaporean landowner.
25. The run started after rumours abounded that Khoo was channelling bank funds to his own companies.
26. Bumiputra Malaysia Finance (BMF) was Bank Bumiputra's Hong Kong-based subsidiary. Petronas had to bailout Bank Bumiputra in 1984 following this scandal, when it pumped RM2 billion into the ailing institution. Petronas then paid PNB RM1 billion and took over the BMF-related loans. For details about this scandal, which implicated a number of senior UMNO leaders, see Lim (1986).

27. During this period, another enterprise that had a huge stake in Sime Bank was KUB Bhd, a cooperative-based company that was owned by UMNO members. When KUB encountered financial difficulties, it was taken over by MoF Inc.
28. Maika Holdings, a holding company controlled by the Malaysian Indian Congress (MIC), a member of the ruling BN coalition, then reportedly held an 8% stake in UAB.
29. When this consolidation exercise was proposed, Multi-Purpose Bank, a relatively small financial enterprise in terms of assets and number of branches, was given anchor bank status. One major shareholder of the bank in the 1980s, then known as the Malaysian French Bank, was Daim. He later entered into a deal with the MPHB group, then controlled by the MCA, a BN member, involving the exchange of his huge interest in the Malaysian French Bank for a controlling stake in UMBC. The Malaysian French Bank was renamed Multi-Purpose Bank, while the MPHB group eventually fell under the control of T.K. Lim. Although Lim was then associated with Daim, he later forged close ties with Anwar. Not long after Anwar was removed from office in 1998, Lim lost control of the MPHB group to businessmen reputedly associated with Daim (Gomez and Jomo 1997).
30. Multi-Purpose Bank was given anchor status, although other institutions to be merged with it included the much larger RHB Bank and the International Bank Malaysia (IBM). Daim had acquired a stake in IBM before he was asked to rejoin the cabinet in 1998 to help Mahathir deal with the currency crisis.
31. Another major bank in the Multi-Purpose Bank group was PhileoAllied Bank, then controlled by Tong Kooi Ong, who was closely associated with Anwar. Tong only got involved in the banking sector in 1994, but he quickly developed the PhileoAllied Bank into a dynamic, technologically innovative organization.
32. For details about the political controversy that erupted following this bank consolidation exercise, see Gomez's (2001) article entitled "Why Mahathir Axed Daim" in the *Far Eastern Economic Review*.
33. Khazanah also has a small stake in Malayan Banking through its interest in ValueCap Sdn Bhd.
34. PERKIM, or the Muslim Welfare Organization Malaysia, is a religious and social welfare body. It was founded in 1960 by Malaysia's first Prime Minister, Tunku Abdul Rahman.
35. Corporate Profile, Bank Islam: http://www.bankislam.com.my/home/corporate-info/about-us/corporate-profile/.
36. Company Profile, MBSB: http://www.mbsb.com.my/about_profile.html.
37. *MBSB 2013 Annual Report*.

38. In 2005, 50% of total assets and 78% of total loans in the financial system were from commercial banks. See: http://www.bis.org/review/r050923e.pdf.
39. For SME Bank's history, see: http://www.smebank.com.my/history/.
40. See: http://www.matrade.gov.my/cms_matrade/content.jsp?id=com.tms.cms.article.Article_6c865731-7f000010-290f290f-db521d8a.
41. Not all DFIs are members of ADFIM. For instance, LTH is considered a non-prescribed DFI by Bank Negara but it is not a member of ADFIM. See: http://adfim.com.my/dfi-data/; http://www.bnm.gov.my/index.php?ch=li&cat=dfi&type=DFI&fund=0&cu=0.
42. Its subsidiaries include MIDF Amanah Investment Bank, MIDF Asset Management and MIDF Amanah Capital. See: http://www.midf.com.my/index.php/about-us-corporate-information/about-us- groups-corporate-structure.
43. CGC, incorporated in 1972, helps young SMEs gain access to credit facilities by providing them credit guarantees. Bank Pembangunan provides financial and advisory services to nurture and develop new entrepreneurs. See: http://www.smebank.com.my/history/.
44. In 2002, the six prescribed DFIs were Bank Pembangunan, Bank Industri, Bank Simpanan Nasional, Bank Rakyat, EXIM Bank and MECIB. By 2013, they were Bank Pembangunan, Agrobank, Bank Simpanan Nasional, Bank Rakyat, EXIM Bank and SME Bank.
45. "Development Financial Institution", Bank Negara Malaysia: http://www.bnm.gov.my/index.php?ch=en_policy&pg=en_policy_dfi.
46. See Gomez (1990) for an in-depth discussion of ownership and control of the media companies through Fleet Group in the 1970s and 1980s.
47. For Syed Anwar's account of his tenure at MRCB, see Nor Mohamed (2016: 56–61).
48. *Media Prima Annual Report 2004.*
49. For an in-depth account of Nor Mohamed Yakcop's role as Economic Advisor and his attempt to reform ailing GLCs with the help of young professionals groomed by him, such as Shahril and Abdul Rahman, see Chap. 4.
50. Bloomberg Terminal Public-Listed Companies by Market Capitalization for 2013.
51. It is ranked 107 by market capitalization in Bloomberg's list of quoted firms.
52. Wan Azmi had been groomed by former Finance Minister Daim in the 1980s and emerged in the 1990s as a major figure in the corporate sector (Gomez 1990). Wan Azmi's reputation as a corporate captain diminished following the 1997 currency crisis.
53. Louis Dreyfus, a leading multinational firm in agribusiness, was targeted as a strategic cornerstone investor. However, Dreyfus did not invest in FGV at the time of the IPO (see *Financial Times* 21 June 2012).

54. In 2017, Shahrir Abdul Samad replaced Isa Samad as Chairman of FELDA. However, Isa remained as Chairman of FGV. Shahrir is also from UMNO and serves as the Member of Parliament for Johor Baru.
55. Waqaf An-Nur Corporation, a company limited by guarantee, manages the assets and shares of companies owned by Johor Corp that are endowed for waqaf. Source: Johor Corp website.
56. "Corporate Profile", Tenaga Nasional: https://www.tnb.com.my/about-tnb/corporate-profile/.
57. *Telekom 2013 Annual Report.*
58. "Group Profile", Axiata: https://www.axiata.com/corporate/group-profile/.
59. "TKR 2012: Telekom Malaysia Demerger", Khazanah, 1 July 2013: http://www.khazanah.com.my/About-Khazanah/Our-Case-Studies/Khazanah-360/TKR2012-Telekom-Malaysia-Demerger.
60. *Petronas Chemicals Annual Report 2013.*
61. See: http://www.mymesra.com.my/About_Us-@-Overview.aspx.
62. See: https://www.petronasgas.com/aboutus/Pages/default.aspx.
63. *UMW Oil & Gas Corp Annual Report 2013.*
64. *IHH Annual Report 2015.*
65. MAS lost its public listing on 31 December 2014. Since the company has undergone numerous name changes, it is referred to here as Malaysian Airline System Bhd, MAS.
66. See: http://www.misc.com.my/About_MISC-@-Our_Milestones.aspx.
67. Mirzan is the son of former Prime Minister Mahathir. This further increased Petronas' stake in MISC.
68. In 2015, MoF Inc. divested its entire stake in Bursa to KWAP, giving this GLIC its first majority interest in a top 100 publicly listed enterprise.
69. It is crucial for the government that MoF Inc. has direct ownership of Petronas because the national oil corporation declares huge dividends annually. Importantly, too, the GLCs mentioned here are but a few of Petronas' major subsidiaries.

CHAPTER 4

GLIC Control

The Control Mechanisms

A variety of control mechanisms serve as crucial tools through which GLICs can structure, coordinate and shape the functioning of the GLCs, and in the process the corporate sector. Importantly, too, the government does not need equity ownership to control an enterprise if it decides to impose a golden share. Having a golden share confers on the government enormous influence over an enterprise. Control of the banking and media sectors, as noted in Chap. 3, are also core control mechanisms. There are other mechanisms available to the government to control the GLICs, and through them the GLCs: legislation, business groups, public policies and directorships.

The law serves as a major control mechanism, as legislation regulating the functioning of the GLICs assigns the Minister of Finance enormous control over these institutions and, by extension, the GLCs. The laws overseeing the functioning of the GLICs ensure that they function well, with oversight authority in the hands of the Minister of Finance as well as other relevant ministers in the case of LTH and LTAT, who ultimately have to report to the cabinet and the Prime Minister. These laws only have the capacity to limit the effects of self-interested transactions of the controlling shareholders to some degree. This situation does not necessarily apply to the Companies Act and the listing regulations of the Bursa Malaysia that oversee the functioning of the GLCs.[1]

E.T. Gomez et al., *Minister of Finance Incorporated*,
DOI 10.1007/978-981-10-4897-5_4

Public policies undoubtedly matter and function as a key control mechanism, as they justify the intervention of GLICs and GLCs in the corporate sector, primarily through affirmative action-based plans such as the New Economic Policy (NEP), the Bumiputera Commercial & Industrial Community (BCIC) and, most recently, the Bumiputera Economic Empowerment (BEE) policy. These policies, along with privatization, industrialization and vendor development programmes, have functioned as instruments to create Bumiputera corporate captains. Although government enterprises were privatized, a number of them were renationalized following the currency crisis in 1997 and now function as prominent GLC-based business groups.

Business groups are an institutional form of control employed by GLICs to manoeuvre the functioning of publicly listed and unquoted GLCs that have an extensive presence in the economy. These business groups multi-task; while active in the corporate sector, they also implement social and political dictates of government leaders. The shareholding structure of GLC-based business groups in the top 100 indicate that a minimum of three GLICs have an equity stake in the leading GLCs at any one time. However, in most GLCs, one GLIC has a majority interest, evident in companies controlled by Khazanah, PNB, LTAT and LTH.

Directorships are a vital control mechanism. Directors with a common bond can create informal communication channels between companies that allow them to formulate agreements in their mutual interest (Mariolis 1975). When directors of different companies share a common bond to a person or institution at the apex of a pyramid, this person or institution could secure decisions that undermine the interests of minority shareholders. These control mechanisms merit review in terms of how they are employed by the GLICs.

Legislation and Governance Structure

Figure 4.1 indicates that the GLICs are under direct executive and legislative control, with enormous influence centred in the office of the Minister of Finance. This minister has direct control of MoF Inc., the government's primary holding company, given its control over Khazanah and PNB, both incorporated as companies and Malaysia's leading investment holding enterprises. MoF Inc. directly controls Khazanah and PNB through equity ownership. Although not part of the executive, the Yayasan Pelaburan Bumiputera (YPB, or Bumiputera Investment Foundation) has a board

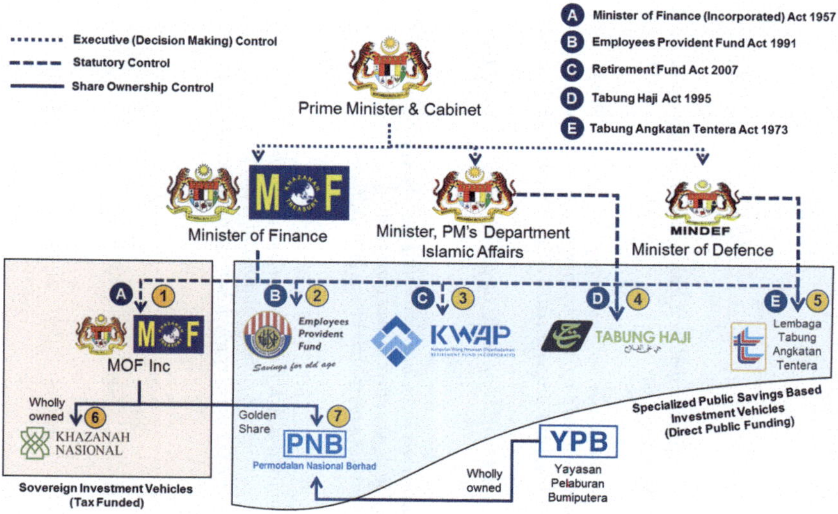

Fig. 4.1 Ownership and control structure of GLICs

of trustees which comprise the Prime Minister, Deputy Prime Minister, Minister of Finance II, Minister of International Trade and Industry and the Chairman of PNB. LTH and LTAT, both statutory bodies, are notable as, respectively, they also have the Minister in the Prime Minister's Department in charge of Islamic Affairs and the Minister of Defence in the controlling seat.[2] EPF and KWAP, also statutory bodies that function as pension/savings-based institutions, are controlled by the Minister of Finance.

The provisions in law for LTH and LTAT are unique, with each having two ministers in control, along with the Minister of Finance. In these two GLICs, the Minister of Finance has control over key matters, such as investment decisions, borrowing approval and profit declaration. A summary of the legislative power of the ministers is provided in Table 4.1, along with the laws overseeing the GLICs that function as statutory bodies.

Three issues can be noted from Table 4.1. First, there is room for portability and ambiguity in the definition of "Minister" in legislation pertaining to EPF, LTH and LTAT. The EPF Act defines the term "Minister" as the minister in charge of matters relating to this GLIC. The Tabung Haji Act defines "Minister" as the one responsible for pilgrimage issues. The Tabung Angkatan Tentera Act does not define the term. While one

Table 4.1 GLIC laws assigning ministers control

Legislation and GLICs	*Powers of ministers*
Minister of Finance (Incorporation) Act 1957 (MoF Inc.)	***Incorporation of Minister of Finance*** *3. (1) The **Minister** for the time being charged with responsibility for finance shall be a body corporate under the name of "**Minister of Finance**" (hereinafter called "the Corporation").* ***Powers of Corporation*** *4. The Corporation may enter into contracts and may acquire, purchase, take, hold and enjoy movable and immovable property of every description, and may convey, assign, surrender and yield up, charge, mortgage, demise, reassign, transfer or otherwise dispose of, or deal with, any movable or immovable property vested in the Corporation upon such terms as to the Corporation seems fit*
Employees Provident Fund Act 1991 (KWSP)	***"Minister"** means the **Minister** charged with responsibility for matters relating to the Employees Provident Fund Board;* i.e. ***Minister of Finance*** ***Power of Minister to give directions*** *11. The **Minister** may give to the Board directions of a general nature not inconsistent with the provisions of this Act as to the exercise of the functions and powers of the Board and the Board shall give effect to those directions* *12. The Board shall furnish the Minister with such information relating to its activities as he may, from time to time, require* ***Power of the Board to establish a corporation or a company*** *26C. (1) The Board may, in exercising the investment powers under this Act, from time to time, with the special approval of the **Minister**—(c) take over any company, to carry out, administer, conduct and manage any project, joint venture, privatisation programme, scheme, enterprise or any other matters which have been planned or undertaken by the Board*

Retirement Fund Act 2007 (KWAP)	***"Minister"*** *means the* ***Minister*** *charged with the responsibility for finance;* i.e. ***Minister of Finance*** ***Functions and powers of the Retirement Fund (Incorporated)*** *(3) The Retirement Fund (Incorporated) with the approval of the* ***Minister****, may —* *(a) enter into any joint venture, undertaking or any other form of co-operation or arrangement for the sharing of profits or carry on its activities in association with, or otherwise, any public authority or government body carrying on or engaging in any such activities;* *(b) by order published in the Gazette, establish a corporation by such name as the Retirement Fund (Incorporated) may think fit, to carry out and manage any project, scheme or enterprise which has been planned or undertaken by the Retirement Fund (Incorporated) in furtherance of its functions under this Act, and the corporation may so do either by itself or by entering into partnership or any arrangement for sharing of profits, co-operation, joint venture or otherwise; and…*
Tabung Haji Act 1995 (LTH)	***"Minister"*** *means the Minister charged with the responsibility for pilgrimage control;* i.e. ***Minister in charge of Islamic Affairs, Prime Minister's Department*** *(3) The Lembaga may, with the approval of the* ***Minister*** *—* *(a) enter into any partnership, joint venture, undertaking or any other form of co-operation or arrangement for the sharing of profits or carry on its activities in association with, or otherwise, any person, public authority or government carrying on or engaging in any such activities;* *(b) take or otherwise acquire shares and securities in any public authority, corporation or other body and may sell, hold or re-issue such shares or securities or otherwise dispose of or deal with them;* *(c) establish a corporation by such name as the Lembaga may think fit to carry out and have the charge, conduct and management of any project, scheme or enterprise which has been planned or undertaken by the Lembaga; or* ***Power of Minister to give directions and require information*** *10. (1) The* ***Minister*** *may give to the Lembaga such directions of a general character not inconsistent with this Act relating to the performance of the Lembaga's functions and the Lembaga shall give effect to all such directions* ***Financing or financial assistance*** *(2) No guarantee or indemnity letter shall be issued by the Lembaga or any corporation established under this Act without the written approval of the* ***Minister of Finance*** ***Borrowing powers*** *18. The Lembaga may, with the approval of the* ***Minister*** *and* ***Minister of Finance*** *and upon such terms and conditions and for such period as they may approve, borrow any sums required by the Lembaga for the purposes of this Act*

(*continued*)

Table 4.1 (continued)

Legislation and GLICs	*Powers of ministers*
Tabung Angkatan Tentera Act 1973 (LTAT)	***"Minister"*** *is not defined* ***Power of Minister in relation to the Lembaga*** *7. (1) The **Minister** may give to the Lembaga such directions of a general character not inconsistent with the provisions of this Act as relates to the exercise and performance of its functions and the Lembaga shall give effect to all such directions* *(2) The Lembaga shall furnish the **Minister** with such returns, accounts and other information with respect to the property and activities of the Lembaga as he may from time to time require* ***Declaration of profit*** *11. (1) Subject to the provisions of this section, the Lembaga may on or before 31st day of December in any year after considering the recommendation of any actuary approved by the **Minister of Finance** declare a rate of profit on the contributions in respect of that year* *14. The Lembaga may, with the approval of the **Minister and the Minister of Finance**, borrow any sums required by the Lembaga for the purpose of this Act and on such terms and conditions and for such period as the **Minister of Finance** may approve* ***Investment by Lembaga*** *15. (1) The Lembaga may on the advice given by the Investment Panel invest moneys which are in the Tabung and in the Reserve Fund to the extent and in the manner following: (b) not more than thirty per centum thereof—(i) in business and commercial enterprises which are not listed and quoted on any stock exchange established in Malaysia: Provided that the total amount of moneys so invested in any one such enterprise shall not exceed thirty per centum of the total amount of shareholders' fund of that enterprise at the time of the investment unless prior written approval of the **Minister and the Minister of Finance** is obtained to invest in excess of such percentage; (iv) in investments in securities or any other forms of investment outside Malaysia: Provided that the prior written approval of the **Minister and the Minister of Finance** shall be obtained both in respect of the security or other forms of investment to be undertaken as well as the total amount of moneys to be invested in any such security or investment (vi) in any other investment within Malaysia: Provided that the prior written approval of the **Minister and the Minister of Finance** shall be obtained in respect of the investment to be undertaken as well as the total amount of moneys to be invested*

Note: Khazanah and PNB are not discussed here because they are not statutory bodies

can assume that the Minister of Finance oversees EPF, the Minister in charge of Islamic Affairs in the Prime Minister's Department manages pilgrimage matters and the Minister of Defence controls LTAT, these roles can be shifted to other ministers. For example, if the government decides to put pilgrimage issues under the authority of the Minister of Foreign Affairs, then power over LTH will be transferred to him from the Minister in charge of Islamic Affairs. Since the Tabung Angkatan Tentera Act does not define "minister", there is no guarantee that the Minister of Defence has permanent control over LTAT.

Second, all acts give the respective ministers wide powers. The EPF, LTAT and LTH legislation empower the relevant ministers to issue directions to the board. Besides that, the minister can obtain any information from the board at any time. Powers held by the minister include providing approval to incorporate and acquire companies, purchase shares and securities, borrow money, provide financing and dictate investment decisions.

Third, through these laws, the Minister of Finance has some involvement in GLICs under the authority of other ministers. LTH, though under the Minister in charge of Islamic Affairs, needs approval from the Minister of Finance before providing financing or borrowing money. LTAT, under the Minister of Defence, requires the Minister of Finance's approval before it can declare its annual profit, borrow money and undertake investments. In fact, the Statutory Bodies (Power to Borrow) Act does not allow a statutory body to borrow money without the prior approval of that body's minister and the Minister of Finance.

Another aspect of these laws as a control mechanism is that concerning the appointment of directors of GLICs. Through these laws, the Minister of Finance, with the Minister of Defence and the Minister for Islamic Affairs, has the authority to appoint people of their choice as members of the board of directors of these GLICs. Table 4.2 provides a list of legislation assigning powers to the relevant minister to appoint directors of GLICs.

Table 4.2 indicates that these laws assign the respective ministers almost total control over the appointment of board members. The respective ministers for these GLICs appoint the chairmen of their boards. All boards have representatives from other government institutions such as Bank Negara and the Ministry of Finance. However, the power to appoint these bureaucrats also lies with the minister in question.

Accountability mechanisms are laid out in these laws. For statutory-based GLICs, accountability is required as stated in the Statutory Bodies

Table 4.2 Legislation on appointment of GLIC directors

No.	*Legislation and GLICs*	*Appointment of directors*
1.	Minister of Finance (Incorporation) Act 1957 (MoF Inc.)	No board of directors
2.	Employees Provident Fund Act 1991 (KWSP)	***"Minister"*** *means the* ***Minister*** *charged with responsibility for matters relating to the Employees Provident Fund Board;* i.e. ***Minister of Finance*** ***Power of Minister to appoint directors*** *4. (1) The Board shall consist of:* *(a) a Chairman;* *(b) a Deputy Chairman to be appointed from amongst the persons referred to in subparagraph (d)(i):* *(c) the chief executive officer, who shall be an ex-officio member; and* *(d) not more than eighteen other members of whom –* *(2) Where the Chairman is not a representative of the Ministry of Finance, the Minister shall appoint a representative of the Ministry of Finance to be a member of the Board under subparagraph (1)(d)(I) who shall also be appointed the Deputy Chairman.* *(3) Members of the Board shall be* ***appointed by the Minister*** *and, subject to sections 6 and 7 shall, unless they sooner resign or their appointment is sooner revoked, hold office for such term as the Minister may determine*
3.	Retirement Fund Act 2007 (KWAP)	***"Minister"*** *means the* ***Minister*** *charged with the responsibility for finance;* i.e. ***Minister of Finance*** ***Power of Minister to appoint Directors*** *4. The Board shall consist of the following members who shall be* ***appointed by the Minister****:* *a) a Chairman who shall be the Secretary General of the Ministry of Finance;* *b) a representative from the Central Bank of Malaysia;* *c) a representative from the Ministry of Finance;* *d) the Chief Executive Officer who shall be an ex-officio member;* *e) three representatives of the Government of Malaysia;* *f) three other persons from the private sector with experience and expertise in business or finance;* *g) a person who,* ***in the opinion of the Minister*** *shall fairly represent the contributories to the Fund other than representatives of the Government of Malaysia*

4.	Tabung Haji Act 1995 (LTH)	***"Minister"*** *means the Minister charged with the responsibility for pilgrimage control;* i.e. ***Minister in charge of Islamic Affairs, Prime Minister's Department*** *6. (1) the Lembaga shall consist of the following members:* *a) a Chairman who shall be* ***appointed by the Minister;*** *b) a representative of the Prime Minister's Department;* *c) a representative of the treasury;* *d) not more than seven other members who shall* ***be appointed by the Minister***
5.	Tabung Angkatan Tentera Act 1973 (LTAT)	***"Minister" is not defined*** *(3) The Lembaga shall consist of:* *a) a Chairman who shall be the Secretary General of the Ministry of Defence or such other person as may be* ***appointed by the Minister;*** *b) a Deputy Chairman who shall be a representative of the Ministry of Defence;* *c) the Deputy Secretary General to the Treasury;* *d) the Chief Executive who shall be an ex-officio member;* *e) four members to be* ***appointed by the Minister*** *to represent the contributors, one of whom shall be the Chief of the Armed Forces Staff;* *f) such other members not exceeding four in number to be* ***appointed by the Minister***

(Accounts and Annual Reports) Act 1980. Under this Act, all statutory bodies

> shall keep or shall cause to be kept proper accounts and other records in respect of its operations in accordance with generally accepted accounting principles and shall cause to be prepared a statement of its accounts in respect of each financial year and shall, within six months after the end of that financial year or such extension thereof as may be granted under section 9, submit the same to the Auditor General for audit.

The Auditor General can audit these statutory bodies according to the Audit Act 1957. Every statutory body must submit its audited accounts to the relevant minister. The minister is then required to table these audited statements in parliament. The Statutory Bodies (Accounts and Annual Reports) Act empowers the minister to "make rules for the purpose of carrying out or giving effect to any provisions of this Act". Another law, laid down in the Statutory Bodies (Discipline and Surcharge) Act, spells out punishable crimes by statutory body directors and officers and the creation of disciplinary committees to judge the offenders. However, this Act also empowers the Prime Minister to exempt any statutory body from the provisions of this legislation. As of 2006, three GLICs—EPF, LTAT and LTH—were exempted from this Act.[3]

The minister is also responsible for the appointment of the members of investment panels, a core institution within the governance structure of the GLIC. The laws overseeing the EPF, LTAT and KWAP have provisions for the creation of an investment panel and the appointment of its members. Khazanah does not have an investment panel of the sort that exists at LTH, LTAT, KWAP and EPF. However, Khazanah has a team of investment directors within its larger Senior Leadership Team.[4] PNB, similar to Khazanah, does not have an investment panel. Instead, PNB has investment committees under its subsidiary, the unit trust manager, Amanah Saham Nasional Bhd (ASNB).[5] Only the LTH legislation does not mention the need to appoint an investment panel. However, LTH established its investment panel in 2001.[6] The investment panel is a vital advisory institution, independent of the directors of these GLICs, as it is responsible for proposing the areas of investment. Table 4.3 provides a list—and brief profile—of the members of these investment panels in each of the seven GLICs.

The appointment of members of these investment panels is the prerogative of the minister. Tables 4.3 and 4.4 indicate that these investment

Table 4.3 Investment panels of GLICs, 2013

GLIC	*Name*	*Background*	*Profile*
Khazanah	Azman Mokhtar	Corporate	• Managing Director (MD) of Khazanah • Refer to Table 4.9 for more details
	Ganen Sarvananthan	Corporate	• Head of Investments • Executive Director, MD's Office • Former Director of Equity Capital Markets, UBS (Hong Kong)
	Joseph Dominic Silva	Corporate	• Executive Director, Investments • 12 years at ABN Amro and other financial institutions
	Ben Chan	Corporate	• Executive Director, Investments • Former Director of Research in several investment houses
	Noorazman Aziz	Corporate	• Executive Director, Investments • Former MD of Fajar Capital Ltd. (Labuan) • Worked at Citigroup, Bank Islam, Kuala Lumpur Stock Exchange and Labuan Offshore
	Tengku Azmil Zahruddin	Corporate	• Executive Director, Investments • Former MD of Malaysia Airline System and Penerbangan Malaysia • Worked for PricewaterhouseCoopers (London and Hong Kong)
	Hisham Hamdan	Corporate	• Executive Director, Investments • Head of Khazanah Research & Investment Strategy • Worked at Sime Darby
	Kenneth Shen	Corporate	• Executive Director, Investments • Former Adviser to the CEO of Qatar Investment Authority • Worked at Salomon Brothers (Hong Kong) and Lehman Brothers (New York)
	Shahazwan Harris	Corporate	• Executive Director, Investments • Worked at PA Consulting and Boston Consulting Group
	Zaida Khalida Shaari	Corporate	• Executive Director, Investments • Former Company Secretary and Head of Legal Department at PNB

(*continued*)

Table 4.3 (continued)

GLIC	*Name*	*Background*	*Profile*
PNB	Ahmad Sarji	Ex-Bureaucrat	• Chairman of PNB and ASNB • Investment Committee of ASN, ASN 2, ASN 3, ASG-Pendidikan, ASG-Kesihatan, ASG-Persaraan, ASB, ASM, ASD and AS 1Malaysia[a] • Refer to Table 4.13 for more details
	Hamad Kama Piah	Corporate	• CEO of PNB & ASNB • Investment Committee of ASN, ASN 2, ASN 3, ASG-Pendidikan, ASG-Kesihatan, ASG-Persaraan, ASB, ASM, ASD and AS 1Malaysia • Refer to Table 4.9 for more details
	Desa Pachi	Corporate	• Director of ASNB • Investment Committee of ASN, ASN 2, ASN 3, ASG-Pendidikan, ASG-Kesihatan, ASG-Persaraan, ASB, ASM, ASD and AS 1Malaysia
	Wan Abdul Aziz Wan Abdullah	Ex-Bureaucrat	• Director of PNB • Investment Committee of ASN, ASN 2, ASN 3, ASG-Pendidikan, ASG-Kesihatan, ASG-Persaraan, ASB, ASM, ASD and AS 1Malaysia • Refer to Table 4.13 for more details
	Abdul Halim Ismail	Corporate	• Investment Committee of ASN, ASN 2, ASN 3, ASG-Pendidikan, ASG-Kesihatan, ASG-Persaraan, ASB, ASM, ASD, AS 1Malaysia and ASW 2020 • Much experience in matters of Islamic Banking, Takaful and Capital Market
	Faizah Tahir	Ex-Bureaucrat	• Former Secretary General of the Ministry of Women, Family and Community Development • Investment Committee of Amanah Saham Wawasan 2020 (ASW 2020)
	Idris Kechot	Corporate	• Director of ASNB • Investment Committee of ASW 2020 • Joined PNB as Investment Analyst, since 1983 • Joined Investment Division as Equity Dealer in 1988
	Cheng Kee Check	Corporate	• Partner at Messrs. Skrine since 1997 • Investment Committee of ASW 2020 • Much experience in legal and corporate advisory

EPF	Samsudin Osman	Ex-Bureaucrat	• Chairman of EPF Board of Directors and Investment Panel • Refer to Table 4.13 for more details
	Zauyah Desa	Bureaucrat	• Member of KWAP Investment Panel • Alternate Director of EPF • Secretary of Loans Management, Financial Market and Actuary Division, Ministry of Finance • Worked for Hashim & Lim Consultancy • Director of Prasarana, BSN, Malaysia Debt Ventures, Johor Corporation, Amanah Raya
	Shamsiah Yunus	Corporate	• Bank Negara Malaysia Deputy Governor • Responsible for divisions that supervise banks and financial institutions
	Nazir Razak	Corporate	• MD of CIMB Group
	Azlan Hashim	Corporate	• Director of Khazanah • KWAP Investment Panel • Refer to Table 4.9 for more details
	David Lau Nai Pek	Corporate	• Retired from Shell after 30 years (2011) • Director of Axiata, Malaysia Airline System, Shell Refining Company, KKB Engineering
	Shahril Ridza	Corporate	• CEO of EPF • Refer to Table 4.9 for more details

(*continued*)

Table 4.3 (continued)

GLIC	*Name*	*Background*	*Profile*
LTH	Azizan Abd Rahman	Corporate	• Chairman of Investment Panel • Chairman of Eastern & Oriental, TH Heavy Engineering • Director of Apex Quality Holdings, TH Plantations • Worked at Ministry of Home Affairs before entering the shipping and securities industry • Former President of Malaysian Stockbrokers Association • Helped restructure Tongkah Holdings, Bina Darulaman, MBf Holdings
	Sheikh Ghazali	Bureaucrat	• Former Director General/Sharie Chief Judge, Malaysian Shariah Judicial Department • Served in many Islamic finance and Shariah advisory councils
	Zahridah Ismail	Corporate	• 22 years in the banking sector • Former Director of RHB Bank • Worked at MIDA, Bank Rakyat, Kwong Yik Bank
	Mohzani Abdul Wahab	Corporate	• Director of Celcom Axiata and Boustead Plantations • Former Director of Pavilion REIT Management, Hong Leong Investment Bank, Shell Refining Company
	Abdul Kadir	Corporate	• Partner of Messrs. Kadir, Andri & Partners • Chairman of TIME dotCom • Director of non-listed UEM Group of Companies, Danajamin • Member of Corporate Debt Restructuring Committee • Chairman of Federation of Investment Managers Malaysia
	Syed Elias Alhabshi	Corporate	• Former CEO of ASEAN Finance Corporation • Former Director of Babcock & Brown, Hong Leong Capital • Former Advisor of PhileoAllied Bank • Worked for Malayan Banking, Bank Bumiputra and Merill Lynch

KWAP	Mohd Irwan Serigar Abdullah	Bureaucrat	• Chairman of KWAP Board of Directors and Investment Panel • Director of LTH • Secretary-General of Treasury, Ministry of Finance
	Che Zakiah Che Din	Corporate	• Director of Financial Conglomerates Supervision Department, Bank Negara Malaysia
	Zauyah Desa	Bureaucrat	• Also in EPF Investment Panel (listed above)
	Azlan Hashim	Corporate	• Also in EPF Investment Panel (listed above)
	Cheah Teak Kuang	Corporate	• Deputy Chairman of AmBank (M) Bhd, AmInvestment Bank, AmIslamic Bank • Director of Danajamin, Cagamas Holdings, IOI Corporation, UMW Oil & Gas, AmFraser International Pte Ltd. (Singapore), AmFraser Securities Pte Ltd. (Singapore), PT AmCapital (Indonesia) • Chairman of Berjaya Sports Toto • Former MD of AmBank Group
	Abdul Farid Alias	Corporate	• CEO of Malayan Banking • Worked at Malayan Banking, JP Morgan, Malaysian International Merchant Bankers, Khazanah
	Wan Kamaruzaman Wan Ahmad	Corporate	• CEO of KWAP • Refer to Table 4.9 for more details
LTAT	Ghazali Seth	Ex-Bureaucrat	• Chairman of Investment Panel • Former Chief of Armed Forces
	Zulkifeli Zin	Bureaucrat	• Director of LTAT • Chief of Armed Forces
	Fauziah Yaacob	Bureaucrat	• Director of LTAT • Deputy Secretary General, Ministry of Finance
	Aziz Ibrahim	Corporate	• Ministerial appointee as provided by the LTAT Act as a member with experience in finance and business
	Abdul Rahman Abdul Hamid	Corporate	• Ministerial appointee as provided by the LTAT Act as a member with experience in finance and business

Source: 2013 GLIC annual reports (The information on the investment committee of ASNB was obtained from the ASNB Master Prospectus 2013/2014 (*Amanah Saham Nasional Berhad, 2013*))

[a]These are unit trusts managed by ASNB, owned by PNB

Table 4.4 Breakdown of representation of GLIC investment panels, 2013

GLIC	*Corporate professionals*	*Bureaucrats*	*Ex-bureaucrats*
Khazanah	10	0	0
PNB	5	0	3
EPF	5	1	1
LTH	5	1	0
KWAP	5	2	0
LTAT	2	2	1
Total	32	6	5

Source: 2013 GLIC annual reports

panels are occupied by people with significant experience in the corporate sector, suggesting professional oversight of the investments by the GLICs. About one-third of these panel members are sitting and former bureaucrats (see Table 4.4).

Many of the managing directors (MDs) of the GLICs are on their respective investment panels. They include Azman Mokhtar (Khazanah), Hamad Kama Piah (PNB), Shahril Ridza (EPF) and Wan Kamaruzaman (KWAP). Some of the chairmen, for example Ahmad Sarji (PNB), Samsudin Osman (EPF) and Irwan Serigar (KWAP), are also on investment panels. Only a small number of the other GLIC directors are on their investment panels, such as Wan Abdul Aziz (PNB), Zulkifeli Zin and Fauziah Yaacob (LTAT). Two people, Azlan Hashim and Zauyah Desa, appear on more than one investment panel. Azlan, a Khazanah director, is present on those of EPF and KWAP. Zauyah Desa, an alternate director of EPF and Deputy Secretary-General of Ministry of Finance, is a member of the EPF and KWAP investment panels. Most MDs of GLICs are on their respective investment panels. The MD can report the findings of the investment panels directly to the board of directors. Even if the board of directors has the final say on investments, the investment panels will have played an important first step in determining the risks of potential investments. The importance of investment panels is seen in the presence of GLIC chairmen on some investment panels, although several GLICs do not conform to this pattern. The chairmen and MDs of LTH and LTAT are not on their investment panels. The absence of Khazanah's Chairman, Prime Minister Najib Razak, from the investment panel is obviously due to his governmental duties.[7]

These investment panels are dominated by experienced corporate professionals and include prominent figures such as Nazir Razak and Abdul Farid Alias (see Table 4.4).[8] No UMNO member is present on these panels. While experienced professionals from the financial sector constitute a large segment of LTH's investment panel, the absence of both the chairman and the MD raises doubts about the importance of this advisory committee to the management. LTH has been involved in several scandals regarding its investments.[9]

Holding Companies and Business Groups

The GLICs function primarily as investment holding companies, with a business group control structure that serves as an important mechanism for one institution to control a large number of enterprises. Figures 4.2, 4.3, 4.4, 4.5, 4.6, 4.7 and 4.8 outline the corporate holdings structures of the seven GLICs in 2013. These figures indicate that a number of quoted GLCs come under the umbrella of each GLIC. These quoted GLCs, in turn, function as business groups, involving the use of a holding company—and, in some cases, cross-holdings—reflecting that this is an extremely important corporate control mechanism. Collectively, the GLICs have common shareholdings of a range of publicly listed firms, although in numerous cases one of them has majority ownership. Block shareholding of listed enterprises, including through obscure private firms, is common among the GLICs. Block shareholdings help shield the collective majority ownership that GLICs have over major quoted companies.

It is clear that MoF Inc. functions largely as a holding company. Its primary modes of corporate control are through majority equity ownership and golden shares (see Fig. 4.2). A unique feature of MoF Inc. is its ownership of two other major GLICs, Khazanah and PNB, both of them companies (the other GLICs are statutory bodies). MoF Inc.'s ownership of Khazanah and PNB is through majority shareholding and one share respectively.[10] MoF Inc. also has direct majority ownership of two unlisted holding companies, AmanahRaya, the leading trustee company, and Petronas, the huge national oil corporation.

MoF Inc. does not have a direct majority shareholding in any of the GLCs among the top 100, but it does have minority interest in two GLCs, that is, Bursa (16%) and IJM Corp (0.16%).[11] MoF Inc.'s direct interest in other GLCs among the top 100 is through golden shares, a feature unique to this GLIC. This allows MoF Inc. to have control over a large number

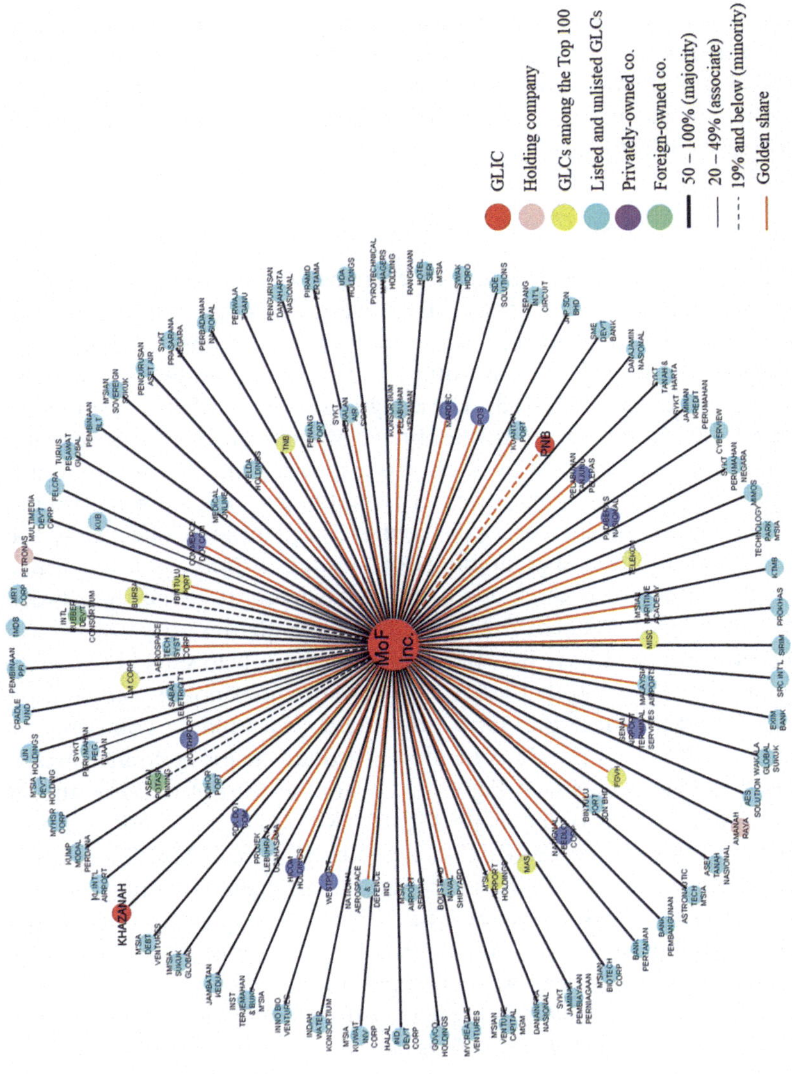

Fig. 4.2 MoF Inc.'s ownership structure, 2013/2016

of companies without any significant equity holdings. The golden share is used in strategic sectors, such as airports, seaports, telecommunications, utilities, healthcare and agriculture. Ownership of private companies is only through the golden share mechanism.

Two interesting points can be noted in Fig. 4.2. First, that an associate company of MoF Inc. is KUB, a listed GLC formerly owned by UMNO and bailed out after the 1997 currency crisis. Second, MoF Inc. has an interest in two foreign-owned enterprises, Asian Potash and IRCO, both agriculture-based companies. Asian Potash, based in Thailand, manufactures potash fertilizers, while IRCO is jointly owned with partners from Thailand and Indonesia to promote the rubber industry. MoF Inc. owned 9.6% and 22% of Asean Potash and IRCO respectively.

Figure 4.3 indicates that PNB uses the model of investing in a large number of publicly listed companies, although, unlike MoF Inc., it prefers largely to remain a non-majority shareholder. PNB's shareholdings in quoted companies are primarily through ASNB. PNB has an associate interest in SP Setia but the volume of shares it owns here is high, at 48.76%. ASNB owns another 15% of SP Setia's equity. PNB, along with ASNB, also has a majority interest in two other companies in the top 100, Sime Darby (51.66%) and Malayan Banking (48.02%). PNB and ASNB collectively own a minority interest in a number of GLCs among the top 100.

PNB, through ASNB, has an interest in a number of publicly listed companies. ASNB has a direct interest in UMW Holdings (49%), Telekom (19%), UMW Oil (8%), Gamuda (12%), IJM Corporation (15%), Tenaga (12%), Axiata (14%), MISC (8%) and Malaysia Airports (15%). PNB, through ASNB, has associate shareholdings in three privately owned quoted companies, MMC Corp, Digi and Capitaland. As for foreign-owned publicly listed companies, ASNB is an associate shareholder in Dutch Lady and Fraser & Neave Holdings, both in the food and beverages business. PNB, through ASNB, owns a minority interest in four privately owned publicly listed companies, Sapura Kencana, Bumi Armada, Maxis and Sunway REIT; all are top 100 companies. ASNB's equity interests in enterprises that are publicly listed are far more extensive than what is shown in Fig. 4.3, which captures its ties with only those GLCs in the top 100.

Khazanah, as a sovereign wealth fund, does not discriminate about where it can achieve value and invests both as a majority and minority shareholder, though usually preferring to own more than 10% of any company in which it invests; it is also active in joint-ventures (see Fig. 4.4).

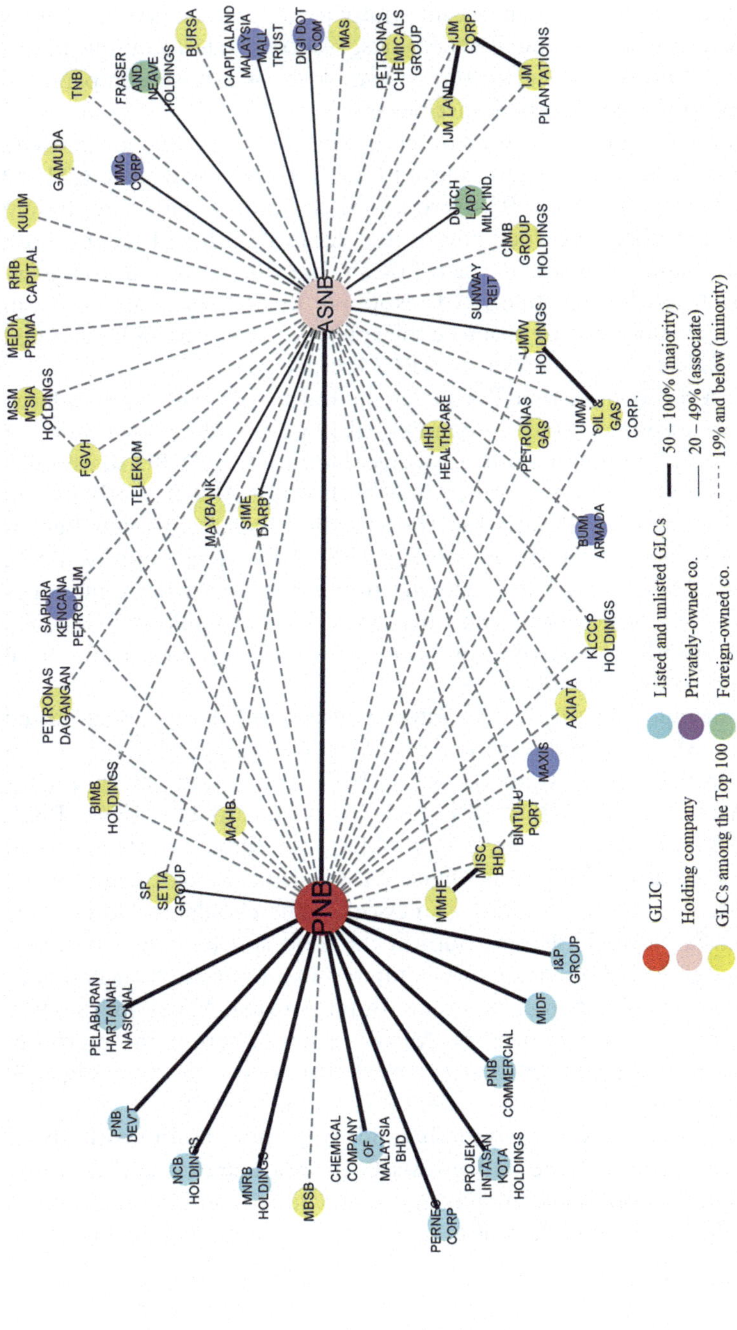

Fig. 4.3 PNB's ownership structure, 2013

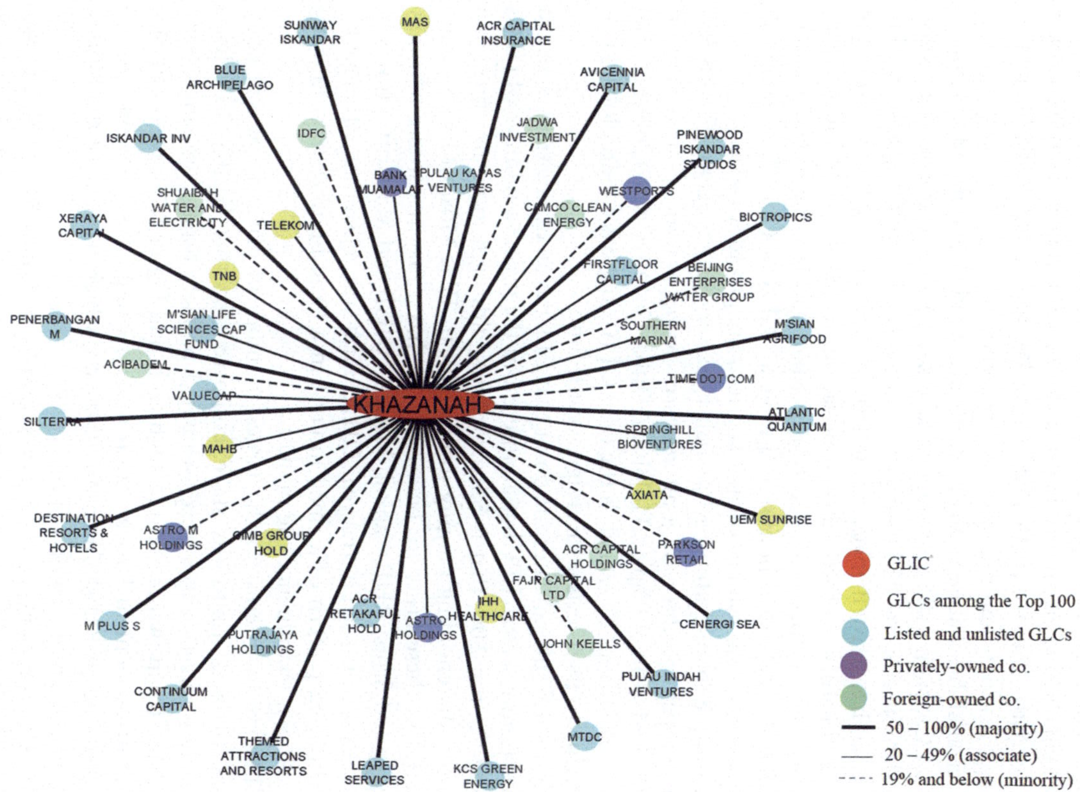

Fig. 4.4 Khazanah's ownership structure, 2013

For GLCs among the top 100, Khazanah owns only eight, having a substantial interest in UEM Sunrise, Malaysia Airlines, CIMB Group, IHH Healthcare, Malaysia Airports, Axiata, Tenaga Nasional and Telekom.[12] Khazanah also has an interest in privately owned publicly listed companies such as Astro, Parkson, TIME dotCom, Westports and Bank Muamalat, through associate and minority level shareholding.

Khazanah has a huge equity interests in a number of unlisted but important GLCs, such as Penerbangan Malaysia, Sunway Iskandar, Pinewood Iskandar, Silterra and M Plus.[13] These majority shareholdings suggest that Khazanah has active managerial control of these enterprises. A number of these companies are focused on innovation, technology and life sciences, all fairly new sectors in the economy. Khazanah has the lowest number of minority level shareholdings among all GLICs. Out of 11 minority companies, six are foreign owned and four are privately owned.

A unique feature about Khazanah is its serious engagement with foreign companies, through joint-ventures with prominent firms such as Temasek Holdings, Capital Holdings, Dubai Group, Camco International and Kuok Group. Khazanah is the only GLIC that has a high global presence, due to its role as a sovereign wealth fund.

Figure 4.5 substantiates the point that EPF has an extensive presence in the corporate sector. EPF has an interest in the greatest number of GLCs among the top 100, that is 35 companies, although most are through a minority shareholding ranging from 0.25% to 17%. Most of EPF's equity holdings in these firms are below 10%. It has a majority interest in only four quoted firms: RHB Capital, MRCB, MBSB and Malakoff. However, Malakoff is not listed in the year 2013, but it was relisted in 2015. EPF's shareholding pattern of a small interest in a large number of companies may allow it to influence the market.

EPF has an interest in the largest number of privately owned companies, through a minority stake, compared to other GLICs. EPF has a minority interest in four foreign-owned publicly listed companies, with less than 10% in two of them (Dutch Lady and Fraser & Neave). EPF also has an investment in Lafarge, a prominent company in the construction industry, and in British American Tobacco, which has one of the highest stock prices among quoted firms.

KWAP's corporate structure is very similar to that of EPF, with an interest in a large number of the top 100 (see Fig. 4.6). However, KWAP has no majority interest in a quoted company. It has a minority interest in 28 GLCs among the top 100, ranging from 0.14% to 8%. Since KWAP is a much smaller fund compared to EPF, it owns stakes in far fewer companies.

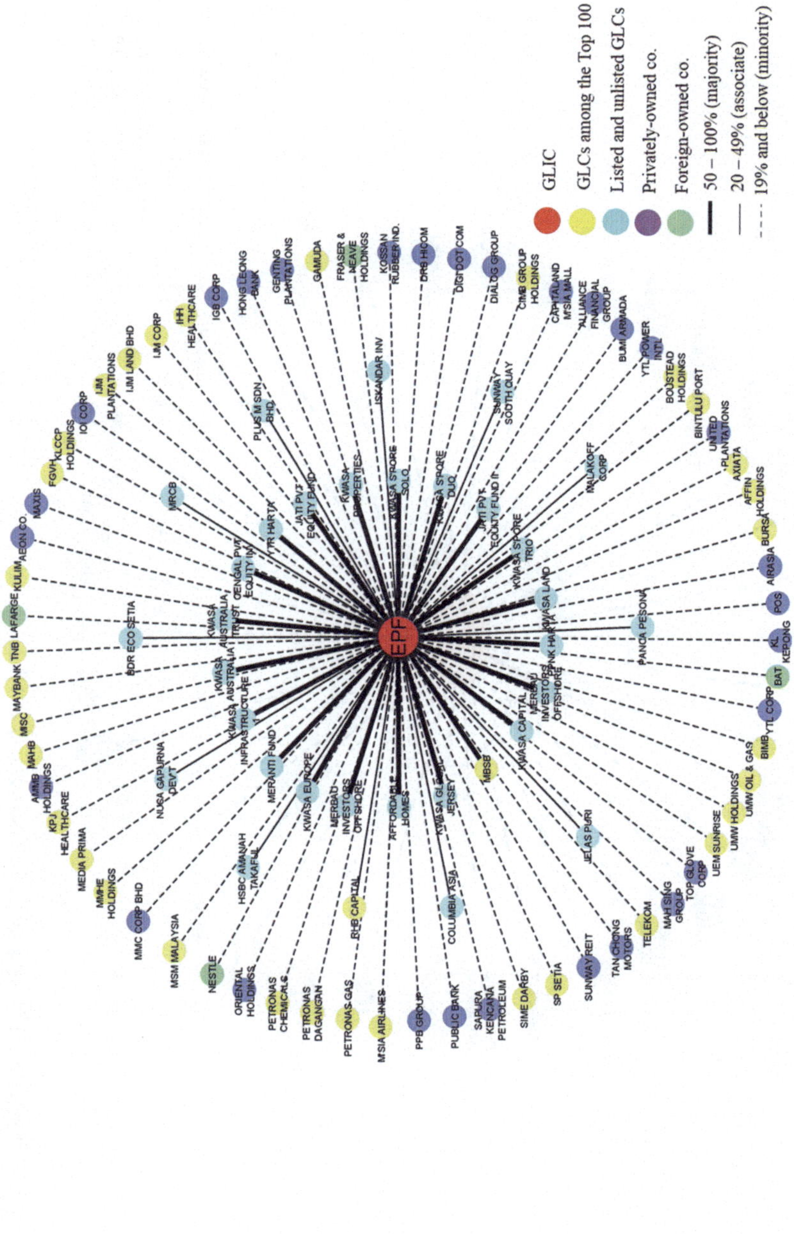

Fig. 4.5 EPF's ownership structure, 2013

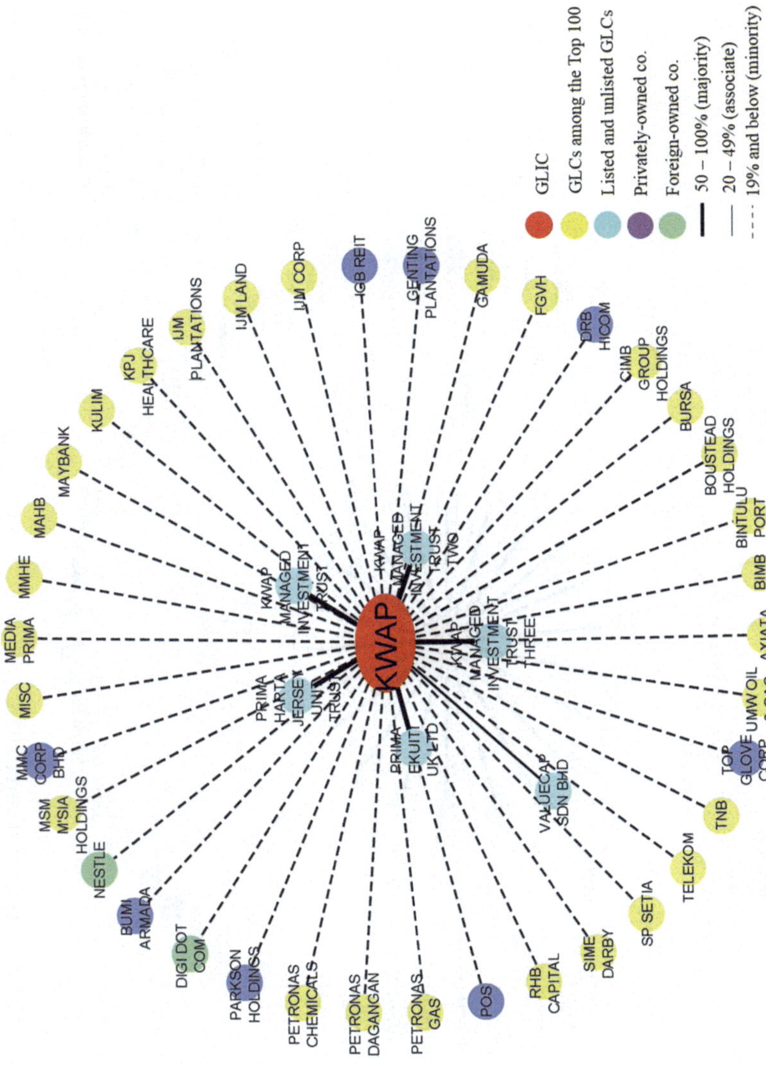

Fig. 4.6 KWAP's ownership structure, 2013

KWAP has a minority interest in eight privately owned and two foreign-owned companies, Nestlé and Digi Dotcom, the latter among the top ten firms on the Bursa, based on the market capitalization. KWAP has only five wholly owned subsidiaries that focus on their core business. ValueCap Sdn Bhd is the only company in which KWAP has an associate shareholding.

LTAT has majority control of two prominent GLCs, Affin Holdings and Boustead Holdings (see Fig. 4.7). LTAT also has a majority interest in Pharmaniaga through Boustead Holdings, the only quoted firm in the LTAT stable that is not a top 100 enterprise. Almost all other companies in the LTAT group in which it has a majority interest are private limited firms that are involved in a diverse range of sectors, such as plantations, communications and biotechnology. Among publicly listed companies, 12 GLCs in the top 100 are companies in which LTAT has a minority interest, ranging from 0.12% to 1.2%, a very small figure compared to the other GLICs' ownership of minority shareholdings in leading GLCs. LTAT owns the equity of six privately owned companies at the associate level. LTAT has no equity interest in foreign companies other than its direct interest in Chery Holdings, a subsidiary of the China-based auto manufacturer.

LTAT's main subsidiaries concurrently own an interest in other firms, indicating an interlocking stock ownership pattern, an uncommon trend among the GLICs. The interesting feature of this group is that LTAT owns Boustead and Affin, while Boustead in turn owns Affin. A similar ownership pattern is evident between PNB and IJM Corporation, IJM Plantations, and IJM Land, although LTAT is actively involved in the management of the Boustead-Affin group. This type of control facilitates the movement of resources within its network of firms.

LTH operates in the same way as LTAT in that they both function like a diversified business group (see Fig. 4.8). Both GLICs own and control a large number of private companies that are involved in a wide range of sectors including plantations, infrastructure development and engineering. In Fig. 4.8, LTH's corporate structure indicates its control of a banking enterprise, BIMB Holdings, with a 55% stake. LTH has a majority interest in three other publicly listed companies that are not in the top 100, TH Plantations Bhd, TH Heavy Engineering Bhd and Theta Edge Bhd, involved in plantations, offshore heavy engineering and as an ICT solutions and service provider respectively. LTH, like EPF and KWAP, has an interest in a number of blue-chip GLCs. It also has an interest in foreign firms that are involved in property development and investment holdings. The other GLCs in the top 100 in which LTH has a shareholding are merely minority interests, with equity holdings ranging from 0.05% to 10%.

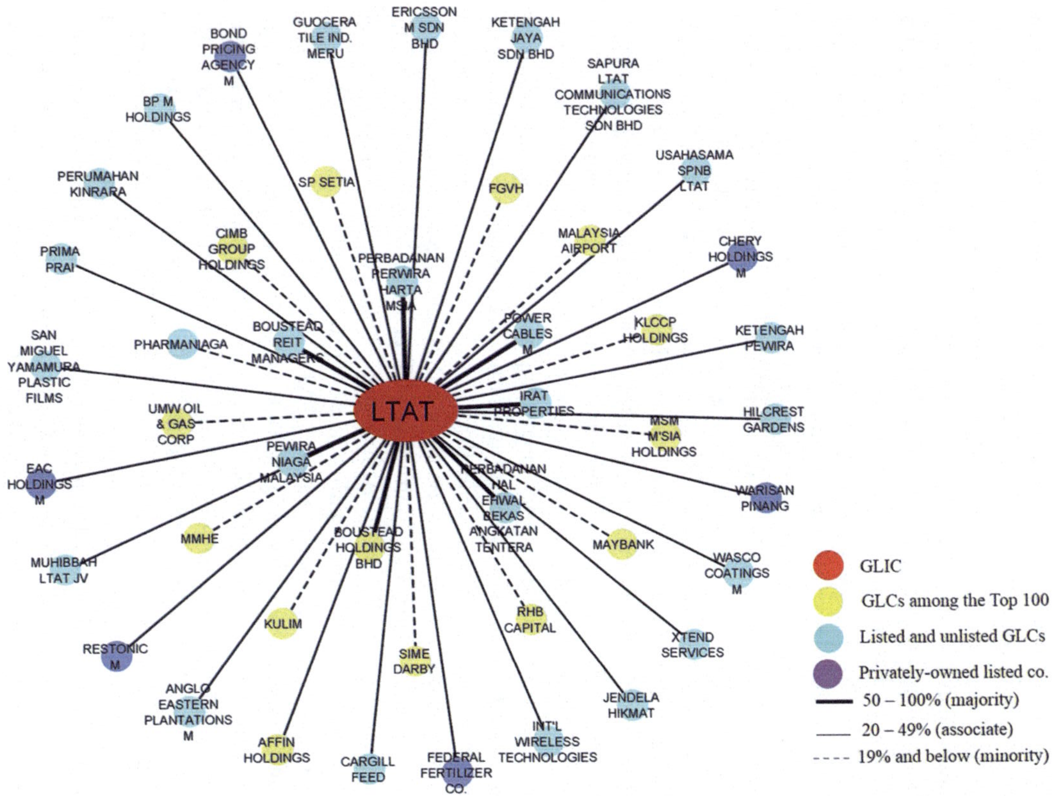

Fig. 4.7 LTAT's ownership structure, 2013

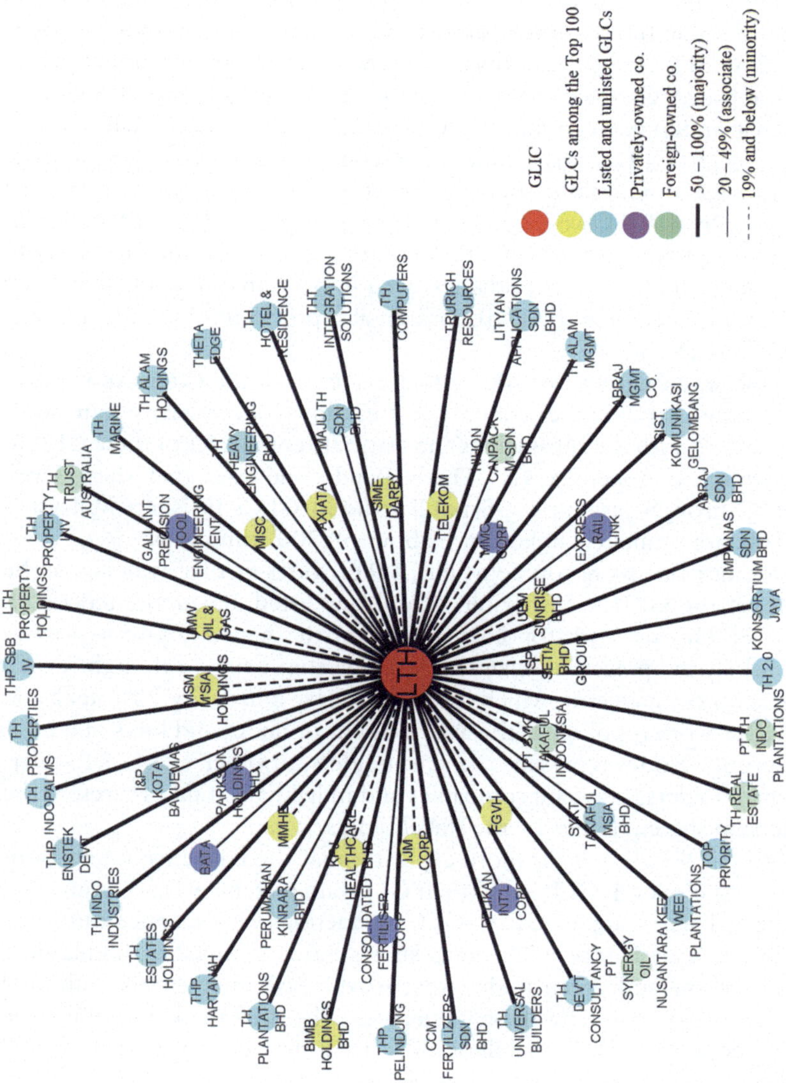

Fig. 4.8 LTH's ownership structure, 2013

Among the notable private companies in which LTH has a stake are Bata (20%), a leading household name in the shoe manufacturing industry, and Express Rail Link (40%), a concession company related to the Kuala Lumpur International Airport express and transit railway services, owned by YTL Corporation Bhd. LTH owns Pelikan International (31%), an established German stationery brand, and Nihon Canpack (40%), a firm that undertakes can-filling beverage services for Nestlé Malaysia.

All seven GLICs share one core control trait: all these business groups have a pyramid ownership structure pattern, a point reinforced in Appendix 4.1. However, the extent of their pyramiding differs significantly, depending on the GLCs they control. GLCs that function as banks have a large number of subsidiaries, seen in particular in companies such as Malayan Banking and CIMB, though also prevalent in the plantations-based Sime Darby.

These seven figures provide further evidence of the extensive involvement of the GLICs in the economy. A breakdown of these corporate holdings, dealing with the subsidiaries and associate companies of these GLICs, is provided in Appendix 4.1. This appendix indicates that these seven GLICs, through just those 35 publicly listed GLCs in Bursa Malaysia's top 100, are ultimately linked with about 68,300 companies!

Through a network topology, Fig. 4.9 provides further evidence of the extent of the GLICs' ownership of publicly listed and unquoted GLCs in 2013. This network topology builds on the figures above as well as Fig. 3.1 in the preceding chapter on ownership issues, although it only focuses on companies in which the GLICs have a majority 20% stake and more. Network topology is the arrangement of nodes and links of a business group. Nodes represent the stakeholders, in other words, subsidiaries, shareholders, associate companies and individuals. Links represent the ownership shareholdings by the stakeholders.

Figure 4.9 indicates far more explicitly that the collective interactions between these seven GLICs and their GLCs are extremely far-reaching and complex. These complex GLIC–GLC interactions were mapped out using a network analysis tool.[14] This map shows 3,621 companies, highlighted in red, yellow and green nodes, that have 4,262 interactions, indicated through the lines linking these companies. The total market capital value of this network is RM720 billion. The total market capital value for all publicly listed companies on Bursa Malaysia for 2013 was RM1.7 trillion, with the 35 GLCs accounting for 42% of this value. A detailed analysis of Fig. 4.9 is provided in Box 4.1.

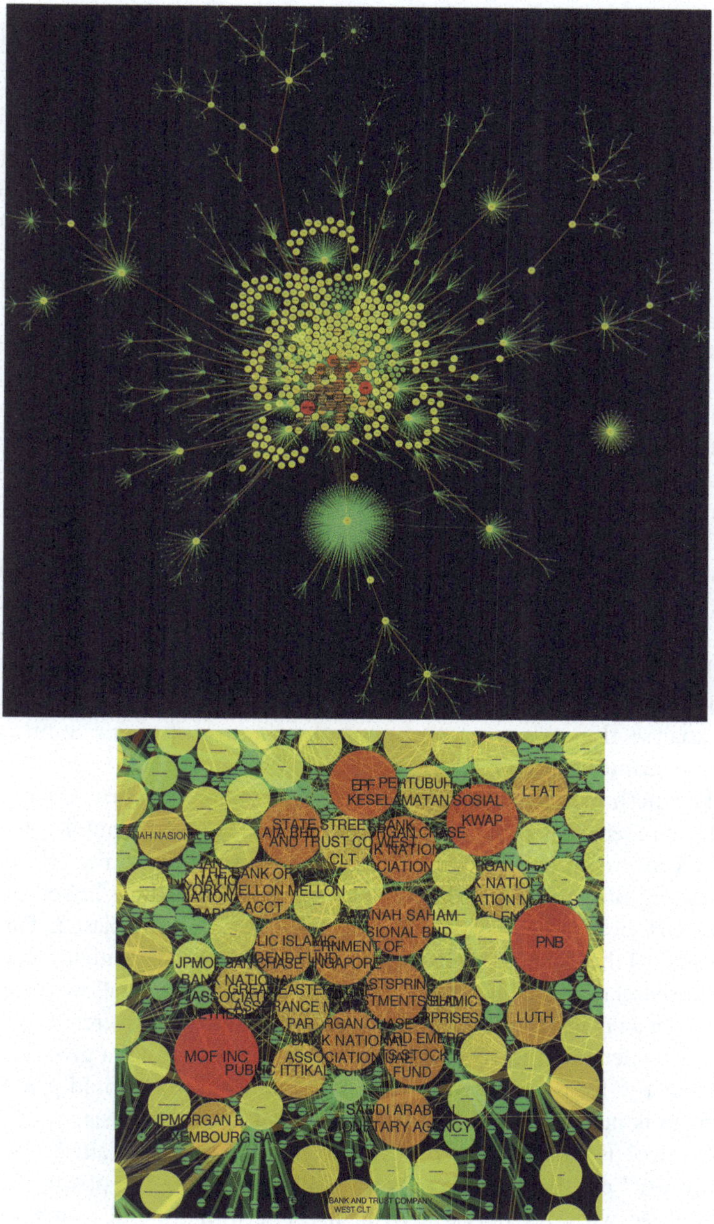

Fig. 4.9 Network topology of the seven GLICs and GLCs in the top 100, 2013 (20% stake or more)

Box 4.1 Understanding the Network Topology of the Seven GLICs (J.M. Roda, Norfaryanti Kamaruddin and E.T. Gomez)

Computational progress in recent years now allows for the application of network metrics to measure control within vast shareholding networks of modern intricate ownership structures (Battiston 2004). Among these metrics, some provide a means to identify the ultimate controlling shareholders within a network of companies. Others allow for a measurement of the power and influence of a shareholding entity over the whole corporate structure to which it is connected.[15] Analysts routinely use company databases such as those provided by Bursa Malaysia, Bloomberg, Thomson Reuters and Bureau Van Dijk when obtaining information to analyse shareholding patterns. These databases may differ slightly in coverage and scope, but they are all fairly similar when used to analyse the major corporate structures of a country or business sector.

Glattfelder (2010) first used these databases to identify the nexus of companies controlling the world financial network. Vitali, Glattfelder and Battiston (2011) found, through computation, that a small group of 147 transnational corporations controlled 40% of the world's financial network. In Malaysia, similar network metrics and methods were employed for the first time by Roda, Norfaryanti and Tobias (2015) to analyse the ownership and control structure of major Southeast Asian agribusiness companies.

The method of Roda et al. (2015) is applied here to analyse Malaysia's corporate sector, with specific focus on the GLICs and the publicly listed GLCs they own and control. This method is sensitive to the selection threshold of shareholding links: when selecting companies linked by at least 10% ownership (and above), the results are critically biased. This is because of the existence of feedback loops of control through interlaced cross-shareholdings. These cross-shareholding structures allow companies to legally increase their control while displaying low percentages of direct ownership. However, by selecting all companies of a given database or the firms linked by at least 1% ownership, this would give the same rankings for the top five controlling entities in Malaysia.

Control is measured through a specific algorithm called "beta-centrality" or "Bonacich's power" which measures the power of an enterprise within a network of firms. The initial applications were developed to assess social networks (Bonacich 1987). This algorithm

(*continued*)

Box 4.1 (continued)

stems from well-known centrality measures developed by Freeman (1977). These measures were derived from the fundamentals of graph theory (Sabidussi 1966). Bonacich's power algorithm, used as a measure of power, has been employed in numerous studies about social networks, social situations, computer networks and information networks and its reliability has been largely acknowledged (Yan and Ding 2009; Friedl and Heidemann 2010; Rodan 2011).

Figure 4.9 presents the companies of Malaysia's corporate sector as nodes, whose size and colour are proportional to their individual power over the network. For example, a large red node has more power over the network than a medium-sized yellow node, while a small green node has the least power over the network. The thickness of the links are proportional to the ownership shares (from 0.00001% to 100%), while the colour of the links are proportional to their "intensity": if one link acts as the only bridge between two large groups, it becomes red.

Bonacich's power computation suggests that nine government bodies control 23.6% of the influence in Malaysia's corporate sector. The most powerful institution is MoF Inc., with 4.9% of the power over the Malaysian corporate sector, followed by PNB (4.2%), KWAP (3.4%), EPF (3.1%) and ASNB (2.7%). The other four government-linked bodies are LTH (1.6%), LTAT (1.5%), SOCSO (1.2%) and Khazanah (1%). Interestingly, JP Morgan Chase Bank National Association USA (2.7%) and AIA Bhd (2.5%) figure highly in this computation, indicating the growing ownership of domestic equity by foreign enterprises (see the full listing below).

According to this listing, a core of 26 corporations controls 54% of the power over the Malaysian corporate sector. This core is represented by red to light orange nodes at the centre of Fig. 4.9, the 26th corporation being Khazanah (1%). Among the corporations in this core, nine are GLICs and government-linked agencies, such as SOCSO, that control 23.6% of the power. Fourteen other corporations are foreign and control 25.3% of the power. Among these, the overwhelming influence of JP Morgan appears through different instances, that is, JP Morgan located in the United States, United Arab Emirates, Norway, Luxembourg, Netherlands and Saudi Arabia. In total, JP Morgan controls 11% of the power over the Malaysian corporate sector. The influence of Singapore-based public and private institutions is also extremely high.

(*continued*)

Box 4.1 (continued)

Rank	*Corporation/institution*	*Influence over corporate Malaysia*	
		By entity	*Cumulative*
1	MoF Inc.	4.90%	4.90%
2	PNB	4.20%	9.10%
3	KWAP	3.40%	12.60%
4	EPF	3.10%	15.60%
5	ASNB	2.70%	18.30%
6	JP Morgan Chase Bank National Association USA	2.70%	20.90%
7	AIA Bhd	2.50%	23.40%
8	Eastspring Investments Bhd	2.40%	25.80%
9	Government of Singapore	2.20%	28.00%
10	Vanguard Emerging Markets Stock Index Fund	2.20%	30.20%
11	JP Morgan Chase Bank National Association UAE	2.20%	32.40%
12	Saudi Arabian Monetary Agency	2.10%	34.50%
13	Public Islamic Dividend Fund	2.00%	36.50%
14	The Bank of New York Mellon Acct	1.80%	38.30%
15	LTH	1.60%	39.90%
16	Public Islamic Select Enterprises Fund	1.50%	41.40%
17	LTAT	1.50%	42.90%
18	Public Ittikal Fund	1.50%	44.50%
19	JP Morgan Chase Bank National Association Norges BK Lend	1.40%	45.80%
20	JP Morgan Bank Luxembourg SA	1.30%	47.20%
21	Great Eastern Life Assurance (M) Bhd	1.30%	48.50%
22	Pertubuhan Keselamatan Sosial (SOCSO)	1.20%	49.60%
23	JP Morgan Chase Bank National Association Netherlands	1.10%	50.80%
24	State Street Bank and Trust Co West CLT	1.10%	51.90%
25	JP Morgan Chase Bank National Association Saudi Arabia	1.00%	52.90%
26	Khazanah	1.00%	53.90%

Note: Power was measured employing Bonacich's power algorithm

References

Battiston, Stefano. 2004. Inner Structure of Capital Control Networks. *Physica A* 338 (1–2): 107–112.

Bonacich, Philip. 1987. Power and Centrality: A Family of Measures. *American Journal of Sociology* 92 (5): 1170–1182.

(*continued*)

Box 4.1 (continued)

Freeman, Linton C. 1977. A Set of Measures of Centrality Based on Betweenness. *Sociometry* 40 (1): 35.
Friedl, Dipl-Math Bettina and Julia Heidemann. 2010. A Critical Review of Centrality Measures in Social Networks. *Business & Information Systems Engineering* 2 (6): 371–85.
Glattfelder, James B. 2010. Ownership Networks and Corporate Control: Mapping Economic Power in a Globalised World. Doctoral Thesis. Zurich: Technische Hochschule ETH Zürich.
Roda, Jean-Marc, Norfaryanti Kamaruddin and Rafael Tobias. 2015. Deciphering Corporate Governance and Environmental Commitments Among Southeast Asian Transnationals: Uptake of Sustainability Certification. *Forests* 6 (5): 1454–1475.
Rodan, Simon. 2011. Choosing the 'B' Parameter When Using the Bonacich Power Measure. *Journal of Social Structure* 12: 1–23.
Sabidussi, Gert. 1966. The Centrality Index of a Graph. *Psychometrika* 31 (4): 581–603.
Vitali, Stefania, James B. Glattfelder and Stefano Battiston. 2011. The Network of Global Corporate Control. *PloS One* 6 (10): 1–6.
Yan, Erjia and Ying Ding. 2009. Applying Centrality Measures to Impact Analysis: A Co-authorship Network Analysis. *Journal of the American Society for Information Science and Technology* 60 (10): 2107–2118.

The range of interactions in Fig. 4.9 highlights the extent of GLIC ownership of GLCs and their subsidiaries and associate companies. The lines that connect them represent their interactions or control through shareholdings. Appendix 4.1 lists, in numbers, the total volume of companies associated with the 35 publicly listed GLCs controlled by the seven GLICs, going down ten levels. As already mentioned, about 68,300 quoted and unquoted companies are linked with these GLCs. Figure 4.9 and Appendix 4.1 reveal that this GLIC–GLC system comprises a vast number of companies interconnected through equity ownership.

The decision-making control lines are linked strongly to the seven GLICs. They are at the top of the pyramidal structure, which spearheads the direction of the GLCs under their control. Most of these massive and complex interlocking relationships occur at the core of the network, which is there most heavy and condensed. The centre of this network system is similar to what Glattfelder (2010) refers to as the strongly connected component (SCC). In this study, the SCC refers to strong relationships between the GLCs and GLICs, derived from their shareholding ties. Decision-making control is situated in the SCC. The flow of control is not one way; it is intertwined within the GLICs and GLCs in the SCC. However, concentration of control in the SCC varies between the GLICs and GLCs. The variations in control concentration are due to the objectives and functions of the GLIC. What Fig. 4.9 confirms is that among the GLICs, MoF Inc. has the largest volume of control through equity shareholdings, even before including the company-based Khazanah and PNB, which it owns. The other GLICs are, as mentioned, statutory bodies and controlled by MoF Inc. through legislation.

What can also be gauged from Fig. 4.9 is the decision-making control mechanism, one that flows from centre, or the core, to the outer, middle and peripheral segments of this network. This flow indicates that decision-making powers are centralized in the SCC. Decisions emanating from the SCC, whether sound business resolutions or those that serve vested political interests, have serious implications for the whole network. Inappropriate control or governance of the GLICs and their GLCs could thus lead to systemic risks.

The 23.6% control of government bodies over the corporate sector carries heavy responsibilities and potential risks in terms of decision-making. This heaviness can increase substantially the volume of time taken to make decisions. The pyramidal structure leads to layer upon layer of decision-making, which contributes to the length of time taken to make decisions. This heaviness further implies less flexibility to react to internal or external changes in the market, more so since these 23.6% of interactions mean that the GLCs have a large number of stakeholders to manage. However, this lengthy decision-making process helps ensure proper governance when GLICs carry out their social responsibilities. However, since power is concentrated in the centre, specifically in MoF Inc., this also suggests that one institution can issue decisions by which all GLICs and GLCs have to abide.

All 35 publicly listed GLCs are interconnected to each other through their links with the seven GLICs. Most of these listed GLCs are situated at the core of the network, further indicating also contribution to the economy. A few extremely large GLCs appear at the outer core, due to their extensive networks with their huge numbers of subsidiaries and associate companies. For instance, the highly diversified Sime Darby has a huge group of companies under its control, a result of its merger with two other major plantations-based enterprises in 2007. Sime Darby can thus be seen as a "semi-GLIC", given its size and structure, as it stands apart from the core and the SCC. Boustead, another well-diversified plantations enterprise, is not as huge as Sime Darby but can also be considered as a "stand-alone GLIC", given its circular shareholding interactions with LTAT and publicly listed Affin Holdings, the owner of a major bank. While Boustead may appear small in size, given its ties with

LTAT and Affin Holdings, this business group is a significant player in the Malaysian economy.

Figures 3.1, 4.9 and those above pertaining to the seven GLICs provide insights into how ownership and control patterns are structured and decision-making power is concentrated. Ownership and control patterns among the GLICs and GLCs are structured differently. The ownership structure depends on the size of the GLC, its core business activities and when it was established. Ownership and control are concentrated differently too. Some GLICs and GLCs have significant and concentrated control, others do not share this feature. For example, in the plantations sector, PNB has substantial and concentrated shareholding of Sime Darby, as does LTAT of Boustead and Johor Corp of Kulim. Although PNB's shareholdings are indirectly held through various enterprises such as ASNB, the interlocking ties through its pyramidal structure could provide this GLIC the control to inform decision-making. FGV has a different model. MoF Inc. has a golden share in FGV which in turn has its own pyramidal structure. FGV's shareholding structure is different from that of other plantations-based GLCs; its shares are widely dispersed, for reasons detailed in Chap. 3.

Directorships

In Malaysian corporate history, there are two major types of directorate ties. First, there are ownership ties, where businesses are jointly controlled by a common shareholder, a trend common in the 1990s.[16] Second, multiple ties, in which two companies share one person as a member of their respective boards. The large voting rights of these common directors allow for greater internal corporate control, leading to greater inter-company transactions that need not necessarily be beneficial to all the shareholders of a firm, particularly minority shareholders.

UMNO-Linked Listed Firms in 1990s

Just prior to the 1997 currency crisis, a number of well-connected Bumiputeras had emerged as owners and directors of publicly listed companies. Table 4.5 provides a list of businesspeople who had served as directors, as well as equity owners, of quoted companies, along with information about their backgrounds. Table 4.5 indicates that some of these directors were said in the market to be close associates of key UMNO

Table 4.5 UMNO-linked directors of listed firms, 1996

Director	*Company*	*Background*
Halim Saad	Renong United Engineers (M) (UEM) Kinta Kellas Time Engineering Ho Hup Construction Faber Group FCW Holdings Park May Crest Petroleum	Daim protégé. Halim publicly admitted in 1998 that he held UMNO's vast corporate assets in trust for the party. He worked for Daim when the latter was in charge of a government-owned company, Peremba
Tajudin Ramli	Malaysia Airlines Malaysian Helicopter Services Technology Resources Industries (TRI)	Daim protégé; worked for him in Peremba
Wan Azmi Wan Hamzah	RJ Reynolds Land & General Rohas-Euco Industries Bell & Order Systematic Education Group	Daim protégé; worked for him in Peremba
Samsudin Abu Hassan	Granite Industries Austral Amalgamated Dataprep Holdings	Daim protégé; worked for him in Peremba
Ahmad Sebi Abu Bakar	Advance Synergy Prime Utilities United Merchant Group Ban Hin Lee Bank	Daim protégé, though also associated with Anwar; his contemporary at University of Malaya

Tunku Abdullah	Malaysian Assurance Alliance Melewar Corporation George Town Holdings Aokam Perdana Malayan Cement MBF Capital MBF Holdings	Former UMNO MP. Close Mahathir associate
Yahya Ahmad (died 1997)	HICOM Holdings Diversified Resources Gadek (M) Gadek Capital Edaran Otomobil Nasional (EON) Perusahaan Otomobil Nasional (Proton) Kedah Cement Holdings Cycle and Carriage Bintang Golden Pharos Uniphoenix Corporation	Mahathir's protégé. Anwar's school contemporary
Tengku Adnan Mansor	Star Publications Berjaya Group Berjaya Singer Berjaya Industrial EMC Logistics Minho Dunham-Bush	Former UMNO Youth Treasurer and Supreme Council member. (He is presently a member of the cabinet and UMNO's Secretary General)

(*continued*)

Table 4.5 (continued)

Director	*Company*	*Background*
Rashid Hussain	Rashid Hussain	Daim associate; connected with Anwar
	DCB Bank	
	Kwong Yik Bank	
A. Kadir Jasin	New Straits Times	Anwar aided their takeover of NSTP and TV3 in 1993
Nazri Abdullah	TV3	
Mohd Nor Mutalib	Malaysian Resources Corp	
Khalid Ahmad	(MRCB)	
	Malakoff	
	Commerce Asset Holdings	
Abdul Mulok Damit	Pengkalen Industrial Holdings	UMNO MP; Daim associate
	Construction & Supplies House	
Ishak Ismail	KFC Holdings	Former secretary of Anwar's UMNO division
	Idris Hydraulics	
	Golden Plus Holdings	
	Ayamas Food Corporation	
	Best World Land	
	Promet	
	Pintaras Jaya	
	Scientex Incorporated	
	Gemtech Resources	
Mohamed Sarit Yusoh	KFC Holdings	Former political secretary to Anwar
	Ayamas Food Corporation	
	Golden Plus Holdings	
	Malayawata Steel	
	Khee San	
	Goh Ban Huat	
	Syarikat Kurnia Setia	

Amin Shah Omar Shah	PSC Industries	Active in UMNO. Daim protégé
	Setron	
	Atacorp Holdings	
	Kedah Cement Holdings	
	Daibochi Plastics & Packaging Industry	
Basir Ismail	Cycle & Carriage	Mahathir's close associate
	Cycle & Carriage Bintang	
	Cold Storage	
	United Plantations	
	Fima Corporation	
Mohd Noor Yusof	Datuk Keramat Holdings	Former political secretary to Mahathir. Had majority ownership of UMBC before divesting it to Sime Darby
	George Town Holdings	
Kamaruddin Jaffar	Sabah Shipyard	Kelantan UMNO leader; Anwar confidant
	Wing Teik Holdings	
	Westmont Industries	
	Inch Kenneth Kajang Rubber	
	Mercury Industries	
Kamaruddin Mohamad Nor	Eastern & Oriental	Kelantan UMNO leader; Anwar confidant
	Dialog Group	
Shuaib Lazim	Ekran	Closely associated with Mahathir and Daim. Former UMNO state assemblyman
	George Town Holdings	
Annuar Othman	Konsortium Perkapalan	Ex-Daim protégé at Peremba. Former UMNO business trustee
Hassan Abas	Cycle & Carriage Bintang	Daim protégé at Peremba
Shamsuddin Kadir	Sapura Holdings	Mahathir associate
	Uniphone Telecommunications	

(*continued*)

Table 4.5 (continued)

Director	*Company*	*Background*
Azman Hashim	AAMB Holdings	UMNO member. Founding director of Fleet Holdings, UMNO's main investment holdings company
	Arab-Malaysia Corporation	
	Arab-Malaysia Finance	
	Arab-Malaysia First Property Trust	
	Arab-Malaysia Development	
	South Peninsular Industries	
Ibrahim Abdul Rahman	Industrial Oxygen Inc.	Anwar's father. Former UMNO MP
Mirzan Mahathir	Mamee-Double Decker	Mahathir's first son
	Lion Corporation	
	Dataprep Holdings	
	Konsortium Holdings	
	Kig Glass Industrial	
	Sunway Building Technology	
	Worldwide Holdings	
	Artwright Holdings	
Mokhzani Mahathir	Tongkah Holdings	Mahathir's second son
	Technology Resources Industries	
	Parkway Holdings	
	Pantai Hospital	
	Ucm Industrial Corporation	
Mukhriz Mahathir	Reliance Pacific	Mahathir's third son
Ahmad Zahid Hamidi	Kretam Holdings	Anwar associate; UMNO Youth Head until Anwar's expulsion. (Deputy Prime Minister of Malaysia since 2015)

Source: Gomez 2002: 87–90

leaders, such as former Finance Minister Daim Zainuddin, or were closely aligned to then Prime Minister Mahathir Mohamad and then Deputy Prime Minister and Finance Minister Anwar Ibrahim. Among the most prominent of the Bumiputera corporate captains were Rashid Hussain, Halim Saad, Tajudin Ramli, Wan Azmi Wan Hamzah, Samsudin Abu Hassan, Ahmad Sebi Abu Bakar, Yahya Ahmad, Amin Shah Omar Shah and Azman Hashim. Significantly, too, a number of UMNO politicians who were closely aligned with Anwar had emerged as corporate players of major publicly listed companies. These politicians included Kamaruddin Jaffar, Kamaruddin Mohamad Nor, Ishak Ismail, Abdul Mulok Damit and Mohamed Sarit Yusoh. This list of prominent business figures includes Mahathir's three sons, Mirzan, Mokhzani and Mukhriz.

UMNO's Presence Declines

By 2013, two major changes had occurred in the corporate sector in terms of the presence of UMNO-linked people as owners and directors of the top 100 publicly listed companies. A review of the list of directors of publicly listed companies in 2013 indicates little evidence that UMNO members had ownership and control of these firms. UMNO members also do not appear prominently as directors of publicly listed GLCs. Among the list of directors of the GLICs and GLCs of the top 100 companies, there were only a few UMNO members (see Table 4.6).

An important fact emerges from Table 4.6: the directors of these GLICs are from four distinct areas: UMNO, the corporate sector, the bureaucracy and non-governmental organizations (NGOs).[17] The largest

Table 4.6 Distribution of GLIC directors according to background, 2013

GLIC	*Corporate professionals*	*Bureaucrats*	*Ex-bureaucrats*	*NGO*	*UMNO*
Khazanah	6	0	0	0	3
PNB	2	0	4	0	0
EPF	6	5	2	5	0
LTH	2	3	1	0	4
KWAP	5	5	0	1	0
LTAT	2	6	1	0	0
Total	23	19	8	6	7

Source: 2013 GLIC annual reports

group of directors are members of the corporate sector. The second largest component of directors are bureaucrats, both serving and retired public servants. The rest of the directors, constituting a small number, are UMNO members and NGO representatives. In each of the six GLICs, the distribution of directors from these four categories of directors varies considerably.[18]

Table 4.6 further indicates that all Khazanah directors have had experience in the corporate sector, except for Najib who serves as its chairman in his capacity as prime minister. The other two men listed as directors with an affiliation to UMNO are Nor Mohamed Yakcop and Ahmad Husni Hanadzlah.[19] Both men have a background in the corporate sector but are listed under UMNO in Table 4.6, given their party membership. They sat on Khazanah's board as they held ministerial appointments in 2013 (see Table 4.7). PNB's board has the smallest number of directors, a mere six, and four of them are former bureaucrats while the other two are from the corporate sector. EPF has the largest board of directors, whose 18 members constitute a balanced mix of people from the public and private sectors, as well as NGOs. EPF's board of directors features the highest number of NGO (five) and East Malaysian (six) representatives.[20] KWAP's board of directors is similar in diversity as EPF's, albeit smaller in size. LTAT's nine directors comprise primarily bureaucrats, from the Ministries of Finance and Defence, and representatives of the armed forces, while two members are from the corporate sector; all directors are appointed by the minister of defence. LTH presents the most interesting list of directors as its board of ten members not only has bureaucratic and corporate sector representation, it also has the largest number of UMNO members, four in total. Only Khazanah and LTH have UMNO members as directors. However, as mentioned, the UMNO members on Khazanah's board served there in their capacity as cabinet ministers. Table 4.7 provides a profile of the UMNO members who sat on the board of directors of GLICs and GLCs in 2013.

Table 4.7 indicates that UMNO members served as directors of GLICs and GLCs. However, some of these UMNO-linked directors are no longer prominent party leaders. Abdul Ghani Othman, the UMNO Chief Minister of the state of Johor from 1995 to 2013, was appointed Chairman of Sime Darby after he failed to win a parliamentary seat in the 2013 General Election. Another former UMNO leader who holds an important corporate position is Isa Abdul Samad, who served as the Chief Minister of the state of Negeri Sembilan. Isa Samad is the Chairman

Table 4.7 UMNO members who are directors of GLICs-GLCs, 2013

Name	*GLICs/GLCs*	*Background*
Najib Razak	Khazanah	• Prime Minister and Finance Minister • UMNO President • UMNO MP for Pekan constituency • Former Chief Minister of Pahang • Held several ministerial posts including Culture, Youth and Sports, Defence and Education • 1MDB Chair Advisor
Nor Mohamed Yakcop	Khazanah	• Former Economic Planning Unit Minister in the Prime Minister's Department • Former Minister of Finance II • Former Special Economic Advisor to Mahathir • Served over 30 years in Bank Negara Malaysia • Former UMNO MP for Tasek Gelugor • 1MDB Advisor
Ahmad Husni Hanadzlah	Khazanah	• Former Minister of Finance II • UMNO MP for Tambun
Azeez Rahim	LTH	• UMNO MP for Baling • UMNO Supreme Council • Founder of Kelab Putera 1Malaysia • Chairman of Yayasan Pembangunan Rakyat Baling
Badruddin Amiruldin	LTH	• UMNO—Permanent Chairman • Former UMNO MP for Yan/Jerai • Former Kedah State Speaker • Chairman of Federal Agricultural Marketing Authority (FAMA)

(*continued*)

Table 4.7 (continued)

Name	*GLICs/GLCs*	*Background*
Mohamad Aziz	LTH	• UMNO—Permanent Deputy Chair • Johor State Speaker • Former UMNO MP for Seri Gading • Former UMNO State Assemblyman for Parit Yaani • Former Johor Exco Member
Rosni Sohar	LTH	• UMNO State Assemblywoman for Hulu Bernam • UMNO Supreme Council member • Wanita UMNO Assistant Secretary
Isa Abdul Samad	FGV MSM Malaysia	• Former Chief Minister of Negeri Sembilan • Former MP for Jempol • Former Minister of Federal Territories • Former Vice-President of UMNO
Abdul Ghani Othman	Sime Darby	• Former MP for Ledang • Former Minister of Youth and Sports • Former Chief Minister of Johor • Former Johor Corporation Chairman
Abdul Manaf Hashim	Tenaga Nasional	• State Assemblyman for Pengkalan Baharu, Perak • Member of Suruhanjaya Perkhidmatan Awam Negeri Perak
Hashim Ismail	Bintulu Port Holdings	• Former UMNO MP for Ledang • Former Parliamentary Secretary to the Ministry of Finance
Noor Ehsanuddin Mohd	MSM Malaysia	• UMNO MP for Kota Tinggi
Harun Narrashid	FGV	• Former Director, Seranta Federal Land Development Authority (FELDA), Prime Minister's Department

Source: 2013 GLIC and GLC annual reports

of FGV. Sime Darby and FGV, both GLCs, are major corporations in the plantations sector. Abdul Ghani and Isa Samad reputedly had little influence in UMNO by 2013.

Najib appears here only by virtue of the fact that he, as the sitting prime minister, oversees the running of Malaysia's sovereign wealth fund, Khazanah. Given Khazanah's prominent role in the economy and the corporate sector, its UMNO-linked directors, besides Najib, were Nor Mohamed Yakcop and Ahmad Husni Hanadzlah, both men with much experience in the corporate sector prior to their entry into politics. Nor Mohamed, who spent about 30 years with Bank Negara, the central bank, subsequently served as Special Economic Advisor to the Prime Minister, Minister of Finance II and Minister in charge of the Economic Planning Unit in the Prime Minister's Department (Wong 2011). Ahmad Husni served as Minister of Finance II, Deputy Minister of Finance I and Deputy Minister of International Trade and Industry. Ahmad Husni stood down as a cabinet minister in 2016. He has also served as director in a number of financial institutions and state-level GLCs.[21]

While Khazanah's UMNO-linked directors were appointed by virtue of their government positions, but their counterparts in LTH were not appointed for the same reason. Unlike Nor Mohamed and Ahmad Husni, the UMNO members in LTH—Azeez Rahim, Badruddin Amiruldin, Mohamad Aziz and Rosni Sohar—have had no experience of employment in the corporate sector. All four are career politicians who appeared to serve as directors of LTH because of their party affiliation.

Furthermore, UMNO members on the board of LTH have held senior party positions.[22] Azeez Rahim is a member of UMNO's Supreme Council. Badruddin Amiruldin serves as the UMNO Permanent Chairman. Mohamad Aziz is the UMNO Permanent Deputy Chairman. Rosni Sohar is the Assistant Secretary of UMNO Wanita (the Women's wing) and was appointed to the UMNO Supreme Council in 2013 (*mStar Online* 22 November 2013).

Noor Ehsanuddin was involved with Kelab UMNO Luar Negara (UMNO Overseas Club) during his varsity days in the United States. He worked as an engineer in the private sector before he was appointed as Director of Seranta FELDA in the Prime Minister's Department in 2008. He was also appointed in the same year to the Majlis Latihan Khidmat Negara (National Service Training Council) (*Agenda Daily* 5 August 2014). Both positions gave Ehsanuddin wide outreach to rural youth (*Free Malaysia Today* 6 March 2016). Abdul Manaf Hashim is currently the State Assemblyman for Pengkalan Baharu in the state of Perak. He has had experience in the private and public sectors. He has been a member of the Suruhanjaya Perkhidmatan Awam Negeri Perak (Perak State Public Service Commission) since 2009.[23] LTH, who had the largest number of UMNO members as directors, has been involved in several controversial corporate affairs.[24]

Rise of the Corporate Professionals

As for multiple directorships in GLICs and GLCs in the top 100 in 2013, UMNO members had no presence (see Table 4.8). Most directors are from the corporate sector, followed by serving and former bureaucrats. The large number of corporate professionals suggests the serious government intent for professional management of the GLCs. These corporate professionals have extensive experience in the private sector, including in major firms (see Table 4.9).

Table 4.9 indicates that Khazanah has the highest number of corporate professionals as multiple directors. Md Nor Md Yusof, Azlan Hashim and Azman Mokhtar, all well-qualified individuals, are dispersed strategically without overlap. Md Nor is in CIMB Group and Malaysia Airlines, Azlan is in IHH Healthcare and Azman in Axiata. Khazanah has a significant stake in all three companies. Of the number of corporate professionals who serve as directors at EPF and KWAP, surprisingly, only one of them has multiple directorships. Shahril Ridza holds directorships in EPF, MBSB and Media Prima. However, EPF has a high proportion of bureaucrats as multiple directors (see Table 4.9).

Most multiple directorships involve people in companies under the same parent company (intra-GLIC). This applies, in particular, to all the MDs. For example, Azman Mokhtar of Khazanah is also on the board of directors of Axiata. Lodin Wok Kamaruddin of LTAT is a director of Boustead, Affin and several of their subsidiaries. Hamad Kama Piah of PNB is a director of Sime Darby. Shahril Ridza of EPF sits on the boards of Media Prima and MBSB. These MDs are presumably present in those

Table 4.8 Multiple directorships in GLICs and top 100 GLCs, 2013

	Corporate professionals	*Bureaucrats*	*Ex-bureaucrats*	*UMNO*
GLIC—GLC	9	5	4	0

Table 4.9 Multiple directorships (GLIC-GLC) of corporate professionals

Name	*GLIC/GLC*	*Background*	*Notes*
Md Nor Md Yusof	**Khazanah** CIMB Group Malaysia Airlines	Commerce	• Former Advisor to Minister of Finance • Former Chairman of Securities Commission • Former CEO of Bank of Commerce • Chartered Accountant
Azlan Hashim	**Khazanah** IHH Healthcare	Accounting	• Former CEO of Bumiputera Merchant Bankers • Former Chairman of Bursa Malaysia • Former MD of Amanah Capital Malaysia • Chartered Accountant
Azman Mokhtar	**Khazanah** Axiata	Accounting	• Khazanah Managing Director • Co-founder and Former MD of BinaFikir Sdn Bhd[a] • Serves in various government bodies including Pemandu, Malaysian Innovation Agency, Bumiputera Agenda Action Council • Worked for Tenaga Nasional, Salomon Smith Barney Malaysia, Union Bank of Switzerland Malaysia • Chartered Accountant and Chartered Financial Analyst
Hamad Kama Piah	**PNB** Sime Darby	Financial Planning	• Served 30 years in PNB in unit trust management • Certified Financial Planner • Member of ASNB Investment Committee
Shahril Ridza Ridzuan	**EPF** Media Prima MBSB	Law	• Credited for restructuring MRCB and Media Prima, as well as the completion of KL Sentral • Worked at Trenergy (M) Bhd, Turnaround Managers Inc. (M) Sdn Bhd, SSR Associates Sdn Bhd, Danaharta

(*continued*)

Table 4.9 (continued)

Name	*GLIC/GLC*	*Background*	*Notes*
Ismee Ismail	**LTH** BIMB FGV	Accounting	• MD of LTH • Former CEO of ECM Libra Securities • Former Chief Accountant of Danaharta • Former Group Accountant of Shell Malaysia Trading • Former General Manager of Arab Malaysia Development • Chartered Institute of Management Accountant
Siow Kim Lun	**KWAP** UMW Holdings	Economics	• Member of Land Public Transport Commission • Worked in Securities Commission
Lodin Wok Kamaruddin	**LTAT** Boustead Affin Holdings	Business Administration	• 1MDB Chairman • Was in LTAT and Boustead during Najib's two stints as Defense Minister (1990–95; 1999–2008) • Perbadanan Kemajuan Bukit Fraser (General Manager)
Ghazali Ali	**LTAT** Boustead	Town Planning	• Fellow, Malaysia Institute of Planners • Former Deputy Director General of Urban Development Authority • Former MD of Syarikat Perumahan Pegawai Kerajaan

Source: 2013 Annual reports of the GLICs and companies mentioned here

Note: Companies with an asterisk are unlisted

[a]BinaFikir was reputedly the firm that helped successfully restructure the ailing airlines, MAS (Wong 2011: 432–434)

subsidiaries in order to ensure their efficient management, besides ensuring that their business plans are aligned with that of the parent company. Of course, this goal can be achieved by placing other directors from the parent company on the boards of their subsidiaries. For example, Md Nor Md Yusof of Khazanah is on the board of directors of two companies under this GLIC's group, CIMB and MAS.

Inter-GLIC directorate links exist as some directors serve on the boards of companies owned by another GLIC or another corporation. Ismee Ismail of LTH is a director of 1MDB, a subsidiary of MoF Inc., and FGV. Siow Kim Lun of KWAP is on the board of UMW Holdings, owned by PNB.

Table 4.10 indicates the rise of professional elites who were responsible for the management of these government-linked companies in 2013. Substantiating the claim that a professional elite is running the GLICs is that all the MDs of these enterprises are corporate figures. This professional elite is, ultimately, responsible to the Minister of Finance. However, the chairmen of the six GLICs are not from the corporate sector. Four of them are serving or former bureaucrats, while the remaining two are from UMNO, including Najib, who chairs the Khazanah board.

For EPF, LTAT and KWAP, as stipulated by their respective laws, the minister in charge of each GLIC can appoint an MD of his choice. These MDs then concurrently serve as ex-officio members of their respective board of directors. For LTH, the MD must come from one of the seven directors also appointed by the minister in charge. Through these laws, the relevant minister has a huge influence over the GLICs, through his selection of the MDs.

It is noteworthy that the MDs of LTH and LTAT, Ismee Ismail and Lodin Wok Kamaruddin respectively, served on the board of 1MDB, the scandal-ridden GLC under the jurisdiction of the Ministry of Finance. Ismee, who became the MD of LTH in 2006, was a board member of Terengganu Investment Authority (TIA) in 2008, an enterprise owned by this state government that was renamed 1MDB in 2009 when it became a federal-owned enterprise (*The Star* 12 May 2009; *The Edge* 14 December 2009).

Table 4.10 Managing directors and chairmen of GLICs, 2013

GLIC	*Managing directors*	*Chairmen*
Khazanah	Azman Mokhtar	Najib Razak
PNB	Hamad Kama Piah	Ahmad Sarji
EPF	Shahril Ridza	Samsudin Osman
LTH	Ismee Ismail	Azeez Rahim
KWAP	Wan Kamaruzaman Wan Ahmad	Irwan Serigar Abdullah
LTAT	Lodin Wok Kamaruddin	Mohd Anwar Mohd Nor

Source: 2013 GLIC annual reports

Note: Refer to Tables 4.7, 4.9, and 4.12 for a profile of these individuals

Lodin replaced Bakke Salleh as Chairman of 1MDB in December 2009 after the latter resigned, reportedly in protest over a business deal between the company and a foreign enterprise named PetroSaudi (*Malay Mail* 11 July 2015). Lodin has served on the boards of LTAT and its primary publicly listed GLC, Boustead, since 1982 and 1984 respectively. When Najib was Defence Minister between 1990 and 1995, and again from 1999 to 2008, Lodin was a member of the boards of directors of both companies. Prior to that, Lodin had served as General Manager of Perbadanan Kemajuan Bukit Fraser in the state of Pahang; during that time, Najib was the Chief Minister of Pahang (*The Star* 4 March 2010).

The New Professional Elite

Nor Mohamed Yakcop, the former Minister of Finance II, had identified and groomed the members of this group of professional elites now leading the GLICs and GLCs. The defining moment that allowed for the rise of this professional elite was when the GLC Transformation Plan was introduced in 2004 by Prime Minister Abdullah Ahmad Badawi (Wong 2011: 379–446).

The reform of the GLICs and GLCs had, in fact, commenced not long after the 1997 crisis, when Prime Minister Mahathir assigned Nor Mohamed this task. Nor Mohamed had played an important role in government under three Prime Ministers, Mahathir, Abdullah and Najib. He joined Bank Negara as a clerk in 1967, after completing his High School Certificate, a pre-university course. The bank gave him a scholarship to read economics at the University of Malaya; he returned to serve his bond in 1972. In 1977, Bank Negara gave him another scholarship to pursue an MBA degree at the Catholic University at Leuven in Belgium, which he obtained in 1979. Nor Mohamed rose rapidly in the bank's hierarchy and by 1989 he was serving as one of its assistant governors (Wong 2011: 55–57). However, in 1994, following hefty speculative activity over the previous two years on the foreign exchange market, Bank Negara registered enormous losses. This episode came to be known as the "Bank Negara forex scandal" as it involved losses amounting to about RM9.3 billion (*Aliran Monthly* Vol. 26(6): 2006).[25] Nor Mohamed resigned from his position at the bank, taking partial responsibility for these losses. He then worked in the private sector, at RHB Securities, then the Abrar financial group and eventually Mun Loong. Nor Mohamed served as Chairman of Mun Loong, a textile firm that had been bought over by Abrar (Wong 2011: 58).

In 1997, following the onset of the currency crisis, Mahathir summoned Nor Mohamed to explain to him the functioning of the forex market.[26] After Mahathir's falling-out with, first, Anwar, the sitting Minister of Finance, and then his replacement, Daim, Nor Mohamed became his close confidant. After Daim's departure, in an unprecedented act, Mahathir appointed himself as Minister of Finance. Nor Mohamed, first assigned the role of Bank Negara Advisor in 1998, was appointed his Economic Advisor in 2000. He would give the Prime Minister daily briefings about the state of the economy (Wong 2011: 308–381; Nor Mohamed 2016: xvi) and, in effect, Nor Mohamed was running the Ministry of Finance.

As advisor to Prime Minister Mahathir, he played a vital role in establishing the Corporate Debt Restructuring Committee (CDRC), Danaharta and Danamodal—institutions that were responsible for restructuring non-performing loans and rescuing debt-ridden companies.[27]

Azman Yahya was appointed Chairman of CDRC, as well as Danaharta when it was incorporated. Azman Yahya later asked Nor Mohamed to consider recruiting capable young professionals such as Shahril Ridza Ridzuan and Abdul Rahman Ahmad who he had trained at Danaharta to turnaround companies mired in corporate debt (Wong 2011: 395–397). Other young executives incorporated by Nor Mohamed to serve in government institutions were Abdul Wahid Omar, Che Khalib Mohamad Noh, Bakke Salleh and Azman Mokhtar (see Table 4.11).[28] Many of these professionals were groomed when they were employed by Danaharta. Regarding the reason for these appointments, Nor Mohamed is quoted as stating: "Our preference is for institutionalising ownership and professionalising management, with a view to providing greater controls, checks and balances and to improve risk management" (*Business Times* (S) 15 January 2003).

When Abdullah became Prime Minister, he appointed Nor Mohamed a senator and then as the Minister of Finance II. In this capacity, he was responsible for implementing Abdullah's GLC Transformation Programme (2005–15), a major endeavour to revamp how the businesses owned by the government were managed. Khazanah was appointed to implement the GLC Transformation Programme. In the 2008 general election, Nor Mohamad was selected to run as a candidate for a parliamentary seat in the state of Penang. He was one of only two UMNO candidates who won parliamentary seats in Penang in that election, with Abdullah taking the other seat. When Najib secured the premiership in 2009, Nor Mohamed was appointed as Economic Planning Unit (EPU) Minister, a post he held until 2013, when he was dropped as a candidate before the

Table 4.11 The professional elite

Name	*Directorships*	*Background*
Nor Mohamed Yakcop	• **Khazanah**	• Former Minister of Finance Minister II and Economic Planning Unit (EPU) Minister • Special Economic Advisor to Mahathir • 1MDB Advisor[a] • Devised the currency peg and currency control proposal during the 1997 Asian currency crisis • In charge of 2005 GLC Transformation Plan. Many young professionals were brought into the GLCs when the plan was implemented • See Table 4.7 for more details
Azman Mokhtar	• **Khazanah** • Axiata • Iskandar Investment*	• Former MD of BinaFikir—involved with the restructuring of Malaysia Airlines[b] • See Table 4.9 for more details
Shahril Ridza	• **EPF** • Media Prima • Danaharta* • MBSB • MRCB	• Worked in Danaharta • See Table 4.9 for more details
Azman Yahya	• **Khazanah** • Ekuinas* • Symphony Life • Scomi Group	• Founding CEO and former Chairman of Danaharta[c] • Former Chairman of Corporate Debt Restructuring Committee (CDRC) • Former CEO of Amanah Merchant Bank • Worked at Bumiputera Merchant Bankers
Azlan Hashim[d]	• **Khazanah** • IHH Healthcare • Scomi Group • SILK Holdings	• Former CEO of Bumiputera Merchant Bankers • Former MD of Amanah Capital • See Table 4.9 for more details

Ismee Ismail	• **LTH** • Syarikat Takaful • BIMB Holdings • TH Plantations • 1MDB • FGV	• 1MDB Founding Director • Former CEO of ECM Libra Securities • Former Director of ECM Libra Capital • Former Chief Accountant of Danaharta • See Table 4.9 for more details[e]
Abdul Rahman Ahmad[f]	• Axiata • Ekuinas* • ICON Offshore* • MRCB	• Director of Ekuinas • Former MD of Media Prima and MRCB • Former Director of SSR Associates • Worked at Trenergy (M)/Turnaround Managers Inc. and Danaharta
Abdul Wahid Omar[g]	• Malayan Banking (until June 2013) • MEPS*	• Appointed Economic Planning Unit Minister in 2013 • Former MD of UEM Group • Former CEO of Telekom and Malayan Banking • Former member of the investment panels of LTH and KWAP
Bakke Salleh	• Sime Darby • Eastern & Oriental	• CEO of Sime Darby • Former Chairman of 1MDB • Former CEO of FGV • Former MD of Felda Holdings and LTH[h] • Former Director of Property Division, Danaharta • Worked with several PNB subsidiaries

(*continued*)

Table 4.11 (continued)

Name	*Directorships*	*Background*
Che Khalib Mohamad Noh	• MMC • Gas Malaysia • Malakoff Corporation* • Bank Muamalat* • Pos Malaysia	• MD of MMC Corporation • Former COO of DRB-HICOM • Former CEO of TNB, KUB Malaysia[i] • Former Director of Khazanah • Worked at Ernst & Young, Bumiputera Merchant Bankers

Source: 2013 GLIC and GLC annual reports

Note: Companies with an asterisk are not publicly listed

[a]1MDB's board of advisors, which included Prime Minister Najib, was dissolved in 2015 (*Bloomberg* 4 May 2016)

[b]Azman Mokhtar and Mohamed Rashdan Yusof, both Cambridge graduates, were founders of BinaFikir, a consultancy firm. They engineered the Widespread Asset Unbundling (WAU) scheme that was used to restructure Malaysia Airlines (MAS). Under the WAU scheme, 73 MAS aircrafts were transferred to a newly formed government SPV, Penerbangan Malaysia Bhd, and were then leased back to MAS to allow the airlines to focus on operations without being distracted by a huge liability. Azman was appointed as MD of Khazanah when it was revamped in 2004 (Wong 2011: 400–407)

[c]Azman Yahya was the first CEO of Danaharta, at the age of 34. He was then CEO of Amanah Merchant Bank (Wong 2011: 357–370)

[d]Azman Yahya credited Azlan Hashim for training this group of young and able professionals. Azman worked under Azlan at Bumiputera Merchant Bankers, where he met Wahid Omar and Che Khalib (*The Star* 10 October 2009)

[e]Abdul Rahman and the names of those below him are not 2013 GLIC directors but they are part of the professional elite

[f]Abdul Rahman, who was appointed CEO of PNB in 2016, has an almost identical background as that of Shahril Ridza. Both went to Cambridge, joined Danaharta at the age of 28, and left to form a consultancy firm, SSR Associates, together with Johan Merican, whom they had met at Cambridge. Rahman and Shahril were introduced to Nor Mohamed Yakcop by Azman Yahya. They assisted Nor Mohamed with the restructuring of the ailing UMNO-linked Renong/UEM group that had been taken over by the government. They were then sent to turn-around another UMNO-linked company, MRCB, which resulted in the creation of the Media Prima Group where its newspaper and television assets were situated. MRCB reconstituted itself as an integrated property and construction company. Its KL Sentral project subsequently came to be seen as a major success (Wong 2011: 382–400)

[g]Abdul Wahid Omar was appointed Chairman of PNB in 2016 (*The Star* 29 July 2016). Wahid was Chief Financial Officer (CFO) at Telekom Malaysia when Nor Mohamed offered him the post of CEO of UEM. Wahid led the relisting of UEM's highway concessionaire, PLUS, and divesting of Time Engineering and TIME dotCom (Wong 2011: 385–90)

[h]Bakke Salleh was appointed as CEO of LTH in October 2001 when the GLIC was facing serious allegations of mismanagement. Under Bakke's management, reforms were instituted that included the setting up of an investment panel that included Wahid Omar to monitor and review all investment proposals. LTH's plantations-based business was successfully listed under his management (Wong 2011: 413–416)

[i]Che Khalib was the CFO of Ranhill Bhd when he was offered the job of CEO of debt-ridden KUB Bhd, UMNO's cooperative-based company. As a director of Khazanah, he was involved with Nor Mohamed in the restructuring of the Renong group. He became the CEO of Tenaga Nasional in 2004 (Wong 2011: 416–418)

general election held that year. Nor Mohamed presently serves as Deputy Chairman of Khazanah, but many of the professionals he brought in and groomed now serve in senior managerial positions in GLICs and GLCs (see Table 4.11).

The Bureaucrats

The second largest group of directors in 2013 were sitting and retired bureaucrats. Bureaucrats, both sitting and retired civil servants, significantly outnumbered UMNO members in the GLICs. The presence of this group in the GLICs and GLCs was perhaps to ensure that these companies fulfilled the country's socioeconomic development aspirations. Senior sitting bureaucrats who were also directors of key GLICs held these positions by virtue of their government positions. Most of these bureaucrats represented the Treasury and other arms of the Ministry of Finance. Among the chairmen of the boards of directors of the six GLICs,[29] only two of them were there by virtue of the government post they held, the Minister of Finance Najib in Khazanah and KWAP's Irwan Serigar Abdullah, the Secretary General of the Ministry of Finance (see Table 4.12). While the MDs of the GLICs were all professionals with corporate sector experience, this was not the case with any of the chairmen.

The relevant GLIC laws confer on the minister full authority to decide on the appointment of chairmen of EPF, LTAT and LTH. KWAP's Chairman, unlike the other three, must always be the Secretary-General of the Ministry of Finance. Hence, the Prime Minister, through each relevant minister, could influence the appointment of the chairmen of these four GLICs. Table 4.13 provides a list of multiple directorships of sitting and former bureaucrats who served on the boards of directors of the six GLICs in 2013.

Inter-GLIC links appear more commonly among bureaucrat directors of GLICs, mostly by virtue of their position. Former bureaucrats, such as Samsudin Osman and Wan Abdul Aziz, are in various companies. Samsudin, the Chairman of EPF, is a director of PNB-owned Sime Darby and LTH-owned BIMB Holdings. Wan Abdul Aziz is a director of PNB, Malaysia Airports, Sime Darby, Bintulu Port and FGV.

Sitting bureaucrats such as Morshidi Abdul Ghani and Sukarti Wakiman of EPF, the State Secretaries of Sarawak and Sabah, are concurrent directors of MAS. From the Treasury, Mat Noor Nawi holds multiple directorships, in EPF, KWAP, Telekom and Bintulu Port. Irwan Serigar Abdullah

Table 4.12 Sitting and former bureaucrats as directors of GLICs, 2013

GLIC	*Director*	*Background*
EPF/KWAP	Mat Noor Nawi	Deputy Secretary General of Treasury (Policy)
EPF	Zainal Rahim Seman	Director General of Ministry of Human Resources
EPF	Mohamad Zabidi Zainal	Director General Public Service Division
EPF	Morshidi Abdul Ghani	Sarawak State Secretary
EPF	Sukarti Wakiman	Sabah State Secretary
LTH/KWAP	Irwan Serigar Abdullah	Secretary General of Treasury
LTH	Othman Mahmood	Senior Deputy Secretary General of the Prime Minister's Department
LTH	Abdul Shukor Husin	Chairman of Universiti Sains Islam Malaysia Chairman of the Fatwa Committee of the National Council for Islamic Affairs Malaysia (MKI)
KWAP	Yeow Chin Kiong	Director of Post Service Division, Public Service Department
KWAP	Idrus Harun	Solicitor General
KWAP	Wan Selamah Wan Sulaiman	Accountant General
LTAT	Ismail Ahmad	Secretary-General of Ministry of Defence
LTAT	Fauziah Yaacob	Deputy Secretary General of Treasury (System and Control)
LTAT	Zulkifeli Zin	Chief of Armed Forces
LTAT	Ahmad Hasbullah Nawawi	Deputy Chief of Army
LTAT	Ahmad Kamarulzaman Ahmad Badaruddin	Deputy Chief of Navy
LTAT	Roslan Saad	Deputy Chief of Air Force
PNB	Ahmad Sarji	Ex-Chief Secretary
PNB	Asmat Kamaluddin	Ex-Secretary General of Ministry of International Trade and Industry (MITI)
PNB	Wan Abdul Aziz Wan Abdullah	Ex-Secretary General of Treasury
PNB	Bujang Mohammed Bujang Nor	Ex-Sarawak State Secretary Ex-Acting Sarawak Head of State[a]
EPF	Samsudin Osman	Ex-Chief Secretary
EPF	Thomas George	Ex-Secretary General of Ministry of Works
LTH	Hashim Meon	Ex-Secretary General of Ministry of Defence
LTAT	Mohd Anwar Mohd Nor	Ex-Chief of Armed Forces

Source: 2013 GLIC annual reports

[a] *Borneo Post* 13 December 2015

Table 4.13 Multiple directorships among sitting and retired bureaucrats, 2013

Name	*GLIC/GLC*	*Background*
Ahmad Sarji	**PNB** PHNB* ASNB*	• Former Chief Secretary of Malaysia • Master's Degree in Public Administration from Harvard University • Former Chairman of the Second National Economic Consultative Council
Wan Abdul Aziz Wan Abdullah	**PNB** Malaysia Airports Sime Darby Bintulu Port FGV Bank Pembangunan*	• Former Secretary General of Treasury • Former Alternate Executive Director of World Bank Group representing the South-East Asia Group
Asmat Kamaluddin	**PNB** UMW UMW Oil & Gas Corp	• Former Secretary General of Ministry of International Trade and Industry (MITI) • Served 35 years in MITI • Appointed by MITI in 2008 to represent Malaysia on the governing board of the Economic Research Institute for ASEAN • Served as Economic Counsellor for Malaysia (Brussels) • Worked with international bodies: ASEAN, WTO and APEC
Samsudin Osman	**EPF** BIMB Holdings Sime Darby	• Former Chief Secretary of Malaysia • Chairman of EPF Investment Panel, Universiti Utara Malaysia • Pro-Chancellor of Universiti Malaysia Terengganu
Mat Noor Nawi	**EPF** **KWAP** Danainfra* Telekom Bank Rakyat* Bintulu Port	• Deputy Secretary General (Policy) under Ministry of Finance

(*continued*)

Table 4.13 (continued)

Name	*GLIC/GLC*	*Background*
Morshidi Abdul Ghani	**EPF** MAS	• State Secretary of Sarawak • Worked in Petronas • Director of Sarawak Economy Development Corporation, Syarikat Sarawak Electricity Supply Corporation
Sukarti Wakiman	**EPF** MAS	• State Secretary of Sabah • Director of Borneo Housing Mortgage Finance, Universiti Malaysia Sabah, Sabah Forest Industries, Warisan Harta Sabah, Tanjung Aru Eco Development
Irwan Serigar Abdullah	**KWAP** **LTH** MAS Petronas* FGV	• Secretary General of Treasury • Extensive experience in Economic Planning Unit (1984–2003) • Master of Science in Energy, Management and Policy from University of Pennsylvania; • PhD in Economics • Director of Inland Revenue Board, FELDA, Bank Negara, Johor Petroleum Development Corporation
Fauziah Yaacob	**LTAT** Telekom	• Deputy Secretary General (Investment) in the Ministry of Finance (Jan 2014) • Director of Iskandar Regional Development Authority and Malaysian Global Innovations and Creativity Centre

Source: 2013 GLIC and GLC annual reports

Note: Companies with an asterisk are unlisted

also represents the Treasury in KWAP, LTH, MAS and FGV. Fauziah Yaacob represents the Treasury in LTAT and Telekom (see Table 4.13).

These bureaucrats, including the retired civil servants, had previously served as senior government officials, and have excellent credentials, with long and proven experience in running ministries (see Table 4.13). It appears that this group has autonomy within the process of collective decision-making on their respective boards.

Conclusion

Business groups are an institutional form of control employed by GLICs to manoeuvre the functioning of publicly listed and unquoted GLCs. Through the business group structure, the seven GLICs have direct and indirect control over a range of companies. Joint stock ownership of quoted GLCs by the GLICs is common and evident in all key sectors. Interestingly, interlocking share ownership is a practice that is not common among the GLICs and the GLCs under their control. Interlocking stock ownership is only evident among companies within large GLCs that operate as business groups. In some cases, obscure private firms are employed to own equity in important companies such as Media Prima, where a number of Malaysia's leading media firms are situated. GLICs, as powerful corporations, need not resort to interlocking stock ownership, a practice common among privately owned business groups.

Major transitions have occurred in terms of directorships, compared to the 1970s, as seen in Lim's (1980) study, and since the early 2000s (Gomez 2002). UMNO members no longer figure prominently as directors of the GLICs and publicly listed GLCs. Multiple directorships are common, although they are most frequent within the GLICs and the publicly listed GLCs they own. It is evident, based on the performance of most quoted GLCs, that the directors are expected to monitor the performance of the managerial team on behalf of the shareholders, particularly minority shareholders. Two other crucial transitions had occurred by 2013. First, there is the rise of professional managers as a managerial elite within the GLICs and their quoted GLCs. Second, there are now decent numbers of ex-bureaucrats on the boards of directors of these GLICs and publicly listed GLCs. Senior sitting bureaucrats who are also directors of key GLICs hold these positions by virtue of the government positions they occupy. These developments, particularly the decline of UMNO members as directors and the rise of a professional elite, are beneficial to the GLICs and GLCs as they reduce political interference in the running of these enterprises. The only exception to these important transitions among the GLICs is LTH, whose board has a large number of UMNO leaders as directors. Interestingly, LTH has been implicated in a number of scandals (see Appendix 2.1).

The much-reduced number of UMNO members on the boards of these GLICs and GLCs suggests, however, that the party's president, concurrently the Prime Minister and Minister of Finance, has enormous influence over the corporate sector, a power that was once far more dispersed among a number of party leaders (see Table 4.5). This group of professionals, as well as sitting and former bureaucrats, has no political influence in spite of its dominant presence in the GLICs and GLCs. These individuals are ultimately responsible to the Minister of Finance, suggesting that they could be subservient to the dictates of political elites. This would be particularly true of former bureaucrats who have served under politicians when they were civil servants. This does not deny the obvious point that these directors are well qualified for the positions they hold, suggesting that they are expected to perform their fiduciary duties.

One phenomenon that has not changed is the practice of "groom and place". In the 1980s, as Table 4.5 indicates, Daim groomed a number of young executives who were placed as owners and directors of key companies associated with UMNO or its leaders. A different trend emerged during the late 1990s. Nor Mohamed groomed a number of professionals who would emerge, not as owners, but as directors and senior management of the GLICs and GLCs. The one exception where Nor Mohamed's protégés do not figure as directors is in LTAT and the GLCs under it. However, it is unlikely that when these young professionals were taken under Nor Mohamed's wing, it was the latter's intention to place them in senior managerial positions in the GLICs and GLCs.

Interestingly, those groomed by Nor Mohamed now also have effective control over the media sector. Shahril and Abdul Rahman serve as shareholders of an obscure holding company, Gabungan Kesturi, a major shareholder of Media Prima, the listed enterprise that has substantial control over the mainstream media. Shahril is the CEO of EPF, the other major shareholder of Media Prima. EPF and Gabungan Kesturi are under the ultimate control of the Minister of Finance.

Apart from these directorships and control of the media, other important control mechanisms in place are the relevant legislation, ownership of the financial sector and the use of business groups and a pyramiding structure with the Minister in Finance at its apex. Najib is well placed to dictate the pattern of development of the corporate sector. In this pyramid structure, one factor appears crucial in terms of control of the GLICs and GLCs through directorships: there is a need to determine who serves as the chairman and MD. While the chairman oversees the board of directors, the MD is responsible for the management of the enterprise. By controlling these two positions, the Minister of Finance can have effective control over the running of the GLICs and GLCs. These seven business groups have extensive ownership of key sectors of the economy, including banking, plantations, media, property development and construction, and oil and gas. The implications of this method of ownership and control of the corporate sector are serious if there are inadequate checks within government, the issue assessed in the next chapter.

Appendices

Appendix 4.1 Total number of companies owned by GLCs among the top 100 ranked by market capitalization going down ten levels

GLCs ranked by market capitalization	*Market capitalization (RM million)*	*Total number of subsidiaries, associate companies and minority interests at all levels*	*Maximum number of levels*
Malayan Banking	88,089	38,068	10
Tenaga Nasional	64,224	64	4
Axiata	58,930	74	4
CIMB	58,898	23,120	10
Sime Darby	57,210	671	7
Petronas Chemicals	55,360	25	1
Petronas Gas	48,044	3	1
IHH Healthcare	31,401	2	2
Petronas Dagangan	31,234	12	2
MISC	25,444	96	2
RHB Capital	20,121	2,966	10
Telekom	19,855	38	3
FGV	16,380	33	5
UMW Holdings	14,090	143	6
Malaysia Airports Holdings	11,092	25	3
Gamuda	11,003	63	3
UEM Sunrise	10,708	134	5
KLCCP Holdings	10,561	KLCCP's subsidiaries, associate companies and minority interests for 2013 were not available in Osiris	

(*continued*)

Appendix 4.1 (continued)

GLCs ranked by market capitalization	*Market capitalization (RM million)*	*Total number of subsidiaries, associate companies and minority interests at all levels*	*Maximum number of levels*
UMW Oil & Gas	8,670	Included in UMW Holdings	
IJM Corporation	8,308	428	7
SP Setia	7,401	91	2
BIMB Holdings	6,781	73	8
Affin Holdings	6,202	Included in Boustead	
Boustead	5,812	1,327	10
MMHE	5,600	Included in MISC	
Malaysian Airline System	5,180	33	2
Kulim (M)	4,399	77	3
Bursa	4,383	631	10
IJM Land	3,975	Included in IJM Corp	
Malaysia Building Society	3,863	15	1
KPJ Healthcare	3,810	59	3
MSM Malaysia	3,515	Included in FGV	
Bintulu Port Holdings	3,450	Included in MISC	
Media Prima	2,883	56	2
IJM Plantations	2,848	Included in IJM Corp	
Total	719,724	68,327	

Source: Osiris (2013)

Appendix 4.1 lists the total number of firms associated with the 35 publicly listed GLCs controlled by the seven GLICs, going down ten levels. What do levels mean? Subsidiaries (50% and above), associate companies (20–49%) and minority interests (19% down to 0.01%) of the 35 GLCs are captured at the first level. At the second level, the subsidiaries, associate companies and minority interests of all companies in the first level are captured. This mode of tabulation carries on for all ten levels. The Osiris search programme provides data up to ten levels.

As Appendix 4.1 indicates, the total market capitalization of the 35 GLCs in 2013 was approximately RM720 billion. Since the total market capitalization of the bourse that year was RM1.702 trillion, the GLICs had, through these 35 GLCs, 42% ownership of the total bourse. In this GLIC-GLC network, there are a total of 68,327 companies (excluding KLCCP Holdings' subsidiaries and associate firms). A majority of these firms are owned indirectly by the GLCs, under the control of the GLICs, through subsidiaries, associate companies and minority interests.

The presence of several levels of companies within this GLIC-GLC network highlights the business group system that is employed, with the presence of a pyramiding structure. This pyramiding happens at various shareholding levels, with the GLIC at the top, down to the GLCs and their subsidiaries and associate companies. Appendix 4.1 stresses the point that not all GLCs have subsidiaries, associate companies and minority interests going down ten levels, an indication also that the size of these business groups varies significantly. For example, among business groups with ten levels, such as Malayan Banking, this GLC owns an unlisted subsidiary, Maybank Kim Eng Securities Pte Ltd., which itself functions as a business group that goes down many levels. Moreover, for this same reason, the Malayan Banking group, through huge subsidiaries such as Maybank Kim Eng Securities, has the largest number of companies linked to it. This pyramiding structure with many layers, including of business groups within business groups, is most obvious in the IJM Corp group, which has two listed subsidiaries, IJM Plantations and IJM Land, each major enterprises in their own right.[30] Both these quoted companies have a large number of subsidiaries, associate companies and minority interest firms.

The various levels occupied by the subsidiaries of the GLCs indicate that some business groups are more pyramidal than others, a trend most obvious in the financial sector. Bank-based GLCs such as Malayan Banking, CIMB, RHB Capital and Affin Holdings have the largest number of companies, going down to ten levels.[31] However, among the top four quoted companies, Tenaga and Axiata have a high market capitalization, but also significantly fewer companies under them than Malayan Banking and CIMB. This is may well be because financial institutions operate in a decentralized way. Centralized models have "free flow of intra-group capital and liquidity with integrated organisational and risk management", while decentralized models are "independently managed affiliates that are financially and operationally self-sufficient" (Fiechter et al. 2011).

What this table indicates is the significant number of ownership and control networks that prevail within large GLIC-based business groups. This table also draws important attention to the business networks that exist between the seven business groups of these GLICs. The networks between and within these business groups all ultimately come under the domain of the Minister of Finance, reinforcing the point about his enormous influence over the corporate sector. Of particular importance is this minister's significant influence over the financial sector, including his control over Malaysia's leading banking institutions.

Appendix 4.2 Directors of GLICs, 2013

Directors of GLICs, 2013

GLIC	Name	Affiliation	Post	Background
Khazanah	Najib Razak	UMNO	Chairman	Politics
	Nor Mohamad Yakcop	UMNO	Deputy Chairman	Economics
	Ahmad Husni Hanadzlah	UMNO	Director	Economics
	Md Nor Md Yusof	Corporate	Director	Commerce
	Azman Yahya	Corporate	Director	Accounting
	Azlan Hashim	Corporate	Director	Accounting
	Arshad Uda	Corporate	Director	Accounting
	Andrew Sheng	Corporate	Director	Accounting
	Azman Mokhtar	Corporate	Managing Director	Accounting
PNB	Ahmad Sarji	Ex-bureaucrat	Chairman	Public Administration
	Hamad Kama Piah	Corporate	CEO	Financial Planning
	Wan Abdul Aziz Wan Abdullah	Ex-bureaucrat	Director	Economics
	Asmat Kamaluddin	Ex-bureaucrat	Director	Economics
	Bujang Mohammed	Ex-bureaucrat	Director	Literature
	Ainum Mohamed Saaid	Corporate	Director	Law
EPF	Samsudin Osman	Ex-bureaucrat	Chairman	Public Administration
	Mat Noor Nawi	Bureaucrat	Deputy Chairman	Policy Economics
	Zabidi Zainal	Bureaucrat	Government Rep	Public Administration
	Zainal Rahim Seman	Bureaucrat	Government Rep	Public Administration
	Morshidi Abdul Ghani	Bureaucrat	Government Rep	Economics
	Sukarti Wakiman	Bureaucrat	Government Rep	Sociology
	Azman Shah Haron	Corporate	Employers' Rep	Hotel Management
	Yong Poh Kon	Corporate	Employers' Rep	Mechanical Engineering
	Hasnol Ayub	Corporate	Employers' Rep	Business Administration
	Abdul Karim Openg	Corporate	Employers' Rep	Economics
	Khalid Atan	NGO	Employees' Rep	NGO
	Lok Yim Pheng	NGO	Employees' Rep	Management
	Catherine Jikunan	NGO	Employees' Rep	Labour Policies
	Hadiah Leen	NGO	Employees' Rep	Business Administration
	Thomas George	Ex-bureaucrat	Professional Rep	Public Administration
	Jafar Abdul Carrim	Corporate	Professional Rep	Civil Engineering
	Lee Lam Thye	NGO	Professional Rep	Politics
	Shahril Ridza Ridzuan	Corporate	CEO	Law
LTH	Azeez Rahim	UMNO	Chairman	Politics
	Ismee Ismail	Corporate	Managing Director	Accounting
	Othman Mahmood	Bureaucrat	PM's Dept Rep	Public Administration
	Irwan Serigar Abdullah	Bureaucrat	MoF Rep	Economics
	Abdul Shukor Husin	Bureaucrat	Director	Islamic Philosophy
	Badruddin Amiruldin	UMNO	Director	Politics
	Hashim Meon	Ex-bureaucrat	Director	Public Administration
	Mohamad Aziz	UMNO	Director	Politics
	Ghazali Awang	Corporate	Director	Accountant
	Rosni Sohar	UMNO	Director	Politics

Appendix 4.2 (continued)

KWAP	Irwan Serigar Abdullah	Bureaucrat	Chairman	Economics
	Muhammad Ibrahim	Corporate	Bank Negara Rep	Accounting
	Mat Noor Nawi	Bureaucrat	MoF Rep	Policy Economics
	Idrus Harun	Bureaucrat	Public Sector Rep	Law
	Yeow Chin Keong	Bureaucrat	Public Sector Rep	History
	Wan Selamah Wan Sulaiman	Bureaucrat	Public Sector Rep	Business Administration
	Siow Kim Lun	Corporate	Private Sector Rep	Economics
	Azmi Abdullah	Corporate	Private Sector Rep	Economics
	Gan Wee Beng	Corporate	Private Sector Rep	Economics
	Azih Muda	NGO	Contributors' Rep	NGO
	Wan Kamaruzaman Wan Ahmad	Corporate	CEO	Economics
LTAT	Mohd Anwar Mohd Nor	Ex-bureaucrat	Chairman	Military
	Ismail Ahmad	Bureaucrat	Mindef Rep	Business Management
	Fauziah Yaacob	Bureaucrat	MoF Rep	Public Administration
	Zulkifeli Zin	Bureaucrat	Chief of Armed Forces	Military
	Ahmad Hasbullah Nawawi	Bureaucrat	Deputy Chief of Army	Military
	Ahmad Kamaruzaman Ahmad Badruddin	Bureaucrat	Deputy Chief of Navy	Military
	Roslan Saad	Bureaucrat	Deputy Chief of Air Force	Military
	Lodin Wok Kamaruddin	Corporate	Managing Director	Business Management
	Ghazali Ali	Corporate	Director	Town Planning

Source: 2013 GLIC annual reports

Notes

1. The Listing Rules (LR) of Bursa Malaysia limit what the GLICs can do. Chapter 10 of the LR has strict stipulations about related party transactions (RPTs). The LR states that persons with an interest in a transaction cannot vote in an RPT exercise. For example, when it was proposed that three major GLC-based financial institutions, MBSB, CIMB and RHB be merged, this segment of the LR was the reason why EPF was prevented from using its rights as majority shareholder to vote in favour of this consolidation exercise. EPF applied to Bursa for exemption from this rule but their application was not approved and the proposed merger was scuttled.
2. According to the Statutory Bodies (Accounts and Annual Reports) Act, GLICs that function in this form must submit to the Auditor General their annual reports, in accordance with general accounting standards.
3. See the Statutory Bodies (Discipline and Surcharge) Act.
4. *Khazanah Nasional Berhad Annual Report 2013.*
5. *Amanah Saham Nasional Annual Report 2013.*
6. *Lembaga Tabung Haji Annual Report 2013.*

7. The MDs of LTH and LTAT, Ismee Ismail and Lodin Kamaruddin, were board members of the controversial GLC, 1MDB, whose advisory board chairman was Prime Minister Najib.
8. Nazir Razak and Abdul Farid Alias are the CEOs of CIMB Group and Malayan Banking respectively.
9. See Appendix 2.1 for a list of corporate controversies involving LTH.
10. MoF Inc.'s one share in PNB functions as a golden share.
11. In 2015, MoF Inc. divested its entire equity in Bursa to another GLIC, KWAP. Following this acquisition, KWAP's stake in Bursa rose to 19.8% (*The Star* 29 July 2015).
12. Khazanah owns Malaysia Airline System and UEM Group as a result of bailouts following the 1997 currency crisis.
13. For further information about these unlisted companies, see Chap. 2, which deals with Khazanah's history.
14. The use of network analysis here is to illustrate the extensive nature of GLIC–GLC interactions. Although this network analysis tool has exceptional mathematical application, it is not the focus of this study. In this book, we employ this tool only for visualization purposes, though some details about this graph are provided in Box 4.1.
15. Strictly speaking, in this mode of analysis, the word "power" refers to the mathematical definition of this concept, used as a measure of the influence of one set of actors or institutions over the rest of the actors and institutions within a network.
16. The studies by Lim (1981), Tan (1982) and Sieh (1982) revealed that interlocking ownership and directorships were important in ownership and control patterns of the corporate sector during the 1970s. However, by 2002, there was considerably less interlocking stock ownership and fewer directorships among Malaysia's leading publicly listed companies. Interlocking stock ownership patterns that existed were those within one group of companies, primarily among Chinese-owned firms (see Gomez 1999).
17. See Appendix 4.2 for details about these directors.
18. For a complete list of 2013 GLIC directors, see Appendix 4.2.
19. Details about the backgrounds of Nor Mohamed Yakcop an Ahmad Husni are provided below.
20. See Appendix 4.2 for details about these directors.
21. Ahmad Husni worked in financial institutions (Bumiputera Merchant Bankers, Asiavest Merchant Bankers, Chase Manhattan Bank), state-level GLCs (Syarikat Majuperak Berhad, Perak Islamic Economic Corporation) and Bumiputera Commerce Bank Bhd. See Sinar Project (2017).
22. See: http://www.umno-online.my/2009/02/24/pemilihan-2008-senarai-nombor-calon/

23. During the 2008 UMNO divisional elections, Beruas UMNO Vice-Chief Azman Noh was charged in court for allegedly offering a bribe in exchange for a vote for him as vice-chief, as well as a vote for Abdul Manaf as division chief (*The Sun* 23 January 2009).
24. For details about controversies involving LTH, see Appendix 2.1.
25. For details about this scandal, see Wain (2009: 166–172). According to Wain (2009: 166), the volume of funds lost was much higher because between 1992 and 1994, Bank Negara had "gambled away between RM16 billion and RM31 billion in the biggest Malaysian scandal of all". Wain (2009: 167) further noted that Bank Negara was speculating so heavily in the forex market in late 1989 that the "U.S. central bank, the Federal Reserve Board, privately asked the Malaysians to cool it. The Bank of England offered similar unsolicited advice."
26. Mahathir's version of this event was: "I tried to understand currency trading. The only person who had experience trading currencies was Tan Sri Nor Mohamed Yakcop" (quoted in *Business Times* (S) 15 January 2003).
27. Nor Mohamed (2016: xvii) claims that he was also responsible for the creation of ValueCap Bhd, an idea he suggested to Mahathir as a means to deal with the prime minister's concern "that the domestic stock market was being manipulated by foreign punters" (Wong 2011: 41–42). ValueCap had an initial fund size of RM5 billion and its primary goal was to add liquidity to the stock market. On this point, one foreign press stated: "Cynics say that is a euphemism for propping up companies like infrastructure giant Renong Bhd and property to power combine Malaysian Resources Corp Bhd, which – despite restructuring – have trouble attracting private investors" (*Business Times* (S) 15 January 2003). Nor Mohamed (2016: xvii), however, would later claim that ValueCap "made a profit of RM250 million for its first year of operations in 2003 and RM8.5 billion for the period 2003 to 2014".
28. For details about these appointments, including personal accounts by these men of their ties to GLICs and GLCs, see Nor Mohamed (2016).
29. MoF Inc. has no board of directors.
30. For the pyramid-style ownership pattern involving IJM Corp, IJM Land and IJM Plantations, see Figs. 3.5 and 3.6.
31. BIMB Holdings is the only bank-based GLC that does not have links with firms going down ten levels, though it still has eight levels. BIMB Holdings' smaller number of companies may be because, unlike the other banks, its expansion abroad is not as extensive.

CHAPTER 5

Conclusion: The Implications

Major Findings

Who Controls Corporate Malaysia Now?

Malaysia's political economy has quietly undergone a major transition that has escaped public attention. Corporate power has shifted from UMNO and well-connected businessmen to the government. Huge business groups controlled by the government have emerged, as can be seen by the dominance that a mere seven GLICs have over the corporate sector. During this transition, one extraordinary outcome was the removal of UMNO and the business associates of party leaders as owners of publicly listed GLCs. UMNO now has direct equity ownership of only one quoted company, the media-based Utusan Melayu, while no UMNO member figures as a major corporate player. A scant number of UMNO members are directors of these government-owned enterprises.[1] These findings are particularly astonishing as UMNO remains a party riddled with money politics, patronage and rent-seeking.[2] The GLICs and the listed companies under their control are now led by well-credentialed, highly competent professionals with no involvement in the political system. These board of directors of these companies are, however, ultimately responsible to the Minister of Finance.

The removal of the hegemonic ruling party, UMNO—and, to a considerable extent, politicians—from the corporate sector has major implications. The power nexus involving politics and business has fundamentally shifted

E.T. Gomez et al., *Minister of Finance Incorporated*,
DOI 10.1007/978-981-10-4897-5_5

at the federal level. If this political business nexus once involved numerous powerful UMNO politicians who had enormous influence over the corporate sector, economic power is now concentrated in the office of the Minister of Finance. If UMNO members once had many sources of patronage, they now have only one source if they wish to obtain access to federal government-generated economic concessions. This is profoundly problematic in terms of public governance as the Minister of Finance concurrently holds the position of Prime Minister, a situation that does not prevail in democracies. This governance structure lays itself open to checks and balances being deeply undermined, opening space for an abuse of power that can have serious implications on the economy and the corporate sector. How did Malaysia get to this point?

Three major events have contributed to these transitions whereby the Prime Minister and GLICs have emerged as economic powerhouses. The first was the implementation of the New Economic Policy (NEP) from 1971 which allowed such enterprises to gradually acquire a major presence in the corporate sector. The involvement of the GLICs in the corporate sector diminished with the active promotion of privatization from the mid-1980s. With this spate of privatizations, major enterprises fell under the ownership and control of UMNO and well-connected businesspeople (see Table 4.5).[3] The second defining event was the 1997 currency crisis and the momentous, even debilitating, intra-elite political feuding that ensued the following year. The GLICs' bailout of ailing well-connected companies and their takeover of firms associated with ousted UMNO leaders led to their re-emergence as major actors in the corporate sector. The third defining moment was when reform of the GLICs and GLCs was initiated by Mahathir Mohamad in the late 1990s though actively implemented by Abdullah Ahmad Badawi from 2003. Najib Razak continued these reforms when he took office in 2009 as Prime Minister. Corporate wealth is now heavily situated in the leading publicly listed GLCs, controlled through block shareholdings by GLICs under the jurisdiction of the Minister of Finance. The vast investment holdings of these GLICs as well as their control over Malaysia's financial sector bestows on the Minister of Finance extensive economic power.

The Ministry sits at the apex of a complex business group structure comprising its holding company, MoF Inc., as well as other GLICs, quoted GLCs and a huge number of unquoted private firms.[4] MoF Inc. is evidently a "super entity", given its enormous influence over the corporate sector through its substantial ownership and control of the other GLICs and the financial sector, comprising Malaysia's leading commercial banks as well as development financial institutions (DFIs). Through the government's ownership of these commercial banks and the DFIs, it can control the economy indirectly by acting as a lender to private firms. This business group structure encompasses multiple layers of publicly listed GLCs with links to a range of unlisted companies, augmenting their control over the economy. MoF Inc.'s vast network of business interactions constitutes only one part of the government's complex system of control over the corporate sector. State governments have a similarly sizeable interest in the corporate sector, and we provide some evidence of this here.[5]

The current concentration of economic power in the office of the Prime Minister is particularly salient because when Najib took office in 2009 he voiced his intention to transfer GLCs to the private sector, arguing that the private sector should function as the primary engine of growth.

Indeed, unlike Prime Minister Mahathir, Najib appeared personally uninterested in business as a government tool for economic and corporate development when he came to power. However, he soon came to realize the significant economic influence that the GLICs have over the corporate sector.

For this reason, the pyramiding structure employed by government to control the GLICs suits Najib, who sits at the apex. Through this system, the GLICs and GLCs can be subjected to considerable abuse. Malaysian history, riddled as it is with a slew of corporate scandals and controversies, shows that this pyramiding system allows the controlling shareholder to secure numerous political and business benefits from the GLICs and GLCs (see Appendix 2.1). Importantly too, the managerial teams of the GLICs and GLCs do not have security of tenure in their positions since the Minister of Finance has the prerogative to remove them at will.

Why This Corporate Control Structure?

The government's focus on nurturing public enterprises in the 1970s, on business groups in the 1980s and 1990s, on SMEs between 2003 and 2009 and on GLCs since 2010 indicates differing modes of governance and enterprise development by political leaders. Implementation of public policies, particularly those that are patronage-based in nature, were at times synchronized, at others syncopated, and quite often abrasive during economic crises which precipitated struggles between political elites over bailouts or access to more rents to fend off insolvency and corporate takeovers. On three occasions, in 1987, 1998 and 2015, after serious economic crises or corporate disputes, a split in UMNO contributed to two important phenomena: the rise of powerful new opposition parties and coalitions and the need for the UMNO president to concentrate power in the office of the Prime Minister.

However, this complex system of ownership and control of the corporate sector is not one that was designed or envisioned by ruling elites. In fact, since the 1980s, all Prime Ministers—Mahathir, Abdullah and Najib—have persistently advocated privatization of the GLCs on the assumption that these enterprises would function far more effectively and productively if under by private ownership (Jomo 1995; Welsh and Chin 2013). Even when the affirmative action-based NEP was conceived in 1970, the plan was to transfer the corporate equity acquired by the GLCs to Bumiputeras in order to redistribute wealth more equitably among the ethnic groups. The new structure of Malaysia's political economy, where control of the corporate sector has shifted from UMNO to the office of the Minister of Finance, served as an important mechanism for Mahathir to retain and consolidate power.

When Mahathir's vision of creating business groups led by corporate captains was dismantled by the 1997 currency crisis, the GLICs and GLCs were deployed to bailout well-connected ailing, debt-ridden enterprises. The bitter feud that ensued between Mahathir and Anwar over such bail-outs (among other things) led to Anwar's ouster from public office and his close business allies losing control of their corporate assets. When a similar feud ensued between Mahathir and Daim, Anwar's replacement as Minister of Finance, companies controlled by his allies and UMNO were channelled to the GLICs and GLCs.[6] Having had persistent feuds with his trusted allies who he had appointed as Minister of Finance, Prime Minister Mahathir then took charge of the ministry. His economic advisor, Nor Mohamed Yakcop, a bureaucrat, was primarily responsible for running the ministry.

UMNO's much reduced presence in business that has quietly unfolded was not in response to criticisms from the opposition or critics of the government. The change was, rather, an outcome of the problems exposed by the 1997 crisis and undertaken to ensure that the GLICs and GLCs, now crucial actors in the corporate sector, contributed far more effectively to economic growth. However, these transitions have also arisen out of the need for the UMNO president to reduce the influence of party warlords. Major businesses once owned by UMNO but now under the GLICs include media companies that own the major newspapers, the *New Straits Times* and *Berita Harian*, as well as TV3, the party's cooperative,

KUB, the huge construction-based UEM Group, the hotel-based Faber Group (now UEM Adgenta) and the Bank of Commerce, now a part of Malaysia's third largest banking enterprise, CIMB Group. Control of these companies ultimately fall under MoF Inc. (see Fig. 3.1). UMNO's involvement in the corporate sector has been reduced to its direct ownership of just one publicly listed enterprise, Utusan Melayu, the publisher of Malaysia's leading Malay newspaper, *Utusan Malaysia*. UMNO has a majority 50% stake in *Utusan Melayu*.[7]

The complex set of inter-organizational relationships created through MoF Inc. allows the Prime Minister access to a range of resources and actors in the corporate sector that could be deployed to serve vested political interests. This power centralization suggests a reluctance by the Prime Minister to create a well-endowed UMNO capitalist class, a phenomenon that emerged when Anwar served as the Minister of Finance and which led to a power struggle between him and Mahathir. The government's control over the corporate sector stems not just from the extensive equity ownership of the seven GLICs. The federal and state governments also have ownership and control of a vast number of unlisted but influential companies.

A practice of "groom and place" had occurred in the 1980s when Finance Minister Daim placed professionals he had trained as executives—as well as owners[8]—of companies associated with UMNO. A similar practice of groom and place emerged in the late 1990s after well-connected companies came under the control of the GLICs, when professionals trained by Nor Mohamed took over the management of these enterprises. However, the rationale behind Nor Mohamad's and Daim's actions differed. As Minister of Finance, Daim, also UMNO's treasurer and a long-standing businessman, appeared intent on securing tight control over the corporate sector to serve his vested business interests (Gomez 1990, 1994). The professional-managerial team groomed by Nor Mohamed was not necessarily trained to manage Malaysia's leading GLICs and GLCs. The professional elite now in charge of the GLICs and GLCs have no dominance over the corporate sector, in spite of the knowledge, information and expertise they have to manage and develop the companies under their control. While the boards of directors of these companies are accountable to the dictates of Minister of Finance, the latter is heavily reliant on them to manage the GLCs in a highly productive and innovative manner and to perpetuate a capitalist system that inspires sufficient confidence to draw domestic and foreign investment. But the government was also aware that having professionals serve as directors of GLICs and GLCs would inspire investor confidence. Such groom and place practice is obvious in the case of Khazanah, PNB and EPF, but not for KWAP, or for LTH, which is controlled by UMNO leaders. Nor is this practice evident in LTAT, long under the control of one man, Lodin Kamaruddin. Clearly, each GLIC is subject to different methods of control.

Of concern, however, is that the ownership and control structure that currently prevails is one that could be open to abuse through the practice of an insider system, facilitated by the directorships ties now in place. The GLIC-based business groups have control over companies through majority equity ownership which accords them significant voting rights. These large shareholdings by related institutions, all ultimately under the control of the Minister of Finance, provides for an insider system of corporate ownership.

Current Ownership and Control Pattern: Possible Repercussions

A key feature of Malaysia's political economy under this GLIC-led framework is that politicians in power can intervene in the economy in distinct ways through different types of business organizations. The seven GLICs fundamentally differ from each other in terms of business ownership methods and there are variations in their holding patterns. MoF Inc., the government's holding company, comes across as a catch-all institution, actively participating in key corporate manoeuvres and having ownership and control of controversial companies such as 1MDB, NFC and UMNO's cooperative, KUB. Khazanah, the sovereign wealth fund, is a policy-based institution, playing a key role in implementing major programmes introduced by the government, including participating in economic corridors to evenly develop all parts of the country, venturing abroad in an attempt to promote the government's business internationalization endeavour, and even taking a lead role in the reforms of the GLICs and GLCs to create better-performing government enterprises. PNB is a portfolio-oriented agency, though also with a policy agenda, particularly to redistribute wealth more equitably between ethnic groups and helping to nurture Bumiputera-owned companies. EPF and KWAP, both savings-cum-pension-based funds, are portfolio-based institutions, with an equity interest in a vast number of companies, but do not seek to control them; nor have they been involved in major corporate takeovers. LTAT is also a savings-cum-pension-based fund, though it functions differently from EPF and KWAP, as it is a GLIC that is actively involved in the management and development of a major business group with control over large businesses such as the plantations-based Boustead, the financial institution Affin Bank, and the drugs-based Pharmaniaga. LTH, though portfolio-based, has attempted an organic form of enterprise development, venturing actively into the development of Islamic-based products and services.

Some GLICs have majority control of quoted GLCs while others, specifically KWAP, do not. The EPF functions like KWAP but appears to have to been forced to take control of RHB Capital from a firm linked with the former Chief Minister of Sarawak, Taib Mahmud. The financial institution under its control, RHB Bank, has long been an enterprise that has come under the control of a number of well-connected people and GLCs. Evidently, the politics of the state has determined how important companies are shifted between institutions and the well-connected, an issue that raises questions about checks and balances in the system, as well as the autonomy of independent investment panels within the GLICs.

With the exception of MoF Inc., the other six GLICs have emerged as major business groups that have majority ownership of Malaysia's leading publicly-listed firms, a process facilitated by relevant legislation and public policies. Through laws that relate to the functioning of the GLICs, the Minister of Finance and MoF Inc. have enormous control over these institutions and, by extension, the corporate sector. These laws can ensure that the GLICs function well, with oversight authority in the hands of the Minister of Finance as well as other ministers in the case of LTH and LTAT. These laws do not, however, have the capacity to limit the effects of self-interested business deals of the controlling shareholders.

Public policies have consistently been used to justify the intervention of GLICs in the corporate sector, primarily through affirmative action-based plans such as the NEP, the Bumiputera Commercial & Industrial Community (BCIC) and, most recently, the Bumiputera Economic Empowerment (BEE) policy. These policies, along with privatization, have functioned as instruments to create Bumiputera corporate captains with a major presence in the economy. In according the Minister of Finance enormous capacity to selectively distribute rents these policies can undermine the performance of the GLICs and GLCs if they are employed for the practice of political patronage. Crucially, too, these policies can discourage private sector investment as private firms may fear expropriation by a strong state if their companies emerge as big businesses. For a similar reason, private companies may be reluctant to work with government-owned business groups in spite of much public rhetoric about public–private partnerships.

The ownership pattern of quoted GLCs by GLICs indicates that a block shareholding structure is in place and that one enterprise, MoF Inc., has enormous business influence. MoF Inc. clearly functions as a "super entity" as it has direct and indirect control over the other six GLICs. In most leading GLCs, three or more GLICs have an equity stake, though one GLIC has a majority interest. This is particularly evident among companies controlled by Khazanah, PNB, LTAT and LTH. The practice of block shareholdings of publicly listed GLCs by GLICs has serious implications for minority shareholders and the economy, in the event of abuse of the companies. Interestingly too, in spite of this block shareholding structure there is little evidence of well-coordinated business deals involving the seven GLICs.

Directorships function as a primary avenue through which the government can dictate decision-making within GLICs and GLCs. A comparison of ownership and directorate patterns in 1996 (prior to 1997 currency crisis) and 2013 revealed a new phenomenon. While GLICs had a rather anonymous, even grey—if competent—image prior to the turn of the century, by 2013, the GLIC/GLC managerial teams comprised well-connected professionals with much experience in the corporate sector. In the boards of directors of the GLICs and GLCs, the number of former bureaucrats has also increased. These ex-civil servants, like the professional elite, have no political influence. They appear to be more conspicuous in the boards of the GLICs and GLCs because of UMNO's declining presence in the corporate sector. They also appear to function as mere figureheads. The most influential decision-makers are the board chairmen and managing directors who, when necessary, take the cue from the Minister of Finance, further indicating his overwhelming influence over the corporate sector. Moreover, the Minister of Finance is ultimately responsible for the appointment of directors to the GLIC and GLC boards.

Since directors of different companies share a common bond with the person or institution at the apex of a pyramid, in this case the Minister of Finance and MoF Inc., this GLIC can secure decisions that favour it, a factor that could undermine the interests of minority shareholders. Through this practice, where directors of different GLCs are appointed by the Minister of Finance, companies in this network can also overcome information asymmetry by securing feedback to improve their position in the market (Mizruchi 1996). Directors with a common bond could facilitate collusion between firms, creating an informal communication channel between them, an inner circle, that could allow companies to make agreements in their mutual interest (Mariolis 1975; Useem 1984).

There is evidence of such inner circles among the GLICs. One inner circle revolves around Nor Mohamad, now the Deputy Chairman of Khazanah. Professional managers he has groomed now lead the GLICs and GLCs. An inner circle is also evident in the media sector. An obscure private firm, Gabungan Kesturi, controls the leading media enterprise, Media Prima, along with PNB. The directors and shareholders of Gabungan Kesturi are Shahril Ridza Ridzuan and Abdul Rahman Ahmad. Shahril is the CEO of EPF, which also owns a huge interest in Media Prima. Rahman was appointed as CEO of PNB in 2016. The use of obscure private companies such as Gabungan Kesturi obscures the identity of the ultimate shareholder, the Minister of Finance, as well as the extent of the state's control over major media companies.

A number of LTH directors, including its chairman, are UMNO members who are elected representatives but hold no position in government. UMNO directors of Khazanah serve in this GLIC as they are the sitting Prime Minister and Minister of Finance II respectively. LTAT is led by Lodin Kamaruddin, a longstanding close business associate of Prime Minister Najib. There is sufficient evidence that these GLICs could be vulnerable to political interference unless sufficient oversight measures and institutional reforms are introduced to ensure they are well insulated from such abuse.

This study's political economy perspective indicates that the core logic of the three main kinds of business groups—portfolio, policy-induced and organic[9]—determine firm strategies of the seven GLICs. But politics matters, influencing how these companies are run. Policies also matter as they shape the different ways in which these seven enterprises are managed. There can be a link, too, between politics and policies, especially redistributive policies and enterprise development strategies, a factor that determines how the GLICs function. This political economic approach indicates that the seven GLICs have been employed differently by the Najib administration. The focus on the politics of the state in the shaping of the GLICs and the GLCs they own indicates that they have not all been abused in a similar manner.

The Complexity of Guardianship

What are the implications of the GLICs' ownership and control of corporate Malaysia when politics features so significantly in its business operations? This question draws attention to the issue of the complexity of guardianship. The fundamental concern about the dominance of the GLICs over the corporate sector rests on the question of whose interests are being guarded.[10] This question must be raised since GLIC–GLC presence in the corporate sector has had contradictory outcomes. On one hand, GLICs and GLCs have been implicated in numerous business scandals (see Appendix 2.1). On the other hand, the leading publicly listed GLCs have been registering impressive turnovers and profits. These companies are professionally managed, which is one reason they have remained, over the past decade, among the top publicly listed companies, with a number of them acquiring a growing regional presence. This state of affairs suggests that these professionals pay careful heed to market trends, ensuring they respond appropriately to ensure the GLCs remain key players in the corporate sector. But since ultimate control of these government enterprises lies with a strong state, they could be easily subjected to corporate abuse, which in turn may lead to major scandals.

The concept of guardianship is thus undeniably closely associated with the politics of UMNO and the implementation of public policies. Through the GLICs and GLCs under his control, the Minister of Finance could use policies to serve political goals, particularly for the practice of selective patronage. Crucially, too, the management team of the GLICs and GLCs is accountable primarily to the holding company at the apex of the pyramid structure, MoF Inc. This is a serious problem as the extensive practice of selective patronage has been justified on the grounds that there is an urgent need to develop Bumiputera enterprises and redistribute corporate wealth more equitably. However, although the common aim of the NEP, BCIC and BEE was to create Bumiputera entrepreneurs, these redistribution policies have not been successful. This is evident in the meagre presence of firms owned by members of this ethnic group in the Bursa Malaysia's top 100 in 2013, which raises concerns about the reasons behind the Prime Minister's insistence on persisting with this policy. The government's own figures on corporate equity ownership patterns between 1969 and 2008 raise doubts about the value of affirmative action in business as a means to create Bumiputera entrepreneurs. Interestingly, between 1969 and 1985, when GLICs were primarily responsible for acquiring and developing corporate wealth on behalf of the Bumiputeras, the volume of equity attributed to this community increased from a mere 1.5% to 19.1%, an increase of 17.6 percentage points (see Table 5.1). Since the

Table 5.1 Share capital ownership (at par value) by ethnic group, 1969–2008 (%)

	1969	*1970*	*1975*	*1980*	*1985*	*1990*	*1995*	*1999*	*2004*	*2006*	*2008*
Bumiputera individuals & trust agencies	1.5	2.4	9.2	12.5	19.1	19.2	20.6	19.1	18.9	19.4	21.9
Chinese	22.8	27.2	n.a	n.a	33.4	45.5	40.9	37.9	39.0	42.4	34.9
Indians	0.9	1.1	n.a	n.a	1.2	1.0	1.5	1.5	1.2	1.1	1.6
Other	–	–	–	–	–	–	–	0.9	0.4	0.4	0.1
Nominee companies	2.1	6.0	n.a	n.a	1.3	8.5	8.3	7.9	8.0	6.6	3.5
Locally controlled firms	10.1	–	–	–	7.2	0.3	1.0	–	–	–	–
Foreigners	62.1	63.4	53.3	42.9	26.0	25.4	27.7	32.7	32.5	30.1	37.9

Note: Par value denotes price at which the share was first issued

mid-1980s, the government's focus through policies such as the BCIC and privatization has been on creating Bumiputera capitalists. By the government's own figures, the volume of equity attributable to Bumiputeras has only increased by 2.7 percentage points between 1990 and 2008.

In fact, in response to the 2008 crisis, Najib announced the end of the policy of affirmative action, only to change tack following criticisms from influential Malay-based groups. Najib went on to introduce what he referred to as "market-friendly" affirmative action in his *10th Malaysia Plan, 2011–2015*. Market-friendly affirmative action was not reviewed in the *11th Malaysia Plan, 2016–2020*, a tacit admission of the failure of the policy. After losing the popular vote in the 2013 general elections and when introducing the BEE a few months later, Najib disclosed that Bumiputera equity holdings in 2011 amounted to 23.5%, an increase of less than 2 percentage points since 2008 in spite of the government's strong endeavour to nurture Malay-owned SMEs.

Table 5.1 further indicates two points: first, the persistent rise of foreign firms, approaching a figure of 38% and reversing the trend seen between 1970 and 1990 when the figure fell from 63.4% to its lowest point of 25.4%. Second, there has been a perceptible fall in Chinese equity ownership, from its peak of 45.5% in 1990 to 34.9% in 2008, a decline of nearly 11 percentage points. This fall raises an important question: have Chinese equity ownership figures fallen because Chinese business owners are reluctant to invest in the economy? After all, the government is well aware, particularly following economic crises in 1986 and 2008, that domestic investors can be impatient with poorly functioning government enterprises, due also to political interference in their management. Interestingly, the government has stopped publicly disclosing such equity ownership figures.

The fall in Chinese equity ownership draws attention to the second issue concerning guardianship and policies, that of property rights. The strong state has the capacity to take over privately owned firms at will. This fear of state expropriation of private firms was exacerbated following the forced consolidation of the banking sector in 1999 when a number of Chinese families lost ownership and control of financial enterprises that they had long nurtured. A similar situation has been evident in the property development and construction sector since 2009. Najib's government has shown a remarkable affinity for the promotion of major infrastructure projects as a means to drive economic growth. And, in spite of the Prime Minister's strong statements about letting private enterprises serve as the primary engine of growth as well as the need to privatize GLCs, four prominent Chinese-owned companies in the property development and construction sector, the IJM group, Gamuda, Sunrise and SP Setia, have fallen under the control of GLICs. The takeover of these construction-based firms suggests that important benefits accrue to the government from its control over such enterprises. It merits mention that small companies owned by UMNO members are active in the construction sector.[11]

What is not disputed about the links between policies, guardianship and property rights is that affirmative action in business does not appear to have fulfilled its goals, even after the transfer of GLCs into private hands. In fact, debates have transpired about the efficacy of affirmative action in business, whether this involves large firms or SMEs.[12] There have also been serious flip-flops about continuing with business-based affirmative action, in 1986 during a recession and more recently, in 2008, following a global financial crisis. The government's repetition of failed policies is because there is a political agenda behind such initiatives, and if the GLICs and GLCs are employed to implement programmes such as the BEE, there may be serious repercussions on the economy.

Conclusion: Implications of Power Concentration

There is now unprecedented political and economic power concentration in the office of the Prime Minister, through MoF Inc. and the GLICs.[13] This is contributing to extremely divisive intra-elite feuds. Prime Minister Najib was compelled to sack his Deputy Prime Minister, Muhyiddin Yassin, in July 2015, as well as other senior UMNO leaders because they had raised queries about how one GLC, 1MDB, was managed.[14] Former Prime Minister Mahathir, who was primarily responsible for creating this complex GLIC-GLC structure, has emerged as Najib's harshest critic. Mahathir has gone on to create, with Muhyiddin and UMNO dissidents, a party that is willing to forge a coalition, or at least an electoral agreement, with opposition parties to unseat Najib as the Prime Minister.

Under Najib, there has been a clear strengthening of the GLICs and GLCs, through takeovers and consolidation exercises, in spite of his extensive rhetoric of the need for "small government". The creation of an organizational structure comprising powerful GLICs is problematic as it is concentrating economic power in the hands of just the Minister of Finance and a coterie of business advisors and professional managers who can be removed at will. The GLICs, given their breadth of ownership and control of the corporate sector and their easy access to funds, whether from the government or from the savings of investors, can shape business behaviour. These institutions have shown a proclivity to take over entrepreneurial companies in spite of the government's professed desire to support dynamic private enterprises. These acts of consolidation can lead to serious repercussions, including creating monopolies or oligopolies, that undermine economic development. In this system, it is extremely difficult for outside investors, particularly domestic firms and minority shareholders, to institute corrective measures if quoted GLCs are abused by the GLICs.

What is particularly noteworthy about these seven GLICs is that even though they are all ultimately under the Minister of Finance, their corporates activities suggest that they tend to act alone, but they are open to acting in a coordinated manner, if necessary. The GLICs are structurally very similar, but operate differently. LTAT and LTH are run independently of the other GLICs even though on major investment decisions final approval is required of the Minister of Finance. Assets are shifted regularly between GLICs, though this usually involves MoF Inc., which has been required to transfer its assets to Khazanah as well as PNB. MoF Inc. has also been required to hold ailing companies, including controversial enterprises such as 1MDB.

Under Najib's administration, state–state relationships have been the basis for the most important corporate deals involving major infrastructure projects. There are growing transnational state–state business links involving GLCs and state-owned enterprises (SOEs) from China. China's SOEs have had a growing presence in major infrastructure projects in the states of Johor, Melaka and Pahang, with an involvement in the 1MDB-linked Bandar Malaysia, a massive development project in the heart of the city of Kuala Lumpur. A matter of related concern is the steady ascendancy of foreign ownership of corporate equity since the late 2000s (see Table 5.1).

The effective functioning of this GLIC–GLC network is also problematic in a situation where the state has been characterized as one that is semi-authoritarian or quasi-democratic, defined as a political system where the independence of oversight institutions to ensure checks and balances have been compromised. The nature of the state, coupled with the government's professed intention to implement selective patronage-based affirmative action, suggests that the possibility of major systemic risks if the GLICs and the GLCs are abused to advance vested political interests. For this reason, the Prime Minister should not simultaneously hold the position of Minister of Finance.

A related concern of such concentration of economic power in the office of the Minister of Finance is what happens when there is a change in leadership or when elites feud. The ownership and control system now in place is an outcome of disputes among politicians in power during the period when Mahathir's premiership. Mahathir's need to institute bail-outs of well-connected businessmen led to the centralization of major enterprises in the hands of the GLICs. There was a relatively arms-length relationship between the GLICs and Abdullah who instituted a major and long-term transformation plan to improve the functioning of such enterprises. Under Najib, numerous controversies have emerged involving the GLICs and GLCs, suggesting that this GLIC–GLC framework is susceptible to abuse. Mahathir's eventual centring of major corporate assets in the hands of the GLICs—not his intent, but an outcome of his fractious administration—as well as Abdullah's reform of the GLICs and GLCs (when professionals were brought in to lead them) may have inadvertently lent itself to serve Najib's political interests.

The key issue about the GLICs is the high level of concentration of corporate ownership in their hands. This can be justifiable, but only if control is dispersed. It is permissible if GLICs rarely intervene in the management of the companies they have an interest in, as they function as trust and pension funds. However, this control is centred in a state where power is concentrated in the office of the Prime Minister via MoF Inc. This issue is particularly problematic during intra-party political contestations as these business groups could be susceptible to the practice of patronage to muster support or create strong factions. These enterprises could also be abused during electoral contests, including during general elections, for example, by undertaking activities in particularly poor under-developed constituencies, ostensibly while implementing corporate social responsibility activities.

Since this is the political economy context in which the GLICs and GLCs operate, institutional reforms to devolve power are imperative. This is because the performance of the GLICs is not simply an outcome of their business decisions but their relationship with the state. In this GLIC–GLC framework, the dynamics of the corporate sector cannot be understood merely by assessing the business strategies of individual government enterprises. The governance structure in place for the GLICs and GLCs must be understood in order to decipher their corporate transactions.

The paradox of the GLICs is that in these ties between government and its business groups, the relationship is not one where no value has been added to these enterprises.[15] The reforms introduced by the GLC Transformation Programme have evidently been of benefit to the GLCs, with improved financial performance of the G20.[16] The business group model can function well as it allows for oversight of the GLCs under the control of the GLICs. Adequate laws are in place to ensure that the GLICs and GLCs are properly managed. The directors are competent, though there are concerns primarily of those on the board of LTH. One core issue of concern remains, however. Ultimate control of these government enterprises is in the hands of the Minister of Finance who is also the Prime Minister.

Political reforms are imperative and need to include the imposition of a stringent institutional check and balance system with independent oversight institutions. Since the GLICs have a huge presence in the corporate sector and the way they function is tied to government programmes, the quality of public policies must be high and their mode of implementation must be subjected to close scrutiny, which suggests that parliamentary action committees, led by members of the opposition, should have oversight of these enterprises. In these institutional reforms, this technocratic professional elite at the epicentre of the GLIC–GLC network can remain, but they must be apolitical and autonomous so that inefficiencies and abuse of power can be weeded out. A clear separation between regulatory and ownership functions is essential to overcome problems of a government that both regulates and owns GLICs and GLCs.

Notes

1. While UMNO's direct and indirect presence in the corporate sector has evidently declined, an important new trend that has emerged is the rise of the opposition in the corporate sector through the appointment of sitting Members of Parliament and State Assemblymen as directors of GLCs controlled by the state governments of Selangor and Penang. Opposition parties have been in control of the Selangor and Penang state governments since 2008 and Kelantan since 1990. This issue will be dealt with in the next study on the role of state-level GLCs in the economy.
2. In one of his final speeches to the party as UMNO President, Abdullah Ahmad Badawi said: "materialism has seeped into the party, making a number of party members greedy and avaricious, hence creating the negative perception that UMNO is a corrupt party" (*The Sun* 29 March 2009). Najib Razak, in his maiden speech as UMNO President, voiced a similar sentiment: "UMNO cannot be seen as a party which is only passionate about struggling

for the interest of a small group. Instead, we want UMNO to be seen, felt and fully trusted as a party that is inclusive and that puts the interests of the people before personal interests. Therefore, the perception that UMNO is a party for people to 'cari makan' (earn a living) must be erased and discarded" (see: http://www.mysinchew.com/node/33169#sthash.WWrLEJq2.dpuf). In 2008, on the issue of money politics, Muhyiddin Yassin, then an UMNO Vice President, is quoted as saying: "We used to be concerned at the division or national levels. Now, it has even reached the branches. If it goes unchecked, UMNO may suffer dire consequences and may disintegrate" (*The Star* 11 August 2008). For an academic discussion of the persistence of money politics in UMNO, as well as the issue of patronage and rent-seeking in government, see Mutalib (2017).

3. For an analysis of UMNO's control over the corporate sector from the 1980s to the late 1990s, see Jesudason (1989), Gomez and Jomo (1997), Searle (1999) and Sloane (1999).
4. Other major government enterprises that can be defined as GLICs and GLCs have not been analysed here. These enterprises include statutory bodies and companies such as SOCSO, ValueCap, Petronas and Ekuinas.
5. An in-depth review of companies owned by the 13 state governments in Malaysia will be undertaken in the next stage of this project.
6. For an in-depth discussion of these events, see Gomez (2006, 2009) and Wain (2009).
7. UMNO's leading partner in the ruling BN coalition, the MCA, owns a majority interest in publicly listed Star Publications, which publishes Malaysia's leading English newspaper, *The Star*.
8. Major business owners such as Tajudin Ramli and Halim Saad would later publicly state they were mere proxies, holding these assets in trust for UMNO or acting on the instructions of Daim and Mahathir. See Mahathir (2011) for his rebuttal of such statements.
9. See Schneider (2009) for an insightful analysis of how government organize and develop business groups in emerging economies.
10. A related question of equal importance is "who will guard the guardians"? (Hurwicz 2008).
11. Funston (2016) notes the huge presence of Class F Contractors among UMNO members.
12. For a review of the failure of affirmative action in business to help nurture Bumiputera-owned SMEs, see Gomez (2012b) and Gomez and Saravanamuttu (2013).
13. For another discussion on the growing concentration of political power in the office of the Prime Minister, see Welsh (2016).
14. These leaders who were removed, first from their government posts and then from UMNO, were the party's Vice President Shafie Apdal, the Minister of Rural & Regional Development, and Mukhriz Mahathir, the

Chief Minister of the state of Kedah. Mukhriz is the son of former Prime Minister Mahathir.

15. However, MoF Inc. and LTH are GLICs that require careful attention. MoF Inc. is where GLCs encountering problems are situated, while LTH continues to be mired in a series of controversies, a problem attributable also to the fact that it remains the only GLIC that is controlled by sitting politicians.
16. According to the GLC Transformation Programme report, the G20's market capitalization increased from RM133.8 billion in May 2004 to RM386.0 billion in July 2015, while their combined net profit grew from RM9.9 billion to RM26.2 billion between 2004 and 2014 (*Putrajaya Committee on GLC High Performance 2015*: 9–13).

Bibliography

Ahmad Faiz Abdul Hamid. 2005. *Malaysia and South-South Cooperation Dring Mahathir's Era: Determining Factors and Implications*. Subang Jaya: Pelanduk Publications.

Ahmad Fauzi Abdul Hamid and Muhamad Takiyuddin Ismail. 2014. Malaysia's General Elections Amidst the Shadow of Re-Mahathirisation. *Kajian Malaysia* 32 (2): 1–24.

Ang, James B. 2008. *Financial Development and Economic Growth in Malaysia*. London: Routledge.

Barber, Michael. 2016. *How to Run a Government: So that Citizens Benefit and Taxpayers Don't Go Crazy*. London: Penguin.

Battiston, Stefano. 2004. Inner Structure of Capital Control Networks. *Physica A* 338 (1–2): 107–112.

Berle, Adolf A. and Gardiner C. Means. 1932. *The Modern Corporation and Private Property*. New York: Harcourt, Brace & World, Inc.

Bertrand, Marianne and Sendhil Mullainathan. 2003. Pyramids. *Journal of the European Economic Association* 1 (2–3): 478–483.

Blair, Margaret M. 1995. *Ownership and Control: Rethinking Corporate Governance for the Twenty-First Century*. Washington, DC: The Brookings Institution.

Bonacich, Philip. 1987. Power and Centrality: A Family of Measures. *American Journal of Sociology* 92 (5): 1170–1182.

Bonbright, J.C. and G.C. Means. 1969. *The Holding Company: Its Public Significance and Its Regulation*. New York: Augustine M. Kelly.

Burnham, James. 1941. *The Managerial Revolution: What Is Happening in the World*. New York: John Day.

E.T. Gomez et al., *Minister of Finance Incorporated*,
DOI 10.1007/978-981-10-4897-5

Burt, Ronald S. 1983. *Corporate Profits and Cooptation: Networks of Market Restraints and Directorate Ties in the American Economy.* New York: Academic Press, Inc.

Case, William. 2009. Electoral Authoritarianism in Malaysia: Trajectory Shift. *The Pacific Review* 22 (3): 311–333.

Centre for Public Policy Analysis. 2006. *Corporate Equity Distribution: Past Trends and Future Policy.* Kuala Lumpur: Centre for Public Policy Analysis.

Chan Chee Khoon. 2010. Re-thinking Health Care and the State. In K.B. Ooi and B.L. Goh (eds). *Pilot Studies for a New Penang.* Singapore: Institute of Southeast Asian Studies: 129–147.

Chandler, Alfred D. Jr. 1977. *The Visible Hand: The Managerial Revolution in American Business.* Cambridge: Harvard University Press.

Chandra Muzaffar. 1977. Some Dominant Concepts and Dissenting Ideas of Malay Rule and Malay Society from the Malacca to the Colonial and Merdeka Periods. PhD dissertation, University of Singapore.

Chang Sea-Jin (ed.). 2006. *Business Groups in East Asia: Financial Crisis, Restructuring, and New Growth.* Oxford: Oxford University Press.

Claessens, S., S. Djankov and L. Lang. 2000. The Separation of Ownership and Control in East Asian Corporations. *Journal of Financial Economics* 58 (1–2): 81–112.

Crouch, Harold. 1992. Authoritarian Trends, the UMNO Split and the Limits of State Power. In Joel S. Kahn and Francis Loh Kok Wah (eds.), *Fragmented Vision: Culture and Politics in Contemporary Malaysia.* Sydney: Allen & Unwin for Asian Studies Association of Australia.

Darity, William Jr. 1986. The Managerial Class and Industrial Policy. *Industrial Relations: A Journal of Economy and Society* 25 (2): 212–227.

Domhoff, William G. 1983. *Who Rules America Now: A View for the '80s.* New York: Simon & Schuster.

Doraisamy, A. 2009. The Gender Implication of Macroeconomic Policy and Performance in Malaysia. In G. Berik, Y. van der Meulen Rodgers and A. Zammit (eds.), *Social Justice and Gender Equality: Rethinking Development Strategies and Macroeconomic Policies.* London: Routledge.

Ehrenreich, Barbara and John Ehrenreich. 1979. The Professional-Managerial Class. In Pat Walker (ed.), *Between Labor and Capital.* Boston, MA: South End Press.

Faccio, Mara and Larry H.P. Lang. 2002. The Ultimate Ownership in Western European Corporations. *Journal of Financial Economics* 65 (3): 365–395.

Faaland, Just, Jack R. Parkinson and Rais B. Saniman. 2003. *Growth and Ethnic Inequality: Malaysia's New Economic Policy.* Kuala Lumpur: Utusan.

Fama, Eugene F. and Michael C. Jensen. 1983. Separation of Ownership and Control. *Journal of Law and Economics* 26 (2): 301–325.

Fiechter, J., I. Otker-Robe, A. Ilyina, M. Hsu, A. Santos and J. Surti. 2011. *Subsidiaries or Branches: Does One Size Fit All?.* IMF Staff Discussion Note SDN/11/04. Retrieved from: https://www.imf.org/external/pubs/ft/sdn/2011/sdn1104.pdf

Ferris, Stephen P., Murali Jagannathan and A.C. Pritchard. 2003. Too Busy to Mind the Business? Monitoring by Directors with Multiple Board Appointments. *Journal of Finance* 58 (3): 1087–1111.

Fligstein, Neil. 2001. *The Architecture of Markets: An Economic Sociology of Twenty-First-Century Capitalist Societies.* Princeton, NJ: Princeton University Press.

Franks, Julian and Colin Mayer. 1997. Corporate Ownership and Control in the UK, Germany and France. *Journal of Applied Corporate Finance* 9 (4): 30–45.

Freeman, Linton C. 1977. A Set of Measures of Centrality Based on Betweenness. *Sociometry* 40 (1): 35.

Friedl, Dipl-Math Bettina and Julia Heidemann. 2010. A Critical Review of Centrality Measures in Social Networks. *Business & Information Systems Engineering* 2 (6): 371–385.

Funston, John. 2016. UMNO – From Hidup Melayu to Ketuanan Melayu. In Bridget Welsh (ed.), *The End of UMNO: Essays on Malaysia's Dominant Party.* Petaling Jaya: SIRD.

Gale, Bruce. 1981. *Politics and Public Enterprise in Malaysia.* Petaling Jaya: Eastern University Press.

Ghemawat, Pankaj and Tarun Khanna. 1998. The Nature of Diversified Business Groups: A Research Design and Two Case Studies. *Journal of Industrial Economics* 46: 35–61.

Gill, Ranjit. 1985. *The Making of Malaysia Inc.: A Twenty-Five Year Review of the Securities Industry of Malaysia and Singapore.* Petaling Jaya: Pelanduk Publications.

Glattfelder, James B. 2010. *Ownership Networks and Corporate Control: Mapping Economic Power in a Globalised World.* Doctoral Thesis. Zurich: Technische Hochschule ETH Zürich.

Golay, Frank H., Ralph Anspach, M. Ruth Pfanner and Elizabeth B. Ayal. 1969. *Under-Development and Economic Nationalism in Southeast Asia.* Ithaca: Cornell University Press.

Gomez, Edmund Terence. 1990. *Politics in Business: UMNO's Corporate Investments.* Kuala Lumpur: Forum.

Gomez, Edmund Terence. 1991. *Money Politics in the Barisan Nasional.* Kuala Lumpur: Forum.

Gomez, Edmund Terence. 1994. *Political Business: Corporate Involvement of Malaysian Political Parties.* Cairns: James Cook University Press.

Gomez, Edmund Terence. 1999. *Chinese Business in Malaysia: Accumulation, Accommodation and Ascendance.* Honolulu: University of Hawaii Press.

Gomez, Edmund Terence. 2001. Why Mahathir Axed Daim. *Far Eastern Economic Review* (5 July): 50–51.

Gomez, Edmund Terence. 2002. Political Business in Malaysia: Party Factionalism, Corporate Development and Economic Crisis. In Edmund Terence Gomez (ed.), *Political Business in East Asia.* London: Routledge: 62–81.

Gomez, Edmund Terence. 2005. The State, Governance and Corruption in Malaysia. In Nicholas Tarling (ed.), *Corruption and Good Governance in Asia.* London: Routledge: 214–244.

Gomez, Edmund Terence. 2006. Malaysian Business Groups: The State and Capital Development in the Post-currency Crisis Period. In Chang (ed.): 119–146.

Gomez, Edmund Terence. 2009. The Rise and Fall of Capital: Corporate Malaysia in Historical Perspective. *Journal of Contemporary Asia* 39 (3): 345–381.

Gomez, Edmund Terence. 2012a. Monetizing Politics: Financing Parties and Elections in Malaysia. *Modern Asian Studies* 46 (5): 1370–1397.

Gomez, Edmund Terence. 2012b. Targeting Horizontal Inequalities: Ethnicity, Equity, and Entrepreneurship in Malaysia. *Asian Economic Papers* 11 (2): 31–57.

Gomez, Edmund Terence. 2016. Resisting the Fall: The Single Dominant Party, Policies and Elections in Malaysia. *Journal of Contemporary Asia* 46 (4): 570–590.

Gomez, Edmund Terence and Jomo K.S. 1997. *Malaysia's Political Economy: Politics, Patronage and Profits*. Cambridge: Cambridge University Press.

Gomez, Edmund Terence and Saravanamuttu, Johan (eds). 2013. *The New Economic Policy in Malaysia: Affirmative Action, Horizontal Inequalities and Social Justice*. Singapore: National University of Singapore Press.

Gomez, Edmund Terence, Elsa Satkunasingam and Lee Hwok Aun. 2015. The State's Business: Government-Linked Companies, the Financial Sector, and Socioeconomic Development in Malaysia. In Edmund Terence Gomez, Francois Bafoil and Cheong Kee Cheok (eds.), *Government-Linked Companies and Sustainable, Equitable Development*. London: Routledge: 103–126.

Gomez, Edmund Terence, Cheong Kee Cheok and Vamsi Vakulabharanam (eds.). 2016a. Special Issue: China, India and Southeast Asia: Paths to Development and State-Society Relations. *The Round Table: The Commonwealth Journal of International Affairs* 105 (6): 597–736.

Gomez, Edmund Terence, Khor Yu Leng and Zhao Fang. 2016b. State, Society and Enterprise Development: Southeast Asia-China Investment Flows. *The Round Table: The Commonwealth Journal of International Affairs* 105 (6): 683–700.

Granovetter, Mark. 1995. Coase Revisited: Business Groups in the Modern Economy. *Industrial and Corporate Change* 4: 93–130.

Heng Pek Koon. 1992. The Chinese Business Elite of Malaysia. In Ruth McVey (ed.), *Southeast Asian Capitalists*. Ithaca: Cornell South East Asian Studies Program.

Hing Ai Yun. 1983. Capitalist Development, Class and Race. In Syed Husin Ali (ed.), *Ethnicity, Class and Development in Malaysia*. Kuala Lumpur: Malaysian Social Science Association.

Horii, Kenzo. 1991. Disintegration of the Colonial Economic Legacies and Social Restructuring in Malaysia. *The Developing Economies* XXIX-4: 281–313.

Hurwicz, Leonid. 2008. But Who Will Guard the Guardians?. *American Economic Review* 98 (3): 577–585.

International Working Group (IWG) of Sovereign Wealth Funds. 2008. Sovereign Wealth Funds: Generally Accepted Principles and Practices – "Santiago Principles". https://www.iwg-swf.org/pubs/eng/santiagoprinciples.pdf

Ismail Md Salleh. 1991. The Privatisation of Public Enterprises: A Case Study of Malaysia. In *Privatisation and Public Enterprise: The Asia-Pacific Experience*. New Delhi: Oxford and IBH Publishing Co. Ltd.

Jensen, Michael C. and William H. Meckling. 1976. Theory of the Firm: Managerial Behavior, Agency Costs and Ownership Structure. *Journal of Financial Economics* 3 (4): 305–360.

Jesudason, James V. 1989. *Ethnicity and the Economy: The State, Chinese Business and Multinationals in Malaysia*. Singapore: Oxford University Press.

Jomo K.S. (ed.). 1995. *Privatizing Malaysia: Rents, Rhetoric, Realities*. Boulder: Westview Press.

Jomo K.S., Greg Felker and Rajah Rasiah (eds.). 1999. *Industrial Technology Development in Malaysia: Industry and Firm Studies*. London: Routledge.

Junid Saham. 1980. *British Industrial Development in Malaysia 1963–71*. Kuala Lumpur: Oxford University Press.

La Porta, Rafael, Florencio Lopez de Silanes and Andrei Shleifer. 1999. Corporate Ownership Around the World. *Journal of Finance* 19 (3): 411–432.

La Porta, Rafael, Florencio Lopez de Silanes, Andrei Shleifer and Robert Vishny. 2000. Investor Protection and Corporate Governance. *Journal of Financial Economics* 58: 3–27.

Lai, Jikon. 2012. Khazanah Nasional: Malaysia's Treasure Trove. *Journal of the Asia Pacific Economy* 17 (2): 236–252.

Lee Hwa Beng and Lee Siew Lian. 2012. *PKFZ: A Nation's Trust Betrayed*. Kuala Lumpur: The Malaysian Insider.

Leff, Nathaniel H. 1978. Industrial Organization and Entrepreneurship in the Developing Countries: The Economic Groups. *Economic Development and Cultural Change* 26: 661–675.

Leutert, Hans-Georg and Ralf Sudhoff. 1999. Technology Capacity Building in the Malaysian Automotive Industry. In Jomo, Felker and Rasiah (eds).

Lim Chong-Yah. 1967. *Economic Development of Modern Malaya*. Kuala Lumpur: Oxford University Press.

Lim Kit Siang. 1986. *BMF: Scandal of Scandals*. Kuala Lumpur: Democratic Action Party.

Lim Mah Hui. 1981. *Ownership and Control of the One Hundred Largest Corporations in Malaysia*. Kuala Lumpur: Oxford University Press.

Lopez, Leslie. 2012. Petronas: Reconciling Tensions Between Company and State. In David G. Victor, David R. Hults and Mark C. Thurber (eds.), *Oil and Governance: State-Owned Enterprises and the World Energy Supply*. Cambridge: Cambridge University Press.

Low Chee Keong. 2000. Corporate Governance in Malaysia. In Low Chee Keong (ed.), *Financial Markets in Malaysia*. Kuala Lumpur: Malaysian Law Journal: 436–449.

Low Kam Yoke. 1985. The Political Economy of Restructuring in Malaysia: A Study of State Policies with Reference to Multinational Corporations. MEc Thesis, University of Malaya.

Mahathir Mohamad. 2011. *A Doctor in the House: The Memoirs of Tun Dr Mahathir Mohamad*. Petaling Jaya: MPH Group Publishing.

Mahfuz, A.H. 1977. Tabung Haji: Institusi Kewangan Bumiputera yang Paling Berjaya. *Dewan Masyarakat* XV (8) (15 August): 46–49.

Malaysia. 1971. *Second Malaysia Plan, 1971–1975*. Kuala Lumpur: Government Printers.

Malaysia. 1989. *Mid-term Review of the Fifth Malaysia Plan, 1986–1990*. Kuala Lumpur: Government Printers.

Malaysia. 1991. *Sixth Malaysia Plan, 1991–1995*. Kuala Lumpur: Government Printers.

Malaysia. 1996. *Seventh Malaysia Plan, 1996–2000*. Kuala Lumpur: Government Printers.

Malaysia. 2001. *Eighth Malaysia Plan, 2000–2005*. Kuala Lumpur: Government Printers.

Malaysia. 2006. *Ninth Malaysia Plan, 2006–2010*. Kuala Lumpur: Government Printers.

Malaysia. 2010a. *Government Transformation Plan*. Kuala Lumpur: Government Printers.

Malaysia. 2010b. *Economic Transformation Plan*. Kuala Lumpur: Government Printers.

Malaysia. 2010c. *Tenth Malaysia Plan, 2011–2015*. Kuala Lumpur: Government Printer.

Malaysia. 2010d. *New Economic Model, I and II*. Kuala Lumpur: Government Printer.

Malaysia. 2015. *Eleventh Malaysia Plan, 2016–2020*. Kuala Lumpur: Percetakan Nasional Malaysia.

Malaysia (Putrajaya Committee on GLC High Performance). 2015. *GLC Transformation Programme Graduation Report*. Kuala Lumpur: Percetakan Nasional Malaysia.

Mariolis, Peter. 1975. Interlocking Directorates and Control of Corporations: The Theory of Bank Control. *Social Science Quarterly* 56 (3): 425–439.

Means, Gordon P. 1991. *Malaysian Politics: The Second Generation*. Singapore: Oxford University Press.

Ministry of Finance. 2011. *Economic Report 2010–11*. Kuala Lumpur: Government Printer.

Mehmet, Ozay. 1986. *Development in Malaysia: Poverty, Wealth and Trusteeship*. London: Croom Helm.

Mizruchi, Mark S. 1996. What Do Interlocks Do? An Analysis, Critique, and Assessment of Research on Interlocking Directorates. *Annual Review of Sociology* 22: 271–298.

Mohamed, S. 1995. MIM Forum With the Employees Provident Fund: The Employees Provident Fund & You Keynote Address. *Malaysian Management Review* 30 (3): 19–27.

Mohd. Saidatulakmal. 2012. Welfare Regime, Social Protection and Poverty Reduction. In Khoo Boo Teik (ed.), *Policy Regimes and the Political Economy of Poverty Reduction in Malaysia*. Basingstoke: Palgrave-Macmillan: 107–144.

Mutalib, Hussin M. 2017. The Other Side of Malaysia's Enviable Economic and Multiethnic Stability: The Obstinate Resilience of 'Money Politics'. *Asian Ethnicity* 18 (1): 54–73.

Nor Mohamed Yakcop. 2016. *Pushing the Boundaries: Stories from the Putrajaya Years (May 2000–May 2013)*. Petaling Jaya: MPH Group Publishing.

Norma Mansor, Sharifah Nabilah Syed Salleh, Tan Lih Yoong, Evangelos Koutronas and Sarala Aikanathan. 2014. Social Security in Malaysia: Stock-take on Players, Available Products and Databases. SSRC Working Paper Series No. 2014–2. Kuala Lumpur: Social Security Research Centre (SSRC), Faculty Economics and Administration, University of Malaya.

Nurul Afzan Najid and Rashidah Abdul Rahman. 2011. Government Ownership and Performance of Malaysian Government-Linked Companies. *International Research Journal of Finance and Economics* 61: 42–56.

OECD. 2013. *OECD Investment Policy Reviews: Malaysia 2013*. OECD Publishing. doi:10.1787/9789264194588-en

Omar, M.A., Muhamad Abduh and Raditya Sukmana. 2013. *Fundamentals of Islamic Money and Capital Markets*. Singapore: John Wiley & Sons.

Ooi Keat Gin. 2009. *Historical Dictionary of Malaysia*. Plymouth: The Scarecrow Press.

Ostwald, Kai. 2013. How to Win a Lost Election: Malapportionment and Malaysia's 2013 General Election. *The Round Table: The Commonwealth Journal of International Affairs* November: 1–12.

Pepinsky, Thomas. 2009. *Economic Crises and the Breakdown of Authoritarian Regimes: Indonesia and Malaysia in Comparative Perspective*. Cambridge: Cambridge University Press.

Puthucheary, James J. 1960. *Ownership and Control in the Malayan Economy*. Singapore: Eastern Universities Press.

Puthucheary, Mavis. 2011. State Economic Development Corporations. In Mahani Zainal Abidin (ed.), *Malaysia: Policies and Issues in Economic Development*. Kuala Lumpur: Institute of Strategic and International Studies: 577–596.

Putrajaya Committee on GLC Transformation (PCG). 2006.

Roda, Jean-Marc, Norfaryanti Kamaruddin and Rafael Tobias. 2015. Deciphering Corporate Governance and Environmental Commitments Among Southeast Asian Transnationals: Uptake of Sustainability Certification. *Forests* 6 (5): 1454–1475.

Rodan, Gary. 2004. *Transparency and Authoritarian Rule in Southeast Asia: Singapore and Malaysia*. London: RoutledgeCurzon.

Rodan, Simon. 2011. Choosing the 'B' Parameter When Using the Bonacich Power Measure. *Journal of Social Structure* 12: 1–23.

Rugayah Mohamed. 1995. Public Enterprise. In Jomo K.S. (ed.), *Privatizing Malaysia: Rents, Rhetoric, Realities*. Boulder: Westview Press.

Sabidussi, Gert. 1966. The Centrality Index of a Graph. *Psychometrika* 31 (4): 581–603.

Salleh, I.M. and S.D. Meyanathan. 1993. *Malaysia: Growth, Equity, and Structural Transformation*. Washington, DC: The World Bank.

Sallehuddin Mohamed. 1995. MIM Forum with the Employees Provident Fund: The Employees Provident Fund & You. *Malaysian Management Review* 30(3): 19–27.

Saravanamuttu, Johan. 2016. *Power Sharing in a Divided Nation: Mediated Communalism and New Politics in Six Decades of Malaysia's Elections*. Singapore: Institute of Southeast Asian Studies.

Schneider, Ben Ross. 2009. A Comparative Political Economy of Diversified Business Groups, or How States Organize Big Business. *Review of International Political Economy* 16 (2): 178–201.

Scott, John. 1985. *Corporations, Classes and Capitalism*. London: Hutchinson.

Searle, Peter. 1999. *The Riddle of Malaysian Capitalism: Rent-Seekers or Real Capitalists*. St Leonards/Honolulu: Allen & Unwin/University of Hawaii Press.

Shirley, Mary M. and John Nellis. 1991. *Public Enterprise Reform: The Lessons of Experience*. Washington, DC: The World Bank.

Sieh-Lee Mei Leng. 1982. *Ownership and Control of Malaysian Manufacturing Corporations*. Kuala Lumpur: UMCB Publications.

Sloane, Patricia. 1999. *Islam, Modernity and Entrepreneurship Among the Malays*. Basingstoke: Macmillan.

Shamsul A.B. 1988. The Battle Royal: The UMNO Elections of 1987. *Southeast Asian Affairs*. Singapore: Institute of Southeast Asian Studies.

Sinar Project. 2017. *Wakil Rakyat: Ahmad Husni Hanadzlah*. Retrieved from Sinar Project. https://mymp.sinarproject.org/ms/wakil-rakyat/ahmad-husni-hanadzlah

Snodgrass, Donald R. 1980. *Inequality and Economic Development in Malaysia*. Kuala Lumpur: Oxford University Press.

Tan Tat Wai. 1982. *Income Distribution and Determination in West Malaysia*. Kuala Lumpur: Oxford University Press.

Tolos, Habibah, Peijie Wang, Miao Zhang and Rory Shand. 2014. Retirement Systems and Pension Reform: A Malaysian Perspective. *International Labour Review* 153 (3): 489–502.

Useem, Michael. 1984. *The Inner Circle: Large Corporations and the Rise of Business Political Activity in the U.S. and U.K.* New York: Oxford University Press.

Vermeulen, Erik P.M. 2012. Beneficial Ownership and Control: A Comparative Study – Disclosure, Information and Enforcement. OECD Russia Corporate Governance Roundtable March 2012 Technical Seminar. OECD.

Vighneswaran Vithiatharan and Edmund Terence Gomez. 2014. Politics, Economic Crises and Corporate Governance Reforms: Regulatory Capture in Malaysia. *Journal of Contemporary Asia* 44 (4): 599–615.

Vitali, Stefania, James B. Glattfelder and Stefano Battiston. 2011. The Network of Global Corporate Control. *PloS One* 6 (10): 1–6.

Wain, Barry. 2009. *Malaysian Maverick: Mahathir Mohamad in Turbulent Times.* Basingstoke: Palgrave-Macmillan.

Weiss, Meredith L. (ed.). 2013. *Electoral Dynamics in Malaysia: Findings from the Grassroots.* SIRD: Petaling Jaya.

Welsh, Bridget and James U.H. Chin (eds.). 2013. *Awakening: The Abdullah Badawi Years in Malaysia.* Petaling Jaya: SIRD.

Welsh, Bridget (ed.). 2016. *The End of UMNO: Essays on Malaysia's Dominant Party.* Petaling Jaya: SIRD.

Witt, Michael A. and Gordon Redding (eds.). 2014. *The Oxford Handbook of Asian Business Systems.* Oxford: Oxford University Press.

Wong Sulong. 2011. *Notes to the Prime Minister.* Petaling Jaya: MPH Group Publishing.

Wong Sulong. 2016. *Being Abdullah Ahmad Badawi: The Authorised Biography.* Petaling Jaya: Pelanduk Publications.

Yan, Erjia and Ying Ding. 2009. Applying Centrality Measures to Impact Analysis: A Co-authorship Network Analysis. *Journal of the American Society for Information Science and Technology* 60 (10): 2107–2118.

Young, Kevin, Willem C.F. Bussink and Parvez Hassan. 1980. *Malaysia: Growth and Equity in a Multi-racial Society.* Baltimore: Johns Hopkins University Press.

Yoshihara, Kunio. 1988. *The Rise of Ersatz Capitalism in Southeast Asia.* Kuala Lumpur: Oxford University Press.

Zainal Aznam Yusof. 1991. Distributional Policies and Programme: The Malaysian Experience. In Lee Kiong Hock and Shyamala Nagaraj (eds.), *The Malaysian Economy Beyond 1990.* Kuala Lumpur: Persatuan Ekonomi Malaysia.

Zakaria Haji Ahmad. 1989. Malaysia: Quasi-Democracy in a Divided Society. In Larry Diamond, Juan J. Linz and Seymour Martin Lipset (eds.), *Democracy in Developing Countries, Volume Three: Asia.* Boulder, CO: Lynne Rienner.

Newspapers and Magazines

Agenda Daily
Aliran Monthly
Asia Asset Management
Asia Times Online
Astro Awani
Bernama
Bloomberg

Borneo Post
Business Times
Business Times (Singapore)
Enterprising Investor
Finance Asia
Financial Times
Focus Malaysia
Forbes Asia
Free Malaysia Today
KiniBiz
Malay Mail
Malay Mail Online
Malaysiakini
Malaysian Management Review
mStar Online
New Straits Times
Pensions & Investments
Reuters
Straits Times (Singapore)
The Australian
The Borneo Post
The Economist
The Edge
The Star
The Sun
The Wall Street Journal
Utusan Online

Index[1]

[1] Note: Page numbers followed by "n" refer to notes.

E.T. Gomez et al., *Minister of Finance Incorporated*,
DOI 10.1007/978-981-10-4897-5

The manufacturer's authorised representative in the EU is Springer Nature Customer Service Centre GmbH, Europaplatz 3, 69115 Heidelberg, Germany. If you have any concerns regarding our products, please contact ProductSafety@springernature.com

Printed and bound by CPI Group (UK) Ltd, Croydon, CR0 4YY
25/09/2026
02222894-0002